Three Hundred Years

of

AMERICAN
PAINTING

Time Incorporated

Editor-in-Chief
HENRY R. LUCE

President
ROY E. LARSEN

———————————

"THREE HUNDRED YEARS OF AMERICAN PAINTING"
was produced by TIME under the general direction of

ROY ALEXANDER, *Managing Editor*
OTTO FUERBRINGER, *Assistant Managing Editor*

The editorial staff for this book:

Senior Editor
EDWARD O. CERF

Art Director
MICHAEL J. PHILLIPS

Research Assistants
RUTH BRINE
ADRIENNE FOULKE, JEAN L. NIESLEY
ROSEMARIE TAURIS ZADIKOV

Production Assistants
ALBERT J. DUNN, ARNOLD DRAPKIN
CHARLES P. JACKSON, EDWARD PUCCIA
DAN P. SIBLEY

Associate Editor
CRANSTON JONES

———————————

Publisher
JAMES A. LINEN

Assistant to the Publisher
FRANK R. SHEA

———————————

Working closely with this editorial staff were TIME's foreign and
domestic correspondents, production department, and copy desk.

Three Hundred Years

of

AMERICAN PAINTING

by

ALEXANDER ELIOT
art editor of TIME

with an introduction by JOHN WALKER
director of the National Gallery

Time Incorporated · New York · 1957

TIME

Book Trade Distribution by Random House, Inc.

ACKNOWLEDGMENTS

THE editors of TIME are indebted to a great many authorities and institutions for their help in preparing this book, in particular to:

•

The museums and collectors credited in the following pages for permission to reproduce the paintings owned by them.

•

The museums and other institutions that provided the material assembled in the section entitled One Hundred Collections of American Painting.

•

The artists interviewed by TIME and quoted herein.

•

The scholars listed in the Bibliography for further quotations and other invaluable material, published and unpublished.

•

And those individuals who have given much helpful advice on the text and the selection of illustrations, notably Holger Cahill; Huntington Cairns, Secretary-Treasurer, National Gallery of Art; William T. Cresmer; Charles Crehore Cunningham, Director, Wadsworth Atheneum, Hartford, Conn.; Samuel Atkins Eliot Jr.; James Thomas Flexner; Samuel Golden, President, American Artists Group; Lloyd Goodrich, Associate Director, Whitney Museum of American Art; Alan D. Gruskin; Robert Beverly Hale, Curator of American Painting and Sculpture, the Metropolitan Museum of Art; Edith Gregor Halpert; Rosalind Irvine, Associate Curator, Whitney Museum of American Art; Oliver Larkin, Professor of Art, Smith College; Jean Lipman; Elizabeth McCausland; Harold McCracken; David M. K. McKibbin, Head of the Art Department, Boston Athenaeum; Barbara Neville Parker; Peter J. Pollock; Harris King Prior, Director, American Federation of Arts; Perry T. Rathbone, Director, Museum of Fine Arts, Boston; Selden Rodman; James Johnson Sweeney, Director, Solomon R. Guggenheim Museum, New York City; Frederick Arnold Sweet, Curator, American Painting and Sculpture, Art Institute of Chicago; Francis Henry Taylor, Director, Worcester Art Museum; Vladimir Visson; John Walker, Director, National Gallery of Art; David H. Wallace; Frederick S. Wight, Professor of Art and Director of Art Galleries, University of California at Los Angeles.

•

TIME of course assumes full responsibility for the final work as a whole.

TABLE OF CONTENTS

Introduction viii

PART THREE

THE WORLD A STAGE

INTRODUCTION

SEVENTY-TWO years ago, Whistler in his famous lecture known as "Ten O'Clock" observed, "Art is upon the Town!" Today he might have added, "especially American art." In New York City alone, an estimated 500 exhibitions of American painting were held last year. Museums are competing with each other to increase their American collections; painters until recently out of fashion, like Remington and the Hudson River School, are now widely acclaimed; attics are being rummaged for primitives, which for years have been flaking and moldering away in dingy neglect; and collectors are speculating on living artists as though they were growth stocks on Wall Street.

Yet it is surprising how little the average person knows about this newly prized commodity, American painting. Abroad we talk of many things—our riches, our natural resources, our comforts, the size of our country and our cities. But we rarely talk about our art. We know too little to be assertive. Yet here pride is justified. We have produced a school of painting which in the past hundred years has been second only to France; today it is challenging even that country for leadership.

Such an evaluation of American painting might be questioned in Europe, and for a simple reason. Some of our greatest artists spent large parts of their lives abroad, and today West, Copley, Stuart, Whistler, and Sargent, for example, are labeled in European museums as "British School," and Mary Cassatt is labeled "French School." This is, in a way, a compliment to their ability, an affirmation of their stature in relation to their European contemporaries. But suppose Nicolas Poussin and Claude Lorrain, who spent just as much of their lives in Italy, were called Italian? What a poor impression one would have of French painting in the seventeenth century. For Europe to arrogate to itself six of our masters cannot but diminish the reputation of the American School. These painters are the displaced persons of the history of art. We need books like this to repatriate our lost artists, to revalidate their citizenship.

But are they really American? Mr. Eliot's answer, well documented in this book, is yes. West in London surrounded himself with his compatriots and helped every American painter who came abroad; Copley longed to return to Boston, and Stuart did come back to paint his greatest pictures in this country. The expatriates of a later age, Mary Cassatt and Sargent, always considered themselves American, just as did the writers Henry James and Edith Wharton. The sole exception is Whistler, and even he did not consider his art British. "There is no such thing as English Art," he once wrote. "You might as well talk of English Mathematics. Art is Art, and Mathematics is Mathematics." Whistler's very rejection of nationalism is in a sense American. We have produced the most complete cosmopolites in the world.

THESE six artists are, without doubt, among the greatest painters we have produced. But actually, we have more to learn from the artists who stayed at home. Their landscapes, which interpret a scenery of infinite variety, are unique. Confronted by a pristine world, a vast unspoiled wilderness, these artists, whether itinerant primitives, or painters of the Hudson River School, or Western pioneers, recorded the beauty of primeval nature with tenderness and love. They saw a paradise that could not last; and as industrialism transformed the countryside, their ardent feelings gave way in later generations to the acrid comments of the social realists and the private intuitions of the abstract expressionists. All these artists who stayed at home and showed the changing character of our country train our eyes to see new beauties in the American scene and make us feel its strange enchantment, whether evoked by virgin forests and endless plains, or by grain elevators, assembly lines, and flashing billboards.

The men and women who created our institutions and safeguarded our freedom also live in the pages of this book. For a part of the originality of American art is due to the fact that portrait painters in this country, regardless of fashionable styles abroad, have rarely been deflected from realism. We have produced the most significant school of bourgeois portraiture since the Dutch artists of the seventeenth century. Like the Dutch, too, our painters mirrored local sports and customs. This has given American painting a documentary significance that irradiates our history. We can often learn more about our past from one canvas than from volumes of printed words.

TODAY as never before, eye and mind have been conditioned to understand pictures. Ours is an age in which the visual image has assumed a new importance as a means of communication. The painter rather than the poet is gaining recognition as the prophet of our time.

When such reservoirs of enjoyment and enlightenment exist in the visual arts, it seems strange that the average person knows less about American painting than about American literature. The explanation is, at least in part, a surprising gap in publications on art. Until a few years ago, though there were myriad books illustrating every aspect of European, Near Eastern, and Far Eastern art, there was no book with adequate reproductions, even in black and white, of our American masterpieces. And until the present volume, there has never been a work reproducing in color the greatest American pictures.

On the other hand, there has been no dearth of writing about American painting. Many of the publications have been scholarly, but very few have been both scholarly and readable, two virtues combined most skillfully in this book. One of its charms is that, whenever possible, the painters are permitted to speak for themselves. The author must have carried out immense research in forgotten memoirs and dusty reviews to catch so many illuminating remarks. And when in the pages of his book the artists speak, how witty and amusing they are. One is reminded that humor is perhaps more characteristic of American painting than of any other school.

Mr. Eliot has also uncovered many anecdotes as fascinating as they are revealing. In this respect his book reminds one of Vasari's *Lives*. Both authors have the knack of making painters live as human beings; and in reading Mr. Eliot's text one realizes that though artists may paint abstract pictures, they are never themselves abstractions.

It is a wonderful panorama that stretches before our eyes. At the beginning are the earliest pictures which can be claimed to be American, and at the end are canvases almost too new to be varnished. The great leaders of American painting are here, but so are the lesser artists, the anonymous primitives, the specialists in genre, the painters of cowboys and the West. And these minor performers are also important. For often they produced the most idiomatic, the most original work of all. Perhaps because in this country the guilds, the academies, the salons were nonexistent or had little authority, there was greater possibility than elsewhere for the artist's eye to retain its freshness of vision and for the artist's personality to develop its own creative idiosyncrasies. American painting has been marked only occasionally by genius, but it has always shown an extraordinary array of richly varied talents.

HOW does our achievement compare to that of a great creative period like the Renaissance? Mr. Berenson's definitive work, *The Italian Painters of the Renaissance*, deals with 158 artists who lived during three centuries. Mr. Eliot's book, covering roughly the same span of time, takes up 147. Thus the number of artists involved is remarkably similar. But there is a great difference in the character of achievement. The Italian Renaissance might be likened to a landscape marked by towering peaks and whole mountain ranges of lofty genius. By comparison, the American artistic scene suggests a gently rolling countryside with meadows and low hills. But both have features of great beauty for all who have acquired a discerning eye.

When this discernment, this connoisseurship, has developed more widely, the painter in this country will gain dignity and stature. His career will be recognized as a serious profession, as has always been the case with artists abroad; and the last traces of his loneliness in the community will vanish. During the Depression the isolation of the artist in America did diminish. The Works Progress Administration and the Treasury Department projects put artists to work in communities throughout the country. Painting murals in courthouses and post offices or recording local arts and crafts, these artists were often the center of controversy, were sometimes admired, sometimes disliked; but everywhere they began to be accepted as a part of American life. With the second World War this program of the Federal Government was abandoned, and it has never been revived. However, industry has tried its hand at patronage of art; and though the marriage of painter and manufacturer has not always been happy, acrimonious divorces have been few. Even more important in bringing about a new respect for the American artist are the articles and reproductions appearing in magazines that reach millions of readers. They have shown that art is not esoteric, not incomprehensible. Consequently, art has begun to play a more vital role in the lives of Americans.

But art could also play a more vital role in our relations with others. The paintings reproduced in this book speak a universal language. They tell objectively and without propaganda the story of this country. They are ambassadors of the American way of life. Widely known, they would help us to gain throughout the world that esteem and sympathy to which all nations aspire.

JOHN WALKER

The National Gallery
Washington, D.C.

PART ONE

M. M. SANFORD'S "WASHINGTON AT PRINCETON" (BEFORE 1850)

THE MAKING OF THE DREAM

*Out of the flesh, out of the minds and hearts
Of thousand upon thousand common men,
Cranks, martyrs, starry-eyed enthusiasts,
Slow-spoken neighbors, hard to push around,
Women whose hands were gentle with their kids
And men with a cold passion for mere justice.
We made this thing, this dream.*

—STEPHEN VINCENT BENET

1

THE AMERICAN VISION

I must soon quit the Scene, but you may live to see our Country flourish, as it will amazingly and rapidly after the War is over. Like a Field of Young Indian Corn, which long Fair weather and Sunshine had enfeebl'd and discolour'd, and which in that weak State, by a Thunder Gust of violent Wind, Hail and Rain seem'd to be threaten'd with absolute Destruction; yet the Storm being once past, it recovers fresh Verdure, shoots up with double Vigour, and delights the Eye not of its Owner only, but of every observing Traveller.

—BENJAMIN FRANKLIN to GEORGE WASHINGTON
March 5, 1780

EVEN Benjamin Franklin would have reason to be astonished by the "double Vigour" of America's growth. At birth, her chief assets were a few wise men in wigs, a few thousand brave men with muskets, a foothold on a savage continent, and an immortal set of ideals. Those ideals remain the constant expression of the American spirit. But everything else about the country has changed mightily, and American painting has grown with the rest, extending the horizons of a flourishing, tumultuous national life. In a continuing harvest of the country's endeavors, it keeps recovering fresh verdure to delight the eye "of every observing Traveller."

The great unifying quality of American painting, and the ultimate source of its strength, has always been its devotion to America and Americans. Unlike such great schools of painting as the Italian Renaissance or the modern School of Paris, which are primarily intellectual and conceived within studio walls, American painting turns outward to embrace the nation. The great American masters—from John Singleton

Copley to Edward Hopper—project an enduring American vision. Their work ranks with that of their contemporaries anywhere. Scores of painters of lesser stature have broadened the native theme, as Frederic Remington did with the now vanished world of the Wild West and John Sloan with turn-of-the-century Greenwich Village. As individuals, American painters from the beginning have rendered an extraordinarily faithful account of their people and their land. Taken as a whole, American painting has produced a rich and fruitful contribution not only to the nation but to the world.

A NATION, like a man, has its several ages, and the painters of each era reflect a different spirit. In the eighteenth century, which gave birth to the nation, America was Protestant, rationalistic, pragmatic, and forward-looking. And so were her artists. The European tradition of painting, which Americans might have been expected to imitate, had two great themes: the Gospels and classical mythology. But America's

2

artists, true children of the new age, rejected both to form the world's most enthusiastically secular school of painting. They aspired to be not mere craftsmen but whole men, and many of them played heroic roles outside their studios. Charles Willson Peale was one who especially embodied the spirit of eighteenth-century America. A saddle maker, he fought in the Revolution and afterwards thrice blessed the New World: with mechanical inventions, a great museum of art and natural history, and splendid pictures.

THE romantic spirit of the nineteenth century, which found its most intense expression in the opening of the West, also inspired artists to participate in great events. John James Audubon, that hawk-eyed traveler of the wilderness, magnificently reflected the new temper. So did the comparatively obscure George Catlin, who wandered the Great Plains all alone on a horse named Charley to record the redskins' vanishing paradise. In Europe, the interests of art and those of science steadily diverged, rending the old culture. Men such as Audubon and Catlin—following their forerunners' reverence for facts—practiced art and science together. They were typically nineteenth-century American romantics in their individualism, their turbulence, and their determination to shape high adventure into fine art.

IN the twentieth century, American art has reached a sort of delta. Its leaders follow a dozen different channels, and each claims his own channel as the main one. The spirit of the age is one of experiment and search. Yet search where they will, American artists as a group still carry with them a native romanticism dating back a century or more, and a consuming interest in the here and now that dates all the way back to the nation's beginnings.

More than ever before, American painters have joined forces with those of Europe, benefiting both. American painting has been vastly enriched by contributions from the Old World. On the other hand, Arthur Dove was painting abstractions on a Connecticut farm before the first abstract canvas was done in Europe by Wassily Kandinsky; Mark Tobey has opened a Northwest Passage between European art and that of the Orient, and the citadel of abstract expressionism is in Manhattan.

IF painting techniques are international almost by definition, subject matter is not. American painting remains unmistakably American, and no other nation's painters have so consciously drawn their inspiration from their native land. Thomas Cole, the founder of the Hudson River School, urged his followers to wed themselves to the American landscape. Thomas Eakins said that to create art worthy of the nation, artists should "peer deeper into the heart of American life." Edward Hopper maintains that a country's art "is greatest when it most reflects the character of its own people."

Such admonitions could be reversed for laymen to show that American painting affords an unexcelled insight into the nation's life, past and present. Vigorous, varied, and spacious as the continent itself, it opens a thousand windows on the American heritage and home.

"MARGARET GIBBS" (1670), ANONYMOUS

CHAPTER I

THE PIONEERS

The land was ours before we were the land's.

—ROBERT FROST

AMERICANS' regard for their pioneers feeds largely on word and spirit. But to reinforce facts in print and feelings in the heart, there is ample testimony by eyewitnesses—the painters who were there. In most cases the documentary value of their work outweighs its aesthetic merit. But whether viewed as art or as history, the colonial canvases that have come down to posterity make a fascinating display.

The first American painters were commercial artists who provided picture signs for stores and taverns, turning the cobbled streets into outdoor picture galleries. They thought of themselves not as artists but as artisans and their paints and brushes as simply the tools of their trade. When their regular business slacked off, they would turn to more prosaic jobs, painting whatever offered from a house to a fire bucket. Occasionally, in that stern and frugal age, they would have the pleasure of a portrait commission.

The results, by European standards, were merely a provincial echo of the late Tudor court style. Being mostly commoners cut off from high life, the Puritans and their Dutch cousins in New Amsterdam had remained unaware of Renaissance art. Instead of trying to paint people in the round, they produced flat, stylized maps of their sitters. This technique of "limning" permitted likenesses of a sort, and an enduring flavor of the times, if little lifelikeness.

Margaret Gibbs, painted in 1670, is one of the earliest surviving Puritan portraits. Typically, seven-year-old Margaret meets the eye not like a real girl in a real world but like a dream of one. Her body looks no thicker than a dress on a clothes hanger. It casts a shadow, yet is itself almost evenly lit. The ringleted hair, silver necklace, lace, drawstrings, and bows are presented separately and distinctly, each with the same cataloguing care. The sweet and serious face lacks solidity; it would be hard to guess how Margaret looked from the side. Her shoes seem not to touch the floor. And though the floor is seen from above, Margaret herself stands at eye level.

But *Margaret Gibbs* is superb, as well as typical, limning at its height. The tessellated floor creates a little stage full of order and repose, and Margaret dominates it effortlessly. She neither looms out of the picture nor shrinks into it. She stands quiet and assured, with soft gestures and thinking eyes, gazing into the world of men.

Ann Pollard, painted in 1721, is less a dream than an apparition, balefully staring down the anonymous artist with her basilisk gaze. Shrewd as a colonial housewife, straight and unyielding as a Puritan divine, and old as the moon, she rises suspicious and eternal out of the night, holding her book like a scepter.

The ancient's haunting memorial was done following her hundredth birthday. One of the original settlers of Boston, she had borne twelve children, kept a tavern, and outlived all her generation. As a "romping girl" of ten, her story went, she was the first of Governor Winthrop's

"ANN POLLARD" (1721), ANONYMOUS

THOMAS SMITH'S SELF-PORTRAIT (CA. 1675)

party to land on the peninsula that became Boston. What had she found the Promised Land to be like? She remembered quite well. It was "very uneven, abounding in small hollows and swamps, covered with blueberries and other bushes."

INTO the calm, flat sea of the limners, Captain Thomas Smith sailed without warning. His self-portrait, done within a few years of the Gibbs canvas, and even earlier than *Ann Pollard*, has little in common with either. Smith thought in terms of shapes, not patterns. By spotlighting his own face, firmly defined with shadows in the foursquare composition, he created an illusion of reality beyond the limner's art.

Historians know almost nothing about Smith beyond the fact that he lived in Boston and Bermuda. But his picture makes plain that he had sailed the sea, that he had seen European and possibly Venetian pictures, that he had fought on water, and that he was a stern, thoughtful man, half in love with death. The poem under the pictured skull reads:

> *Why why should I the World be minding*
> *therein a World of Evils Finding*
>   *Then Farwell World: Farwell thy Jarres*
>   *thy Joies thy Toies thy Wiles thy Warrs*
> *Truth Sounds Retreat: I am not sorye.*
>   *The Eternall Drawes to him my heart*
>   *By Faith (which can thy Force Subvert)*
> *To Crowne me (after Grace) with Glory.*
>   *T.S.*

CAPTAIN Smith's amateur breakthrough was not followed up. It remained for an immigrant professional named John Smibert to put American painting on the path to its first sustained triumph. Smibert's portrait of chubby Joseph Wanton set a new standard for the New World. *Joseph Wanton* is character analysis in the grand manner. Painted about 1735, it shows a Royalist politician whose bland, irresolute features presaged an unheroic future. Wanton actually became Governor of Rhode Island, met the stirrings of the American Revolution with soft talk, and retired the moment the storm broke.

Smibert's own story was just the opposite: a rise from poverty to riches and from obscurity

JOHN SMIBERT'S "JOSEPH WANTON" (CA. 1735)

to honor. The son of an Edinburgh dyer, he was apprenticed to a house painter as a youth, and by odds that should have been the sum of his career. But Smibert's grit and talent got him down to London, where he painted gentlemen's coaches. From London he moved on to Italy, where he copied old masters. There he also made a friend of Bishop George Berkeley, who had written the famous lines:

Westward the course of empire takes its way;
The first four acts already past,
A fifth shall close the drama with the day—
Time's noblest offspring is the last.

Helped by the bishop to emigrate, Smibert set out for New England in 1729, when he was forty. One year later he held the first art exhibition ever recorded in America, and became the toast of Boston. Until Smibert's coming, explained a contemporary versifier:

No heav'nly pencil the free stroke could give,
Nor the warm canvas felt its colors live.
Solid and grave and plain the country stood,
Inelegant, and rigorously good.

Smibert's low birth mattered little in Boston. One patrician, in the tolerating tone of Back

ROBERT FEKE'S "THE REVEREND THOMAS HISCOX" (1745)

JOHN HESSELIUS' "PORTRAIT OF CHARLES CALVERT" (1761)

Bay, pronounced himself "favorably impressed by Mr. S., whose ingenuity is equalled by his industry and surpassed by his deportment." The painter married an heiress and settled down in one of Boston's finest houses—"in Queen Street, between the Town House and the Orange Tree." Besides supplying portraits of Boston's rising merchants, Smibert himself dabbled in trade. He imported engravings and casts of Renaissance works for sale, scattering the fragments of a great tradition in new soil.

AMONG the first painters to feel Smibert's influence, Robert Feke soon surpassed his master. Almost nothing is known of Feke personally, beyond the word picture provided by a Scottish tourist of the time. Feke had "exactly the phiz of a painter, having a long pale face, sharp nose, large eyes—with which he looked upon you steadfastly—long curled black hair, a delicate white hand, and long fingers."

Feke's climactic achievement was his portrait of the Reverend Thomas Hiscox. He painted the

9

JOHN GREENWOOD'S "SEA CAPTAINS

CAROUSING AT SURINAM" (1757–58)

preacher in 1745 with the utmost simplicity and force. Hiscox stands above the viewer as if in a pulpit. Though the minister's hair has a certain flowing grace, the rest of him looks like a bullfrog. The powerful throat seems to be preparing its organ tones; the wide, traplike mouth is about to open. The brilliantly modeled eyes focus with disdain upon someone in the back row—whether a sinner or a sneezer. Taken altogether, the portrait achieves a remarkable sense of immediacy. Instead of an observer regarding the canvas at his leisure, the portrait fixes on him.

THE Southern colonies had fewer painters than New England; rich planters preferred to go direct to England for their likenesses. But some fine examples of early Southern portraiture survive, among them *Charles Calvert*. The picture was painted in 1761 by a Maryland artist named John Hesselius, who later taught the great Charles Willson Peale. Hesselius' five-year-old subject, the great-great-great-grandson of Maryland's founder, stands like a general in full regalia ordering his troops to advance. But Calvert has the dreamy look of a boy who wonders how soon he can go out to play. His slave, kneeling with the drum, seems the better actor.

THE precise opposite of such formal make-believe is *Sea Captains Carousing at Surinam* (1757-58). The canvas calls to mind Cotton Mather's stricture on the salty life: "It is a matter of saddest complaint that there should be no more serious piety in the seafaring tribe."

Painted by John Greenwood, a footloose Boston artist, *Sea Captains* shows the soft underbelly of Puritanism. Surinam, or Dutch Guiana, was a stopping place on the Yankee merchant circuit. Greenwood spent some years there, and evidently liked to splice the main brace when ships from home dropped anchor. He put himself in his picture, rushing, candle in hand, for the door. Among the other portraits is that of Captain Nicholas Cooke, smoking a pipe and talking with Captain Esek Hopkins at the table. The evident ability of these two men to hold their grog was crowned by success in the hard cold-sober world; Cooke became Governor of Rhode Island, and Hopkins commander of the Continental navy. Another Hopkins, Stephen (who was to sign the Declaration of Independence), blesses the oblivious Mr. Jonas Wanton of Newport with rum. Captain Ambrose Page neatly vomits in Wanton's pocket. The time is 2:00 a.m., and things (including Page's pants) are warming up.

CHAPTER II

THE PRODIGIES

Genius is the power of lighting one's own fire.

—JOHN FOSTER

JOHN SINGLETON COPLEY'S
SELF-PORTRAIT MINIATURE (CA. 1760)

MRS. HENRY COPLEY GREENE

SUCH pioneer painters as Smith and Smibert, Feke, Hesselius, and Greenwood helped prepare the American soil for an astonishing spring flowering. The year 1738 saw the birth of two artists—John Singleton Copley in Massachusetts and Benjamin West in Pennsylvania—who were to delight not only America but Europe as well.

The incredible Mr. Copley abruptly became a Mr. at thirteen, when his stepfather died and left him head of the family. The stepfather, a mediocre mezzotint artist and dancing teacher named Peter Pelham, had introduced the boy to the rudiments of his art. Now, to help support his mother and half brother, Copley had to turn himself without delay into a skilled professional. The boy's response to the challenge was more than manly; it was heroic.

A solemn, plump, tightfisted, and deceptively timorous little fellow, Copley at once set up shop as a painter. He started out, sensibly enough, by copying the best art available. Pelham's mezzotints had given him a fuzzy, colorless notion of European painting, along with a stock repertory of poses and backgrounds. Copley had also seen the portraits of Smibert, and John Greenwood was a family friend. Within a decade Copley was painting better pictures than any American before him, and all but a handful since.

Copley's achievement owed at least as much to hard work as to genius. Upbraided once by a selectman for strolling on the Sabbath, his only known offense against propriety, Copley soberly explained that his weekdays were spent entirely in his studio and that, therefore, he had found it healthful to take a constitutional on the one day working was forbidden. He early reached the conclusion that his paintings were "almost always good in proportion to the time I give them, provided I have a subject that is picturesque." Among his most picturesque subjects was

13

COPLEY'S "PAUL REVERE" (CA. 1765)

a Boston merchant named Nicholas Boylston, whom Copley painted in 1767, dressed in a damask banian and cap of the sort gentlemen then wore at home. As the picture shows, the new-rich Yankees could be far from puritanical.

Copley did not appreciate until middle age the advantages of making preliminary drawings. He worked directly on canvas, feeling his way with infinite pains. A contemporary recorded that Copley had "painted a very beautiful head of my mother, who told me that she sat to him fifteen or sixteen times! Six hours at a time!! And that once she had been sitting to him for many hours, when he left the room for a few minutes, but requested that she would not move from her seat during his absence. She had the curiosity, however, to peep at the picture, and found it all rubbed out." The results were worth the labor. As John Adams wrote of Copley's portraits: "You can scarcely help discoursing with them, asking questions and receiving answers."

Paul Revere at his workbench is a case in point. Copley painted it in his twenties, when he had

already reached the peaks. As if to demonstrate his powers, he deliberately multiplied the technical difficulties, painting the close harmonies and color reflections in pleated linen, flesh, and polished silver, and making the teapot tilted in the hand an elaborate illusion of solidity. Yet the overall effect is sympathetic, not showy. Copley had figured out how to paint what he saw, and what he saw was not merely a subject for his brush but a real human being. The silversmith appears to be in the grip of some overriding idea, and looking at the picture is like dropping in on him without disturbing his reverie.

Copley broke precedent by painting Revere in shirtsleeves, Revere being an ardent egalitarian and Copley delighting in light on linen. They probably did not discuss politics during the long sittings. Copley stoutly believed that "political contests are neither pleasing to the artist nor advantageous to the art itself."

He soon became a wealthy man, with three houses and twenty acres on Beacon Hill and a Tory heiress to wife. His humble beginnings and

14

high achievements gave him friends on both sides of the political fence, and he made a brave try at mediating between them before the Boston Tea Party. But he was almost mobbed for his pains. His thoughts turned to the home country he had never seen and the greater honors to be gained abroad. Benjamin West, already an expatriate, kept writing, urging him to come. At thirty-five, on the eve of the Revolution, Copley set sail.

Not half his life had yet run, and most of his worldly triumphs lay ahead; but Copley's chief work was done. He left behind him in America a magnificent portrait gallery that would last as long as paint holds to canvas.

Scholars have long debated whether to place *Mrs. Seymour Fort* toward the end of Copley's American period or the beginning of his English one. Today most believe the latter, although the picture equals the keenest of Copley's American portraits. The epitome of wise, firm, and kindly grandmothers, Mrs. Fort looks a little amused to find herself in such a pretentious setting. Meanwhile, she has her tatting to do—with swollen hands that seem to have once known dishwater.

Brook Watson and the Shark was commissioned by Watson himself, a London businessman who was to become Lord Mayor, to commemorate a leg lost in Havana harbor. Copley used newly acquired techniques in putting together the picture; he began with studies of single figures and then combined their movements as elaborately as a choreographer. The canvas is monumental

COPLEY'S "NICHOLAS BOYLSTON" (CA. 1767)

COPLEY'S "MRS. SEYMOUR FORT" (CA. 1785)

in composition, dramatic in detail. A man overboard confronts the jaws of death. No softening atmosphere veils the facts; there are no historical or literary connotations to lift them to an abstract plane. For sheer pity and terror the picture stands alone in its age. The American Copley had invented romantic horror-painting, though he never followed up his invention. That remained for the Frenchman Jean Louis André Théodore Géricault, whose *Raft of the Medusa* was to come forty years afterwards.

Soon after he arrived in England a complacent Copley had written a letter home to his half brother: "Could anything be more fortunate than the time of my leaving Boston? Poor America. I hope for the best, but I fear the worst. Yet certain I am she will finally emerge from her present calamity and become a mighty empire. And it is a pleasing reflection that I shall stand amongst the first of the artists that shall have led the country to the knowledge and cultivation of the fine arts, [which] will one day shine with a luster not inferior to what they have done in Greece and Rome."

The day King George III admitted in Parliament that the United States of America was now indeed a nation, Copley proudly painted an American flag into one of his pictures. He sold his Beacon Hill estate by mail for five times what he had paid for it, and felt he had the best of both worlds. Then all at once the rosy glow turned to red rage: he learned that Boston's Statehouse was

COPLEY'S "BROOK WATSON AND THE SHARK" (1778)

BENJAMIN WEST'S "PENN'S TREATY WITH THE INDIANS" (1771)

18

to rise next door to what had been his property. Clearly he should have made not a fivefold but a hundredfold profit.

Slowly the painting of Copley's London peers (Romney, Gainsborough, Reynolds, West) corrupted his own homespun realism. To compete in such fast and fashionable company, the old dog learned a pathetic array of new tricks. He kept on painting industriously until death came, at seventy-seven, to even all his accounts. But long before that time Copley's ice-clear eye had veiled, his granite-firm hand had learned to practice soft flamboyance, and all his genius slipped away.

LIKE Sunday's child in the old nursery rhyme, Benjamin West was full of grace. His long life unfolded like a triumphal procession—stately, sunny, splendid, and altogether complacent. Destined for smaller achievements than Copley, he had far greater worldly fame. While Copley sweated to forge his talents, Benjamin West found the skills he needed waiting for his command.

Little Ben grew up in surroundings that were at once pastoral and strictly virtuous. The tenth child of an innkeeper, he was born in a Quaker community west of Philadelphia. Friendly Indians still roamed the region and, according to West, it was they who introduced him to painting, showing him how to mix the red and yellow earths with which they painted their faces. His mother, who, like everyone else, seems to have considered West a genius from birth, provided indigo from her dye vat. The cat unwillingly supplied some hairs for a brush, and West's career was launched. He was then about seven.

West's first models were the few engravings of European pictures and the even fewer and poorer portraits to be seen locally. He absorbed their lessons as easily as breathing. By the time he was thirteen, West had executed a fistful of portrait commissions passably well. At seventeen he was invited to attend Benjamin Franklin's College of Philadelphia as an honorary student. The college being apparently the world's most indulgent, West did not even learn to spell. Instead, he filled his mind with poetry and moral tales, and his creel with fish from the Schuylkill River.

He was handsome, serene, and charming, completely at his ease in the most prosperous and powerful circles of Philadelphia society. In fact his wealthy friends financed his education in Italy. At twenty-one West entered Rome. Welcoming the visitor as a curiosity, the Roman elite leaped to show him their treasures. Confronted with the famed *Apollo Belvedere*, he cried out (with that mingling of reverence and gamesmanship which best became him): "My God, how like a Mohawk warrior!"

West spent three years of study in Italy, mostly under an eclectic named Raphael Mengs, who put him to copying the Renaissance masters. The Quaker in West deplored the Italian emphasis on sensuous delights. Art's purpose, he maintained, was not to please the eye but to elevate the mind. He resolved to subdue the flesh in his own pictures, to be a visual sermonizer. Because this notion reflected the increasingly neoclassic temper of the time, West's new efforts were assessed at his own lofty valuation. At twenty-four he carried his mission to London.

London, like Rome, melted before West's cool blaze. King George III, himself a stuffy young fellow, called West "my friend"—and meant it. West led in the founding of the Royal Academy, and was elected its second president. "To do honor to the office," he announced in his acceptance speech, "I shall presume in the future to wear my hat in this assembly." Johnson's Boswell dedicated a hats-off piece of doggerel to "Our own rare Ben."

West's unfailing good fortune was hardly a true measure of his merits as a painter. But *Penn's Treaty with the Indians*, done when West was thirty-five, does bear out his belief that "the art of painting has powers to dignify man by transmitting to posterity his noble actions." In costuming the participants, West went counter to the neoclassic fashion, which demanded that Roman togas be worn in historical pictures regardless of their time or place. Yet his composition is spacious and serene in the classic manner, and his figures are drawn with classic poise. Paunchy, peaceful Penn dominates without seeming to do so, his hands spread wide in a gesture of giving and taking combined.

Colonel Guy Johnson was one of West's few important portraits. "I am not friendly," he used to say, "to the indiscriminate waste of genius in portrait painting." Apparently West considered Johnson too dramatic a figure to pass up. Johnson was a British colonel assigned to American Indian affairs. His Indian friend was one Joseph Brant, a Mohawk chieftain on a visit to London. Guerrilla fighters both, they were soon to cooperate in harrying the rural Revolutionists of New York and Pennsylvania. With fine instinct for the future, West wrapped them in an atmosphere of gloom, and highlighted the qualities of alertness and calm essential to their bloody business.

As the decades passed, West came to be a proud institution. Fawned upon by thronging visitors, he plied the brush daily in the studio of his grand London mansion. "His liberal mind," an uncritical critic noted, "did not even prohibit the study or practice of his liberal profession on the day set apart for the cessation of labor. To study or exercise his high calling was no labor to him. It was the pleasant exertion of powers given by his Creator to lift his fellow creatures from the pits and quagmires of ignorance."

While West indulged in this "pleasant exertion," his wife would be reading in another part of the house. After forty years of married life, she remarked that she had never seen her husband intoxicated or in a passion.

Greatness, of course, cannot exist without passion, however controlled. Nor without struggle, however hidden. The truth is that West avoided both. Most of his later art, including acres of Biblical scenes commissioned by George III, is pretentious stuff. Few of his contemporaries recognized the fact, though Lord Byron, prophet of a new freedom in the arts, could not fail to see it. He wrote of

> . . . *the dotard West,*
> *Europe's worst daub, poor England's best.*

Fortunately for West's peace of mind—something that becomes increasingly precious with advancing years—he himself remained convinced that he possessed the genius with which the world always credited him. When death at last came, bowing and scraping to summon him home, the king's friend went peacefully and without regret. At eighty-one he felt sure his reputation would live forever.

Soon afterwards, a hotly romantic generation was laughing openly at West's all-too-cool canvases. But there were many who still revered him for kindnesses received. London's most honored artist had also been her most openhearted. He found kind words for everyone, even poor crazy William Blake and those two upstart landscapists Turner and Constable.

More important in the context of American art history, West built a bridge between American and European painting. He filled his house with American pupils, and his pupils with inspiration. In fact, West's generosity of spirit must have overcome his smugness to make him a great teacher, for the next era of American art belonged largely to painters who made the pilgrimage to West's door, seeking help and advice.

WEST'S "COLONEL GUY JOHNSON" (CA. 1775)

CHAPTER III

PEALE AND SONS

The world is my country, all mankind are my brethren, and to do good is my religion.

—THOMAS PAINE

ONE of West's first American students would have been immortal even without the master's aid. Only three years younger than Copley and West, Charles Willson Peale was a slower starter, a less appreciated painter, and a far bigger man. If Benjamin Franklin was the father of American humanism, Jefferson its hero and Tom Paine its voice, Peale was its artist. He had the strength of ten, for his heart was pure and his enthusiasm boundless. A birdlike fellow with wide blue eyes and a long, thin beak, he took to life like a lark to the dawn sky.

Like so many great men of his day, Peale started without any advantages of class or education. His seamstress mother apprenticed him to an Annapolis saddle maker at the age of twelve; eight years later he opened his own saddle shop. Peale soon branched out into watch repairing, silversmithing, and painting, and he boasted that he would rather "practice the use of my tools than ride in a coach drawn by six horses." He traded a saddle to John Hesselius for some lessons in portraiture, and then practiced the art with such flair that he won the backing of a group of Maryland businessmen. When he was twenty-five they sent him to London to study with the already famous West.

During his saddle-making period Peale had brooded much on freedom. Now the Revolution was brewing in his heart. He solemnly refused to tip his hat when King George rode by. Back home in Annapolis after two years, he soon had a reputation for making exact likenesses that brought all the portrait work he could handle. Among his sitters was Colonel George Washington of Mount Vernon, whom Peale was to paint seven times from life. He noted that Washington had "a pig eye" (small and grey) and features flushed with port, but the figure of Apollo.

Peale experimented with making gunpowder and painted the designs of flags for the military companies that were starting to form. Moving to Philadelphia in 1776 he himself joined one, and was elected first lieutenant. Peale rode out of town at the head of eighty-one men. He was wearing a brown uniform and black tricornered hat, and carrying a sword, a musket with telescopic sights of his own invention, a quarter cask of rum, and his painting kit.

Crossing the Delaware, he saw battle at Trenton. Later, standing up to a hot British volley near Princeton, he noted with alarm the "balls which whistled their thousand different notes around our heads and, what is very astonishing, did very little or no harm." After returning the fire three times Peale's men watched the enemy, formed by the college, turn in flight. Jubilantly, he wrote in his diary: "We huzared Victory."

Peale mothered his men through many a long march. Once, when his company deserted him

CHARLES WILLSON PEALE'S
"WASHINGTON, LAFAYETTE, AND AIDE-DE-CAMP TENCH TILGHMAN AT YORKTOWN" (1784)

C. W. PEALE'S "JAMES MADISON" (CA. 1792)

to rob an orchard by the road, Peale had the presence of mind to call after them an order to fall out. He foraged and cooked for his troops, and made fur-lined moccasins to replace their worn-out boots. At Valley Forge he occupied himself with painting miniature portraits, done on ivory, for the soldiers to send back home as mementos. Using bed ticking for canvas, he also portrayed Washington, Lafayette, Nathanael Greene, and dozens of other leaders.

When the tide of war turned in the patriots' favor, Peale returned to Philadelphia to plunge into politics. A fiery Whig, he soon alienated the city's conservative merchants who had bought his paintings. In tones of astonishment Peale apologized for any hard feelings he might have caused, and announced his complete retirement from public life. Then, suffering all the symptoms of a nervous breakdown, he holed up in his house. But the day Colonel Tench Tilghman galloped into town with the news of Cornwallis' surrender, the painter immediately recovered. Peale turned his house into an illuminated victory display, filling windows with oil paintings on paper lit from behind by candles. Portraits of Washington and Rochambeau bore the legend SHINE, VALIANT CHIEFS, and the third-story

windows spelled out the triumphant message: FOR OUR ALLIES HUZZA! HUZZA! HUZZA!

Soon afterwards Peale painted *Washington at Yorktown* for the Maryland Assembly. The portrait is perhaps the most convincing picture now extant of Washington in his prime—a persevering man whose iron will has at last won all. Behind Washington stands Lafayette, who was also a particular friend of Peale's. Hard-riding Colonel Tilghman, the Marylanders' hero, holds the articles of surrender. "To tell the story at first sight," Peale painted the French and American battle flags in the middle ground, flanking two downcast Britons with colors cased.

Despite the glorious issue of the Revolution, Peale had come to loathe war utterly. He was perhaps the first American pacifist to take his position on rationalist rather than on religious grounds. All human violence, Peale argued, is wasteful, cruel, and stupid. He opposed corporal punishment and despised the growing vogue for dueling. Any duelist, he said, "stinks . . . as much while living as he would in four days after being shot."

Peale had built a gallery to house his portraits of thirty-odd Revolutionary heroes, and invited the public in free. Now he needed a lot of money

24

C. W. PEALE'S "JOHN PAUL JONES" (CA. 1781)

C. W. PEALE'S
"ALEXANDER HAMILTON" (CA. 1791)

C. W. PEALE'S
"JOHN ADAMS" (CA. 1791)

C. W. PEALE'S
"EXHUMING THE FIRST AMERICAN MASTODON" (1806–08)

fast, for he had married young and his family was growing prodigiously. (In all, he was to sire seventeen by his first two wives.) Having lost his rich patrons during his brief political life, he turned to the populace for support. His idea was to find a new museum attraction for which he could charge admission.

He found natural history, and an altogether original way of presenting it. Peale conceived of stuffing animals for his museum and placing each one in a still-life setting backed by a picture of its natural environment. A full century ahead of time in his idea, he made it work by sheer force of effort. Tigers, bats, cranes, and poisonous snakes were delivered alive to his door. Killing and stuffing each one, with the help of his family, he slowly built up a display of more than 100,000 items. This, he boasted with some justice, was "the world in miniature"—a new system of visual education.

Peale's distinguished friends shared his enthusiasm. Benjamin Franklin sent the corpse of his Angora cat as a contribution, and Washington forwarded pheasants that Lafayette had sent to him from France. Jefferson and Hamilton, whose portraits Peale included in the art section of the museum, served as directors. But even with all this backing Peale failed in one of his ambitions,

which was to mount likely specimens of "the human animal" for display. He had to make do with a few redskin scalps and skeletons, plus waxwork dummies of humankind.

In 1801 Peale paid a New York State farmer $300, a rifle, and a couple of dresses for an odd heap of bones and permission to dig for more. Forming the first scientific expedition in American history, he invaded the farm to search out and piece together the first mastodon skeleton ever assembled. (Peale called it a mammoth.) With this as the centerpiece of his museum, he soon became rich and even more famous.

Success sobered him. Peale gave up the gold lace he had once affected, and ate sparingly. Tinkering became his chief diversion. Peale had pleased Philadelphia by building a triumphal arch equipped with a drop-on laurel wreath in honor of Washington's inauguration. Just as the general rode beneath, Peale's daughter Angelica pulled a concealed string to score a dead ringer on his wig. But now Peale proceeded to more practical contraptions. He invented a smokeless stove, set elks' teeth in lead to make new dentures for Washington, repaired the hookah that Jefferson smoked when conferring with Indian chiefs. With it all he kept painting and building up his portrait gallery of famous contemporaries, which included *John Adams, James Madison, John Paul Jones,* and half a hundred more.

"Mediocrity," he wrote, "is scarcely admissible in the art of painting. It must be perfect in the representation or it is of no value. But if it can be executed so well as to render it a perfect illusion, there is no price too high can well be set on such a picture." In testing this theory that the true business of painting is to fool the eye, Peale achieved his most charming canvas, the so-called *Staircase Group.* He fitted the picture, portraying two of his sons, into a false doorway at his museum, and equipped it with a projecting bottom step. Washington was said to have nodded politely to the pictured boys as he passed.

FOR all Peale's roving interests, his heart lay most at home. The whole family strenuously pursued a hundred varied projects, from painting and taxidermy to music and horticulture. Not too surprisingly, all six of the Peale boys who survived to full maturity had unusual careers. But only two, hopefully named Rembrandt and Raphaelle, became artists.

Like his father, Rembrandt Peale was a water drinker, and like his father he crossed the sea to study with Benjamin West. If Rembrandt lacked his father's joyful and continuously creative spirit, this only made him easier for the public to understand. The painter of *Thomas Jefferson* was a more popular artist in his own day than Charles Willson ever was.

Raphaelle Peale's character and career were very different from Rembrandt's. He happened to marry the wrong girl, which is a black misfortune for any man, and one generally fatal to drunkards and artists. Being both, Raphaelle suffered bitterly under pretty Patty McGlathery's shrewish tongue, and died, at fifty-one, a broken sot. The boys in the back room mourned Raphaelle's talent for ventriloquism—he had a way of causing a roast to weep and plead at the approach of knife and fork—but few men mourned the loss of his painting skill. Though he was a better fool-the-eye artist than even his father, Raphaelle earned so little by his brush that Patty was forced to keep a boarding house.

Meanwhile, Raphaelle used his art to tease and amuse. One day Patty found on his easel

COURTESY OF THE PHILADELPHIA MUSEUM OF ART, GEORGE W. ELKINS COLLECTION

C. W. PEALE'S
"STAIRCASE GROUP" (CA. 1795)

REMBRANDT PEALE'S
"THOMAS JEFFERSON" (1805)

RAPHAELLE PEALE'S "STILL LIFE WITH CAKE" (1822)

what looked to be a painting of a nude covered over with one of her best napkins. Angrily she snatched at the cloth. Her fingers met nothing but painted canvas. While Patty gaped and blushed in confusion, the company guffawed. *After the Bath* had served its purpose. A hopeless, henpecked boozer, two years from the grave, had painted one of the finest still lifes in history as a practical joke.

OLD Charles Willson Peale had retired to a country estate that compared favorably with Thomas Jefferson's. There he was engaged in experimental farming, and inventing such useful adjuncts to country life as an apple-parer, a corn-planter, and a fly-shooer. Peale had lost his third wife after she insisted on seeing a doctor about her yellow fever. He had shaken off the same illness by himself. Now, at eighty-six, he felt in his prime, and hoped that by staying away from doctors he could extend his own life twenty years or so. Looking to the future as always, he went courting a fourth bride, and undertook it so strenuously that he died during his courtship.

Peale's last words were to one of his daughters: "Sybilla, feel my pulse." When she told him she could feel none, he murmured with characteristic objectivity: "I thought not."

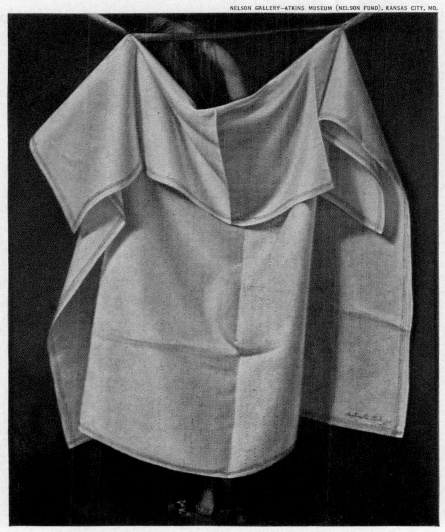

RAPHAELLE PEALE'S "AFTER THE BATH" (1823)

RALPH EARL'S "ROGER SHERMAN" (CA. 1775)

CHAPTER IV

HEIRS TO GLORY

The storm through which we have passed has been tremendous indeed. The tough sides of our Argosy have been thoroughly tried. Her strength has stood the waves into which she was steered with a view to sink her. We shall put her on her republican tack, and she will now show by the beauty of her motion the skill of her builders.

—THOMAS JEFFERSON

PEALE had been in at the birth of America, and played his part with fire, grit, and glee. The next generation of painters were heirs to the glory that Peale had helped to create. The men who forged the young republic are seen largely through the eyes of Ralph Earl, John Trumbull, and Gilbert Stuart.

Ralph Earl, shiftless, sodden, and little more than a hack for much of his life, had already made his greatest contribution with one masterpiece painted at the start of the Revolution. His subject was Roger Sherman of New Haven, who had risen from shoemaking and farming through surveying and storekeeping to politics, publishing, and law. He was the only founding father to sign the four great documents of American independence: the Articles of Association, the Declaration of Independence, the Articles of Confederation, and the Constitution itself.

Truth of characterization is the prime requirement of portraiture—and the most difficult for posterity to appraise. Fortunately, Earl's painting of Sherman can be compared with the word portrait written by one Major William Pierce, a Georgia delegate to the Constitutional Convention. "Mr. Sherman," Pierce observed, "exhibits the oddest-shaped character I ever remember to have met with. He is awkward, unmeaning, and unaccountably strange in his manner. But in his train of thinking there is something regular, deep and comprehensive; yet the oddity of his address, the vulgarisms that accompany his public speaking . . . make everything that is connected with him grotesque and laughable; and yet he deserves infinite praise—no man has a better heart or a clearer head. If he cannot embellish he can furnish thoughts that are wise and useful. He is an able politician and extremely artful in accomplishing any particular object; it is remarked that he seldom fails."

Earl backed this solemn, hard-driving, and hard-thinking patriot into a corner, made him sit in a Windsor chair as unyielding as the man himself, and painted him in a light as searching as Sherman's own mental processes. The harshness of the lighting and the abrupt perspective create a photographic effect, as if Earl had aimed a camera straight at Sherman's wishbone and snapped before the man could open his taut lips to protest. The stubby artisan's hands seem to regret having nothing to do. The too-tight vest underlines the equally constricted features: the brow square-cut as a headstone; weary, wise, button eyes; plow nose, sickle mouth, and firm

31

JOHN TRUMBULL'S "CAPTURE OF THE HESSIANS AT TRENTON" (1784-94)

Gibraltar jaw. It is the granite face of conscience, immovable and unforgettable.

His own conscience Earl seems to have faced down with remarkable ease. During the early days of the Revolution he worked for the British. Deserting his wife and two children when the patriot cause began to prosper, he fled to England. Seven years there, partly under Benjamin West's tutelage, turned him from a powerful primitive painter into a prissy provincial one.

Earl deserted a second wife and more children to return to America. Making small headway in the big cities, he did the rounds of New England towns, portraying the local gentry while he sampled the local cider. Slowly his early directness of vision returned; his portraits improved year by year, though they never again reached the height of *Roger Sherman*. Dispensing with the stock backgrounds that he had learned to use in England—a rich curtain, a classic column—Earl painted the real habitats of his sitters. He posed

a draper with piled bolts of cloth, a country squire at a window overlooking his property. But Earl had a more consuming mission than painting, namely, drinking himself to death. In the neat, white, elm-shaded, one-tavern towns he frequented, this must have been a dismal business. He brought it off as quickly as possible, expiring in 1801 at the age of fifty.

IT was the needlework of John Trumbull's sisters that first attracted him to art. His father found this odd attraction inappropriate on two counts: first, the boy had lost the use of one eye in a childhood accident, and second, he was a gentleman. Picturemaking might be a fit diversion for young ladies and a profitable occupation for suitably skilled laborers. But for the handsome son of the Governor of Connecticut it was unthinkable. So John was packed off to Harvard for polishing. There, however, he called on John Copley, and soon began to paint and copy all the pictures he could. He was one of the first male aristocrats in America to take brush in hand.

At the outbreak of the Revolution, Trumbull put his predilection to use: the self-taught artist proved valuable as a maker of military maps. This talent, plus the influence of his father, who had early joined the rebel cause, helped him rise fast in the Continental ranks. He served for a year and a half, including a few weeks as Washington's aide-de-camp. Then, disappointed that the commission making him a full colonel at the age of twenty was postdated three months, he resigned in a pet. "A soldier's honor," Trumbull haughtily informed Congress, "forbids the idea of giving up the least pretension of rank."

Self-barred from the war, Trumbull dreamed of recording it for posterity. Setting off for London (where he was jailed for a time, in reprisal for the hanging of Major André), he made the usual pilgrimage to the studio of Benjamin West. The master took him in, taught him, and set free Trumbull's prodigious talent.

West urged him to paint small pictures which his one eye could compass; this led Trumbull to compress his heroic, sweeping compositions into canvases more concentrated and powerful than West's own. He also had a happy faculty for making miniature portraits, both from life and from memory. Returning to America after the Revolution, he traveled from New Hampshire to South Carolina portraying the VIPs of a Very Important Period and sketching the quiet battlefields. With this material he composed before the age of forty all his half-dozen important works.

The Capture of the Hessians at Trenton is characteristically grand. The picture contains sixteen portraits and can be read almost as a historical account, but it strikes the eye first as a lucky

TRUMBULL'S "DECLARATION OF INDEPENDENCE" (1786-94)

glimpse of a great moment. The drama eclipses the plot, and particulars are swept up in the general scene as in a whirlwind. Through the clouds of war, between its banners, and over its dead, the victorious Washington comes slowly riding, his hand held out in a generous gesture to the defeated enemy. Placed at center stage and silhouetted against a sword-bright opening in the clouds, he dominates, unifies, calms, and ennobles the stormy whole.

With his *Declaration of Independence* Trumbull achieved a still greater triumph. Here in a canvas only thirty inches wide are no fewer than forty-eight portrait figures, all grouped naturally and convincingly in a manner suited to the solemn occasion (among them, at the table before John Hancock, stand John Adams, Roger Sherman, Robert R. Livingston, Thomas Jefferson, and Benjamin Franklin). The observer is led into the room as if by the hand, and shown far more than he could have seen at any instant of the actual event. Trumbull's subject lacked action, but he managed to convey something of its suppressed excitement in the zigzag arrangement of heads and the winglike banners at the back.

Washington was lavish in his praise of Trumbull's art. Jefferson offered him a sinecure as private secretary to enable him to make more historical pictures. Trumbull refused the offer. Eventually he turned to business and the hack portraiture that was to support his final years. But he could well boast, in a letter to Jefferson, of "having borne personally a humble part in the great events which I was to describe."

LIKE Ralph Earl, Gilbert Stuart was a sinful fellow, and like John Trumbull a proud one. But Stuart's sins were mostly of a jovial sort, and he had plenty of cause to be proud.

Stuart was a big, sloppy man, bulging and gouty with excess. He had red-rimmed eyes of a disconcerting intensity, and a monstrous cherry nose into which he kept stuffing fistfuls of snuff from a snuffbox the size of a hat. When visitors dared to notice his addiction he would explain, in the most courtly accents, that it came from his having been born in a snuff mill.

It was true. Stuart's snuff-grinder father emigrated from Scotland to become the first man of his calling in New England. As improvident as the son was to be, he did badly. Little Gilbert grew up ragged and wild on the Newport, Rhode Island, docks. But when an itinerant Scottish painter named Cosmo Alexander came to town, Stuart begged instruction. He made himself so useful around the studio that Alexander decided to take the fourteen-year-old along as an apprentice. Together they roamed the colonies in search of commissions, and afterwards sailed to Edinburgh. There, when Stuart was just sixteen, his master died. Alone and penniless, Stuart shipped home before the mast, a sea baptism so brutal that he would never afterwards speak of it.

Stuart had learned just enough about portraiture to please the citizens of Newport. The local merchants bought his laborious likenesses with delight, and when the Revolution threatened he was presented with a boat ticket to England, out of harm's way. His pictures could not possibly meet the competition in London, so after a year of proudly avoiding West's studio he gave in to the inevitable and wrote to West: "Destitute of the means of acquiring knowledge, my hopes from home blasted, and incapable of returning thither, pitching headlong into misery, I have only this hope—I pray that it may not be too great—to live and learn without being a burden. Should Mr. West in his abundant kindness think of aught for me, I shall esteem it an obligation which shall bind me forever with gratitude."

West must have been startled to discover that the writer of such abject lines was a sly, vain, gay, clever popinjay—and a brilliant student as well. For the next five years Stuart served as West's chief apprentice, and those years with West were probably the most fateful of his whole life. There in a sober, professional atmosphere the youthful rustic from America blossomed into a superbly cosmopolitan painter.

A born portraitist, Stuart was learning not only from West but from the recurring triumphs of three elegant contemporaries, Reynolds, Romney, and Gainsborough. Indebted as he was to West, he knew the vacuity of West's grandiose compositions, and tartly maintained that "no one would paint history who could do a portrait." Unfashionable as Stuart's view then was, it had a great future. Dr. Samuel Johnson, that

GILBERT STUART'S "THE SKATER" (1782)

STUART'S "JOHN QUINCY ADAMS"
(FINISHED BY THOMAS SULLY IN 1830)

weighty layman, spoke for millions yet unborn when he said: "I'd rather see a portrait of a dog that I know than all the allegorical paintings . . . in the world."

Stuart's near-magic ability to seize a likeness was admired by all, but some whispered that he could not draw (he hardly ever tried it), and that while his heads were remarkable he could never paint a body "below the fifth button." To refute the second charge Stuart at twenty-seven exhibited his masterpiece, *The Skater*. The picture represents one William Grant skating in St. James's Park, with Westminster Abbey in the distance. Studio-posed, it was inspired by a day that the painter and his friend spent on the ice instead of working. Grant appears to be cutting a figure eight, which Stuart repeats throughout the composition. If the luminous, chill landscape —never Stuart's forte—carries small conviction, the figure is splendid. Seldom were manliness and grace more winningly joined.

This one canvas made Stuart's reputation and permitted him to set up shop as a portraitist very nearly on Gainsborough's level. He married a pretty girl of eighteen, leased a palatial house, and plunged happily into coffeehouse society. Like many a self-made gentleman before and since his time, Stuart had learned manners and fine pronunciation by aping the stage (the actor John Philip Kemble was his particular friend and model). When Dr. Johnson rudely inquired where the outlander had learned to speak so well, Stuart shot back: "I can tell you better where I did not learn it. It was not from your dictionary."

Success brought Stuart the opportunity to give full play to his weaknesses. Eating and drinking delighted him so that he spent more time at table than some men do sleeping. The question of getting home at night struck him as immaterial; he alternately bullied and ignored his rapidly expanding family. He was supremely careless about money, and habitually spent more than he made. This last weakness apparently drove Stuart from London. He left England without a word to his friends, owing £80 for snuff alone.

Stuart had no particular desire to return to America. He turned up first in Dublin, but debts soon drove him on. In 1793, when he was thirty-seven, the prodigal settled in New York. Until his

STUART'S "GEORGE WASHINGTON" (1796)

STUART'S "JAMES MONROE" (1817)

death thirty-five years later, he was to remain the foremost portraitist in the land. Yet, though he painted about a thousand portraits at good prices, Stuart died in debt. His family conveniently "forgot" where he was buried; it saved the cost of a headstone.

Within the narrow limits he set himself, Stuart was a master, and he knew it. He heaped insults on merchants who thought themselves too grand for mere artists. Painters who came for instruction were never disappointed, and among his pupils were John Neagle, Thomas Sully, John Vanderlyn, and Washington Allston.

He tried to teach his own method of painting, but it was too personal to be imparted successfully. Stuart proceeded on the principle that it is simplest to explore first the general nature of a phenomenon, and only afterwards inquire into its particular characteristics. He would begin with a vague blob of a head as seen in a dim, dark mirror. The image always had precisely the color of the sitter's flesh, and usually all the other colors in the picture would be keyed to

that. Flesh, Stuart enthusiastically explained, "is like no other substance under heaven. It has all the gaiety of a silk-mercer's shop without its gaudiness and gloss, and all the soberness of old mahogany without its sadness."

Chatting continually to keep his sitter looking lively, he would slowly round out the blob and begin to get the features in focus. Then a few bold highlights and shadows, laid on smartly with no fuss, brought the subject to actuality, as if the sitter suddenly popped up in the cloudy cube of space that Stuart conceived his canvases to be. A swift final glaze added the blush of life. By then it would be lunchtime, and Stuart would quit for the day.

Likely as not, he would never return to that canvas; he was notorious for leaving his portraits unfinished. In the case of *John Quincy Adams*, for example, Stuart was content to get the shrewd face down pat. Thomas Sully later supplied the body and background.

Dissatisfied customers regularly got the back of Stuart's hand. Once when a proud husband

38

complained that Stuart had failed to capture his wife's elusive beauty, the artist snapped back with typical vigor: "What damned business is this of a portrait painter? You bring him a potato and expect he will paint a peach!"

This uncompromising realism extended even to Stuart's portraits of Washington, which he intended as icons of a sort. When he first painted Washington, Stuart made a characteristically cheeky effort to get his man to relax. "Now, sir," he said as he took up his brush, "you must let me forget that you are General Washington and that I am Stuart the painter." After a moment's surprise, Washington's countenance cracked just sufficiently to emit the glacial reply: "Mr. Stuart need never feel the need of forgetting who he is or who General Washington is." The picture, naturally enough, is not one of Stuart's best.

On his second try, Stuart did better. Despite its absurdly regal background, the full-figure Washington looks every inch a human being. But Stuart could not agree with Charles Willson Peale's observation that Washington had the figure of an Apollo. He found the shoulders high and narrow, and the hands and feet rather large. Washington happened to be wearing particularly ill-fitting false teeth, so Stuart painted the mouth and jaw uncomfortably out of shape.

On his third and last try Stuart produced the vibrant bust that stares from every dollar bill today. Martha Washington had commissioned the picture, and Stuart needed an excuse to hold on to it so he could make copies for sale. Telling her the portrait was not ready, he left it unfinished, kept it all the rest of his life and copied it scores of times. The President's wife had to rest content with one of the copies.

The original portrait tallies well with Stuart's own description of Washington: "There were features in his face totally different from what I had observed in any other human being. The sockets of the eyes, for instance, were larger than what I ever met with before, and the upper part of the nose broader. All his features were indicative of the strongest passions; yet like Socrates his judgement and self-command made him appear a man of different cast in the eyes of the world."

Stuart, too, was a man of the strongest passions, but unlike Washington he had very little judgment and practically no self-command. The ultimate seriousness of Stuart's artistic contribution seems to have embarrassed him a bit. He kept a snuff grater behind a curtain in his studio, so that when visitors gushed over his "great" portraits he could play a wry little joke: "Draw the curtain and you will see a grater." Though Stuart's quips and cranks and wanton wiles must often have exasperated his contemporaries, they were not of the kind to disturb posterity. What remains, beyond the brilliant body of his work, is the picture of a narrow, self-willed, exuberant man of compelling genius.

CHAPTER V

THE INTELLECTUALS

Oh, that we could have ivy in America!

—Nathaniel Hawthorne

LIKE all man's greatest ideals, the ideal of equal human rights has always been wide open to misinterpretation. Some artists of the young republic thought that it could be extended to include their own talents, and they fancied themselves as the potential equals of the greatest painters in history. Where there's a will to rival Raphael, they assumed, there must be a way. Such painters as Washington Allston, John Vanderlyn, and Samuel F. B. Morse all overreached themselves in trying to join the immortals. Yet each had his moments of triumph, and for all their weaknesses they brought both European sophistication and their own high-mindedness to American painting.

By the general consent of his peers, Washington Allston was the nation's leading painter. It was something less than a conclusive honor, for American art stood at ebb tide in Allston's day. Possessing one of the finest intellects of his age, Allston saw what was needed to rescue American painting. Painters yet to be born when Allston died owed him a debt of gratitude, not so much for his art as for the example it set. The objective approach to painting, which produced such American giants as Copley and Stuart, was an eighteenth-century ideal. To the new generation of painters coming of age in the nineteenth it became a mere convention. So it was in 1800, when Allston graduated from Harvard. But the young Allston was alive to the romantic spirit of the coming era, and he set himself to painting

subjective pictures, scenes appearing in his inner eye. This was at least as important a discovery for American art as, say, the abstractionist revolution which was to explode a century later.

Allston had been promisingly dreamy from the start. "To go back as far as I can," he wrote, "I remember that I used to draw before I left Carolina, at six years of age . . . and still earlier, that my favorite amusement, much akin to it, was making little landscapes about the roots of an old tree in the country. . . . Another employment was converting the forked stalks of the wild ferns into little men and women, by winding about them different colored yarn."

By selling his share of an ancestral plantation in South Carolina, Allston raised enough money to live and learn for many years in Europe. He was instructed in oil glazing by the British portraitists, and then moved to the Continent, where he explored the magnificent store of treasures that Napoleon had amassed at the Louvre. "Titian, Tintoretto, and Paul Veronese absolutely enchanted me," Allston afterwards wrote of that experience, "for they took away all sense of subject. . . . It was the poetry of color which I felt; procreative in its nature, giving birth to a thousand things which the eye cannot see, and distinct from their cause."

Allston learned another great lesson when he crossed the Alps to Italy. It was simply that the ideas in man's mind can be bodied forth in art. Leonardo da Vinci, who stated this discovery

WASHINGTON ALLSTON'S "MOONLIT LANDSCAPE" (1819)

for the Renaissance, went on to say that the job is not so easily accomplished, since man's ideas can only be expressed in painting "by means of gestures and the movements of the limbs." This task was meat and drink, of course, to Leonardo and the Renaissance masters who followed him. But it was too much for Allston; he never learned to compose a group or draw the human figure adequately. His big pictures in the Renaissance mold were all failures. He could not bring himself to finish *Jason Returning to Demand His Father's Kingdom. The Dead Man Revived in the Tomb by Touching the Bones of the Prophet Elisha* exhausted him, and he never quite recovered from the nervous stomach that he developed in painting it. *Belshazzar's Feast*, which was to have been his masterpiece, became the bane and burden of his old age. Having been paid for it in advance, Allston could not in conscience put *Belshazzar* aside, but labored dutifully over the picture until his dying day. The result is a pretentious ruin, no more.

There is tragedy hidden in Allston's remark to a student: "A painter may be blessed with every gift of nature, but unless he has acquired the art of design he can never express himself. If you would not be tormented by a consciousness of having noble and beautiful conceptions to which you cannot give birth, you must give much of your time to drawing."

While Allston knew his own shortcomings better than anyone else, he had the comfort of a loyal circle of friends. When he settled in England, Wordsworth, Southey, and Washington Irving came to tea. Coleridge once wrote Allston (with the poet's eternal mingling of enthusiasm and tactlessness): "Had I not known the Wordsworths, [I] should have loved & esteemed you *first* and *most*, and as it is, next to them I love & honor you." Allston heartily returned the compliment. It was Coleridge, he noted in grateful recollection, "who taught me this golden rule: *never to judge of any work of art by its defects; a rule as wise as benevolent; and one that while it has spared me much pain, has widened my sphere of pleasure.*"

Allston returned to America in 1818, and he lived in and near Boston until his death in 1843. He met the springtime of transcendentalism in New England, and among his new friends were Emerson, Longfellow, Lowell, William Ellery Channing, and Samuel Atkins Eliot. Emerson, naturally, was the most objective of the lot. "Allston's pictures," he wrote, "are Elysian; fair, serene, but unreal. I extend the remark to all the American geniuses. Irving, Bryant, Greenough, Everett, Channing, even Webster in his recorded eloquence, all lack nerve and dagger."

Allston settled into a cozy, contemplative life that was described in precise detail by one of his students: "Immediately after breakfast [Allston] would light his cigar and take some book on art, which he would read for a while in preparation for his painting. About one o'clock he would enter his studio, put down his pitcher of drinking-water which he always brought with him through the streets from his house. . . . He would take out his picture, place it on his easel, light his cigar, and sit down in front of it, seemingly wrapped in pleasing contemplation of what he expected to do. It is obvious that, with his deliberate preparation, his hours for work in winter were few. After painting he would carefully clean his palette and return to the contemplation of his picture, which would continue generally until quite dark.

"Then with his brushes and his pitcher in his hands, he would start for his house; and so abstracted was he frequently, that upon reaching it, he would return to see whether he had locked his studio door. After readjusting his toilet, he would enter the dining-room, which was also his sitting-room. There he would usually find some friend or friends whose intimacy rendered invitations superfluous, and with whom he would spend an hour or more in cheerful conversation and the enjoyment of a well-provided and tempting table, on which there was always sherry wine."

In such congenial atmosphere Allston turned temporarily away from Renaissance imitations to express his own inner visions, and produced two of his finest paintings. The composition of *Moonlit Landscape* is a simple cross: the moon, its wake, and the foreground figures form a vertical against the dark horizontal of bridge and middle-ground foliage. All color is subordinated to the moon's glow. The moon has become such

ALLSTON'S "SHIP IN A SQUALL" (BEFORE 1837)

a stock item of calendar art that it is hard to conceive of as a subject for a serious painter. But looking at Allston's canvas tends to bring the satellite, controller of tides and loves, back into focus once again.

Ship in a Squall, a preparatory drawing in chalk on dark-painted canvas, may have inspired one of Gilbert Stuart's more crushing vulgarities. "Nobody," Stuart remarked, "could beat Mr. Allston in making water." Yet the sense of mystery in the painting is created with a sure technical control. The ghostly ship, bound for no imaginable harbor, partakes of both sea and sky, for its sails are like the wind and its hull like the waves. The whole shows that when Allston drew only what was in his mind's eye, and stayed away from human figures, he had mastery. It is a haunting work that recalls Allston's most haunting words.

"There is a period of life," he once wrote, "when the ocean of time seems to force upon the mind a barrier against itself, forming, as it were, a permanent beach, on which the advancing years successively break, only to be carried back by a returning current to that furthest deep whence they first flowed. Upon this beach the poetry of life may be said to have its birth; where the real ends and ideal begins."

JOHN Vanderlyn became the first American painter who faced up to naked flesh. Actually he had small choice in the matter; his patron Aaron Burr decided it by sending him to Paris instead of London for training. The sobersided redhead from Kingston, New York, reached the French capital in 1796. Finding himself in the doctrinaire icebox of neoclassicism dominated by Jacques Louis David, Vanderlyn conscientiously acquired its basic asset, which was figure drawing. He also acquired its defects, stale color and chill pretension.

Young Washington Allston became Vanderlyn's close friend, and both moved on to Rome. But the two youths only reinforced each other's yearning to paint great pictures instead of trying for good ones. Vanderlyn's grandiose attempt, *Marius Amidst the Ruins of Carthage*, caught Napoleon's eye. "Give the medal to that," the emperor ordered, and overnight the American's name was made. When Aaron Burr was tried for

43

JOHN VANDERLYN'S "ARIADNE" (1814)

44

treason, Vanderlyn was able to repay Burr's past generosity. The painter helped support his patron in Paris as he himself had been supported by Burr in earlier years.

All that was needed to complete Vanderlyn's good fortune was a reputation in New York to match what he had gained in Paris. He returned to Manhattan in 1815, confidently bearing with him the pictures Paris had admired. Among them was the most skillful nude yet exhibited by an American—a solid, polished essay in sensuality made respectable, he hoped, by its title, *Ariadne*. But *Ariadne* shocked his staid countrymen, who denounced the picture as a deplorable example of European depravity.

Vanderlyn cheerfully produced a second offering. He had brought back detailed perspective drawings of Versailles, which he now proposed to work up into an oil panorama. His admirers raised money for Manhattan's first art museum building, specifically to house the painting. It was a neoclassic, circular structure, a few steps from City Hall, on ground rented from the city for one peppercorn a year. Vanderlyn's circular panorama occupied the whole second floor. His smaller pictures, which he thought finer, were downstairs. Entrance fees were supposed to pay for the maintenance, but hardly anyone entered. Taken over by creditors, the museum eventually became a criminal court. *Versailles* itself went on tour; it was shown in various cities, never successfully. Once it served as a theater backdrop; Manhattan's Metropolitan Museum has it now.

With the commercial failure of the panorama, Vanderlyn had used up most of his luck. And since his was one of those tender talents that blossom only in the sunlight, his force declined with his fortune. Hearing of Allston's death in 1843, Vanderlyn wrote: "When I look back some five or six and thirty years since, when we were both in Rome together and next-door neighbors on the Trinità del Monte, and in the spring of life, full of enthusiasm for our art, and fancying fair prospects awaiting us in after years, it is painful to reflect how far these hopes have been from being realized."

Vanderlyn's own last years grew even more bitter and ever more obscure—a slow, sore fading away into the remote attic of history.

SAMUEL Finley Breese Morse hoped to "be among those who shall revive the splendor of the fifteenth century." Disappointed in his efforts to warm over the past, Morse turned at last to the future, and invented the telegraph.

The son of a stiff-necked Yankee pastor, Morse was taught to beware of fleshly things. He conceived the notion that art can be purely "intellectual." While Morse was at Yale, President Timothy Dwight regularly admonished the students against everything from daydreaming to theatergoing. "Recollect," Dwight would exhort, "that you are to give an account of your conduct at the last day." The high-minded Morse felt quite at home in this atmosphere, and along with art he dabbled in electricity. His father looked on young Sam's idealistic daubing and dabbling with equal alarm. "Your natural disposition," he wrote in a worried parental letter, "renders it proper for me earnestly to recommend to you to attend to one thing at a time."

On graduation, Morse decided that the one thing he really wanted to do was paint. Gilbert Stuart and Washington Allston both encouraged him and helped persuade his father to send him to England in 1811. Old Benjamin West, everyone agreed, was the man to make an artist of the boy. West, of course, suited Morse's untried taste precisely. "There is not a line or a touch in his pictures," Morse wrote in awe, "which he cannot account for on philosophical principles." For himself he added: "I cannot be happy unless I am pursuing the intellectual branch of the art. Portraits have none of it; landscape has some of it; but history has it wholly." His mother voiced her concern at his point of view: "You must not expect to paint anything in this country for which you will receive any money to support you, but portraits."

Mother knew best. After his four-year apprenticeship, Morse came home as an accomplished academician in the West manner. But although his elaborate works were a critical success, they were a financial failure. He had to settle for portrait commissions at fifteen dollars a head. As the years passed he made himself one of the nation's best portraitists, with a sure if somewhat hard grasp of his sitters' characters. Yet he kept complaining that he despised the work. Whenever he

SAMUEL F. B. MORSE'S "THE OLD HOUSE OF REPRESENTATIVES" (1822)

could steal the time to paint a grand canvas, he did. Unfortunately nobody seemed to care.

The best of Morse's big canvases was his *Old House of Representatives*, painted in 1822. He meant it to edify his countrymen, to impress them with the solemnity and splendor of American democracy in action, and to earn money as a touring exhibition. Shown in New Haven, Boston, New York, and elsewhere, the huge canvas attracted but little popular attention; yet it is a remarkable achievement. Morse chose the moment when the Representatives were gathering for evening session and the central chandelier was being lit. He handled the tricky perspective expertly and softened the elaborate architectural details in mellow light. All but one of the eighty-eight assembled legislators actually posed for their portraits, which gave Morse the opportunity of turning his skill at portraiture to great account. He grouped the figures informally so that the eye could play freely among them, yet managed somehow to obtain a portentous effect. History, the canvas seems to say, is made here in this dim, lofty chamber.

Though the public yawned at Morse's efforts, his fellow artists appreciated them. He founded and headed the National Academy. His friends pleaded that he be given a commission to decorate the national Capitol but were turned down. Morse considered the rejection an overwhelming tragedy. "I have too long lived in the hope of doing something for the Capitol," he wrote. "I have studied and traveled to prepare myself, I have made sacrifices of feeling and of pecuniary interests buoyed up with this phantom of hope which is daily growing dimmer and will soon vanish. . . . I see year after year the vigor of my life wasted in this vain expectation; Raphael had accomplished all his wonders and had died some years before my present age; a few more years and my fate in art is decided."

Morse did not wait a few more years. That very year, at the age of forty-one, he abandoned his father's principle of attending to one thing at a time to resume his college-boy tinkering with electricity. The principle of the telegraph was in his head. He knew that someone else would soon invent it if he did not, and he burned to be first. After a decade of striving Morse won through. Sitting anxiously in the gallery of the House of Representatives he had painted twenty years before, he heard the bill passed which authorized him to string an experimental telegraph wire between Washington and Baltimore. In 1844 he flashed the first message over those forty-one miles: WHAT HATH GOD WROUGHT!

So began a second life for Morse, one full of honors and empty of painting. His first wife had died and his children had grown up. Now he bought a Hudson River estate, married a beautiful deaf girl half his age, and raised a second family. He dabbled amateurishly in politics and fought hard to promote his invention and preserve the credit for it. He lived to see a statue of himself erected in Manhattan's Central Park. Yet the failure of his early hopes still rankled.

"Alas," he wrote to his friend James Fenimore Cooper, "the very name of *picture* produces a sadness of heart I cannot describe. Painting has been a smiling mistress to many, but she has been a cruel jilt to me; I did not abandon her, she abandoned me. I have no wish to be remembered as a painter, for I never was a painter; my idea of that profession *was* perhaps too exalted; I may say, *is* too exalted. I leave it to others more worthy to fill the niches of art."

THE HEAD-HUNTERS

*You cannot be too particular in what you do
to see what animal you are putting down.*

—GILBERT STUART

EDWARD GREENE MALBONE'S
"WASHINGTON ALLSTON" (CA. 1800)

MUSEUM OF FINE ARTS, BOSTON

THE heyday of formal, flattering portraiture in America was the early nineteenth century, when family likenesses were considered an almost essential part of the family furniture, and the camera had not yet arrived to challenge the artist. Seeing the money that was to be made in portraits, hundreds of painters naturally turned head-hunter. Their art is a gilt-framed mirror held up to the face of the new nation and to the genius of their master, Gilbert Stuart.

Stuart had given the gospel to his disciples in no uncertain terms: "Most persons in striving after effect lose the likeness, when they should go together. To produce a good effect, you must copy nature: leave nature for an imaginary effect and you lose all." Stuart himself was, of course, a born stylist and he possessed the vast advantage of having learned his craft in London when London was the portrait center of the world. But he came to believe that nature had been his

MALBONE'S "ROBERT MACOMB" (1806) AND "MARY CORNELL PELL" (1806)

only teacher, and by imposing this notion on his worshipers, he turned them from the highroad of imaginative portraiture into the narrow bypath of the literal copyist.

EDWARD Greene Malbone was essentially a copyist like the rest, but the fact that his portraits are in small scale, done on ivory, gives them the charm of distance. Malbone's *Mary Cornell Pell* and *Robert Macomb* look like real people seen through the wrong end of a telescope. His miniature of Washington Allston is a more personal and convincing portrait, capturing the gentle sadness of his good friend.

A bastard, born in Newport, Rhode Island, Malbone had a hard childhood. Somehow he taught himself to paint, and at seventeen he set up shop as a miniaturist in Providence, charging about twenty dollars a picture. Meeting with success, he wrote a proud letter to his father, who had never acknowledged him by name: "I must conclude with making use of that name which I

shall study never to dishonor. Your dutiful son, Edward G. Malbone." The artist traveled to England and afterwards throughout the young republic. He built a solid reputation and raised his price to fifty dollars. Then, at only twenty-nine, he died. But Malbone lives on in scores of heirloom lockets. He was the best miniaturist in American art history, which has rightfully accorded him his miniature niche.

THOMAS Sully of Philadelphia was one of the few to sit at Stuart's feet who openly dared modify the master's precepts. "Resemblance is essential," Sully conceded, "but no fault will be found with the artist—at least by the sitter—if he improve the appearance." By taking great pains always to improve the appearance, Sully cheapened his own great gifts and of course became rich and famous. His parents had been actors, and he himself kept in close contact with the stage. His portraits have dramatic flair, but their weakness is theatricality. Even craggy old

49

THOMAS SULLY'S
"ANDREW JACKSON" (1845)

WILLIAM J. HUBARD'S
"JOHN C. CALHOUN" (1830)

Andrew Jackson, as pictured in Sully's portrait, looks like a gentle ham powdered for the footlights and wigged for the role of Old Hickory.

CHESTER Harding, a tall backwoodsman, was as rugged as Sully was smooth. He worked as farmhand, saloonkeeper, peddler, and chairmaker before trying his hand at portraiture, and failed at everything but the last. His first portrait was of his wife. "I made a thing that looked like her," he wrote. "The moment I saw the likeness I became frantic with delight: it was like the discovery of a new sense; I could think of nothing else." Harding carried his new sense to Boston to submit it to Stuart's refining influence, and only succeeded in taking away a large part of the master's business. American and later English society were charmed more by the frontiersman than the artist. But Harding managed to get many a notable, from Chief Justice John Marshall to Daniel Boone, reasonably well nailed to canvas.

THE age knew at least half a dozen portraitists of Harding's caliber, though none more picturesque or more successful. Typical of the lot were Henry Inman of New York and John Neagle of Philadelphia. Both were solid journeymen portraitists who conscientiously gave their sitters their money's worth. But credit for Neagle's one famous picture should go not so much to Neagle himself as to his subject, the blacksmith Pat Lyon.

No mere horseshoe man, Lyon had a devil of a way with all sorts of ironwork. Once he was commissioned to build a strongbox and did the job with customary thoroughness. Being disappointed in his fee, Lyon snapped the box shut. Since no one else could reopen it, the box stayed shut until Lyon collected double pay. His growing reputation soon had him in trouble. A Philadelphia bank had been robbed, and people said that only Lyon could have got past its locks and bars. Protesting manfully, he was arrested and clapped into Walnut Street jail. Three months later the real robbers were caught, and Lyon released on bail. But he lived under a cloud for seven years more, until he finally brought suit for malicious prosecution and won $9,000 damages.

With his new wealth in hand Lyon hurried round to one of the town's most fashionable portraitists and offered a commission. He had no wish to be portrayed as a gentleman, Lyon informed the startled John Neagle, but as a workingman. Perhaps the first commissioned portrait of its kind, the canvas would have to be splendid as well as precedent-shattering. It was to show the blacksmith life-size, laboring in freedom and honesty at his forge. And in the background would be glimpsed the accursed jail from which Providence and his own sturdy determination had rescued him, its cupola topped by a weather vane of crossed keys.

Given his opportunity, Neagle did nobly. And though his canvas looks staged and has a flattering slickness, its virtues far outweigh its faults. The Walnut Street backdrop gives a fresh-air feeling to what would otherwise seem a Vulcan's cave. The young apprentice nicely complements Lyon's robust maturity. Lyon himself, his big feet spread and firmly planted, his heavy arm and hand holding the hammer with negligent authority, easily dominates the canvas.

WILLIAM James Hubard was on the average level of competence, as his portrait of John C. Calhoun demonstrates. But Hubard's life, an odd fluttering in the wings of history, was

CHESTER HARDING'S
"CHIEF JUSTICE JOHN MARSHALL" (1830)

HENRY INMAN'S
"HENRY CLAY" (CA. 1840)

51

a fascinating one. Although he claimed to be "an Englishman of good descent," Americans were put off by his tangled hair, refused to meet his piercing eye, and declared him a gypsy. Hubard had landed on Manhattan at the age of seventeen in the charge of a promoter named Smith, who set him up on Broadway. For fifty cents' admission to the Hubard Gallery visitors might, in the words of Smith's brochure, "see the exhibition and obtain a correct likeness in bust cut by Master Hubard, who without the least aid from a drawing machine or any kind of outline but merely by a glance at the profile and with a pair of common scissors instantly produces a striking and spirited likeness."

No one knows just when Hubard left Smith and silhouetting to take up portraiture. He did well at his new craft, married into Virginia society, and settled down in Richmond. One of his patrons, the poetaster Mann Valentine, put the painter under a microscope and produced a penetrating description: "Small, delicate-looking, black hair, brown eyes, harelip, Roman nose, large mouth, strongly marked features: when quiet—painful, sad, and thoughtful; when he laughs it is hysterical and rarely with a hearty guffaw." The truism that unskilled portraitists incline to superimpose their own features on those of their sitters is startlingly borne out in the case of Hubard's *Calhoun*. Every feature noted in Valentine's description of the artist (except the harelip) applies to Hubard's painting. And by placing his sitter far down in a dreary darkness, he suggested a feeling of unhappy impotence sharply at variance with Calhoun's own vigorous character.

Hubard's end was almost as strange as his beginning. At forty-six he wearied of painting and became obsessed with the notion that the marble bust of George Washington done by the Frenchman Jean Antoine Houdon ought to be cast in bronze. Building his own foundry, he spent seven years and all his savings to make six reproductions of the bust. At the start of the Civil War he tried to recoup his fortune by turning the foundry into a Confederate arsenal. He began experimenting with the manufacture of explosives, and blew himself up.

JOHN NEAGLE'S "PAT LYON AT THE FORGE" (1827)

"THE SARGENT FAMILY" (1800), ANONYMOUS

54

CHAPTER VII

FROM THE GRASS ROOTS

Liberty, when it begins to take root, is a plant of rapid growth.

—George Washington

WHILE the head-hunters stalked their quarry mainly in the big cities of the East, their country cousins plied the back roads, recording the looks and customs of the nation's frugal rural aristocracy. They did not pretend to equal the gloss and flair of the big-city portraitists, and they charged accordingly for their work, asking about as much for a portrait as a small-town photographer does today. The invention of the daguerreotype was soon to force them out of business, but not before they had produced a mountain of pictures with a peculiar and enduring charm of their own.

A typical example of American folk art in its golden age, from the close of the Revolution to the start of the Civil War, is *The Sargent Family*, painted by an unknown artist in 1800. The picture shines with domestic bliss. But the symmetry of composition and stiffness of drawing add something more: a feeling of weightlessness which

PAUL SEIFERT'S "WISCONSIN FARM SCENE" (1880)

"BLUE EYES" (CA. 1840), ANONYMOUS

denies, and an impression of orderliness which transcends, the world of real people and places.

The artist who painted Elizabeth Fenimore Cooper in 1816 aimed to make a neat delineation of a nice old lady at home in the grandest house west of Albany. But his unintentionally deep perspective swells the room to theater size, and the monumental Mrs. Cooper (her hands and feet tucked out of sight to lighten the artist's task) seems to have floated into position on a cloud. Actually, Mrs. Cooper had come to her new home in just such a sedentary fashion. When her husband decided to move his family into the wilds of western New York, she clutched her eleventh child, James Fenimore, to her breast and refused to budge from her chair. Mr. Cooper hoisted chair, wife, and son together into the wagon.

Blue Eyes, done about 1840, is a disarming attempt to present some honest maiden with no nonsense. But the artist's failures, not his modest success, are what appeal today. They are the cooky-cutter coiffure, the muffin face, and most of all the bright and penetrating blueberry eyes.

NOT all of the grass-roots painters were portraitists, though all were bent on portraying reality. Among the best of the primitive landscapes, *Benjamin Reber's Farm* is a green and gold homage to the rich earth of Pennsylvania. Paul Seifert, who painted *Wisconsin Farm Scene*, had trouble drawing animals and people, and resolved his problem by placing them in profile. Perspective was beyond him, so he ignored it. But he had a relaxed and gracious way of spacing things out in his pictures, and a poetic sense of color. Done on grey cardboard, his farmscape takes its chief tone, as of gathering dusk, directly from his material. He painted the sun and sunset clouds in real gilt, and the metallic paint contrasts with the rest of the picture to point up with startling drama the difference between earth and sky. Gilt is used again with almost magical overtones on the doors of the snow-white house, to which the people are turning at close of day.

Seifert is one of the few nineteenth-century folk artists of whom anything is known. A German immigrant to Wisconsin, he helped support

"ELIZABETH FENIMORE COOPER" (1816), ANONYMOUS

CHARLES HOFMANN'S "BENJAMIN REBER'S FARM" (1872)

HARRIET MOORE'S "RICHARDSON MEMORIAL" (1817)

"MOTHER AND CHILD" (CA. 1810), ANONYMOUS

himself by farmscapes at two dollars and fifty cents apiece and by nostalgic memories of castles on the Rhine (painted on glass, with windows of gold and silver foil) at five dollars. He was also something of a tree expert, a gardener, and a taxidermist. His wife did sewing for the Indians, on occasion, in exchange for venison. His view of his art was typically unassuming: "People like my work, and I like to paint for them."

AMONG the many uses of folk art in the nineteenth century was the so-called "memorial picture," painted to represent eternal mourning for the deceased. With its weeping willows complementing the weeping figures and framing a fancy tomb, the *Richardson Memorial* is a typical example. The inscriptions read: "Sacred to the memory of Miss Nancy Richardson who died August 31st AE 14 years," and "Mrs. Fanny

Richardson who died August 22nd AE 57 years." The memorial was done by a girl of fifteen, who imitated in water color the effect of needlework.

Mother and Child, done on glass, was probably a panel for a clock. It is as peaceful and bare as *Bare Knuckles* is peaceful and crowded. The latter shows that the New York *Mirror* was right when it editorialized in 1835 that "the detestable practise of prize fighting threatens to take root within the soil of our native land." Although done to record a sort of battle royal, the picture has an atmosphere of utter calm. The eyes of the 129 spectators focus as dispassionately as buttons on the six pale males posturing together in spotted pants.

HISTORY was a favorite subject of the backwoods artists. An unknown named M. M. Sanford painted *Washington at Princeton* (*see*

GEORGE A. HAYES'S "BARE KNUCKLES" (CA. 1860)

"GENERAL PUTNAM'S LEAP" (1846), ANONYMOUS

frontispiece) clearly for fun. It has all the school-boy exuberance of a ride on a merry-go-round. But *General Putnam's Leap* and *The Murder of Jane McCrea* were the work of a professional, done to fill the need that comic books and pseudohistorical movies now supply. More than ten feet high, they were part of a set commissioned by one George Mastin, a Genoa, New York, tailor, farmer, phrenologist, violin player, and horse trader. Mastin exhibited the pictures, and his own wares and talents, in barns all over his part of the state. Seen in flickering candlelight and buttressed by proper rhetoric, they must have presented a weird and wonderful view of the nation's early history.

The huge canvases were recently found rolled up in a central New York barn, along with the spiels that Mastin spouted when he showed his pictures. His notes for the Revolutionary War feat of General Putnam read:

General putnam Performed his famous feat
of Riding down the stone stairs at horse neck . . .
and plunged down the Precipice near the church. this
was so steep as to have artificial stairs, composed of

Nearly 100 stone steps for the accommodation of foot
Passengers, the Brittish dragoons, durst not follow
the in tripid horseman down the precipice. . . .

For *The Murder of Jane McCrea*, which was witnessed by a fellow prisoner of the Indians, he wrote:

. . . high words violent gestures. till at Lenghth they
*   Engaged in a furious*
Quarrel. and Beat one another with there muskets
*   in the midst*
of which fray one of the chiefs apparently in a
*   Rage shot Miss Mc*
Crea in the Breast. she in stantly fell and Expired.
*   her hair*
Was long and flowing. the same chief grasped it in
*   his hand.*
Seized his knife and took off the scalp in such a man-
*   ner as to*
include nearly the whole of the hair—then springing
*   from*
the ground, he tosed it in the face of a young war-
*   iorur, who*
stood near him watching the operation.

60

"THE MURDER OF JANE McCREA" (1846), ANONYMOUS

The anonymous painter of *Jane McCrea* had an elegant model; he drew on an elaborate academic picture of the same subject by none other than John Vanderlyn. This may account for the classic immobility of the figures, so different from General Putnam and his dashing horse-descending-a-staircase.

THE most extraordinary painter to spring up from the nation's grass roots was a Pennsylvania Quaker named Edward Hicks. He was born in the midst of the American Revolution, which wiped out his Tory family's fortune. At thirteen he took up the brush—in a carriage maker's shop. Soon afterwards, as Hicks remembered it, he was "introduced by lechers and debauchees into the worst of company and places, both in city and country." A terrible hangover, suffered at twenty, combined with a serious bout of illness, led him to join the sober Society of Friends. Within a decade he became one of the society's

most sought-after preachers. Taking nothing in payment for his sermons, he supported himself by painting whatever was offered to him—carriages, tavern signs and even tables and chests. More than 3,000 country people attended Hicks's funeral in 1849, but they mourned the preacher, not the artist.

Hicks himself scorned the pictures he painted on the side. "If the Christian world was in the real spirit of Christ," he wrote, "I do not believe there would be such a thing as a fine painter in Christendom. It appears clearly to me to be one of those trifling, insignificant arts, which has never been of any substantial advantage to mankind. But as the inseparable companion of voluptuousness and pride, it has presaged the downfall of empires and kingdoms. . . ."

Those few words tell a good deal about the man. Hicks was eloquent, pious, humble, intolerant, the very archetype of the back-country preacher that he was. His dim view of art came

EDWARD HICKS'S "THE PEACEABLE KINGDOM" (CA. 1830)

from looking at engraved copies of paintings, and from the same engravings he drew all the materials for his own perennial minor piece, *The Peaceable Kingdom*. Hicks's present fame rests mainly on that one picture, of which he painted perhaps a hundred versions.

To illustrate the haunting prophecy of Isaiah, Hicks borrowed animals from Bible illustrations, children from engravings done after Raphael, the background scene from a reproduction of Benjamin West's *Penn's Treaty with the Indians*, and the Natural Bridge of Virginia backdrop from still another popular print. That he was able to fit these miscellaneous materials into an emotionally convincing whole is one of the great oddities of American art history. He knew, as he once wrote, that

> *Inferior folks with only munkey's art*
> *May imitate but never life impart.*

He himself imparted life to his art over and over again, devotedly. Religious fervor accomplished what his skill could not. Many of his *Kingdoms* he gave away to friends, explaining that they symbolized among other things the peace of soul that comes to the man who can control his animal passions. With the picture he would often present a poem, also by himself:

> *The wolf with the lambkin dwells in peace*
> *his grim carnivorous thirst for blood will cease;*
> *The beauteous leopard with his restless eye,*
> *shall by the kid in perfect stillness lie;*
>
> *The calf, the fatling and the young lion wild,*
> *shall all be led by one sweet little child;*
> *The cow and the bear shall quietly partake*
> *of the rich food the ear and corn stalk make. . . .*
>
> *The illustrious Penn this heavenly kingdom felt*
> *then with Columbia's native sons he dealt,*
> *Without an oath a lasting treating made*
> *in Christian faith beneath the elm tree's shade.*

Hicks has been compared to the great French primitive, Henri Rousseau—doubtless because both were fond of painting animals. But when the French painter Fernand Léger called Hicks "the finest American of them all," he was either exaggerating out of politeness or indulging the hardy European contempt for the art of the New World. Hicks himself, on the other hand, grossly underrated his own achievements. He wrote in his diary: "Oh, how awful the consideration: I have nothing to depend on but the mercy and forgiveness of God, for I have no works of righteousness of my own. I am nothing but a poor old worthless insignificant painter."

JOHN QUIDOR'S "RIP VAN WINKLE AT NICHOLAS VEDDER'S TAVERN" (1839)

CHAPTER VIII

SENTIMENTAL JOURNEYS

Yes! let the proud despise, the rich deride,
These humble joys, to Competence allied:
To me, they bloom, all fragrant to my heart,
Nor ask the pomp of wealth, nor gloss of art.

—TIMOTHY DWIGHT

SCORES of American artists in the mid-nine-teenth century were painting primarily for lithographic reproduction by Currier & Ives and other smaller firms. To please the broadest possible audience, they pictured common human situations sentimentally and with a touch of humor. Humor seems to escape serious definition, but George Meredith made a fine cast at the meaning of sentimentality when he wrote: "Sentimentalists are they who seek to enjoy without incurring the immense debtorship for a thing done." In painting, unearned emotion sells well. Demanding little of the artist, it requires even less of the observer, and so pleases without disturbing.

JAMES Clonney's *Sleigh Ride* implies, like the verse by Yale's President Timothy Dwight, that humble joys are probably much the best after all. First exhibited at the National Academy of Design in 1845, the canvas has all the cuteness, flatness, and candy-sweetness that characterize its kind. The plumply decorous children with their eternally patient pup are like cardboard cutouts in a window display, set against a skim-milk backdrop and artificial snow.

William Sharp painted his *Railroad Jubilee on Boston Common* in 1851 to celebrate "the final completion of the great lines of railway communication between Boston, the Canadas, and the Great West, and the establishment of American lines of steamers between Boston and Liverpool." Meant for people who had been on the spot, the picture is painstakingly accurate in describing the ordered ranks of soldiers and officials massed on the tawny turf. A fringe of onlookers invites the viewer to step into the scene and reimmerse himself in the golden aura of a fine afternoon.

John Quidor, who painted *Rip Van Winkle at Nicholas Vedder's Tavern* in 1839, was a vastly more accomplished artist than Sharp or Clonney; yet he made his living chiefly by decorating fire engines. His illustrations seem to have been no more than a hobby. But Quidor's canvas, with Rip glooming by his musket under the tree, gives startling life and body to Washington Irving's sleepy lines: "For a while [Rip] used to console himself, when driven from home, by frequenting a kind of perpetual club of the sages, philosophers and other idle personages of the village, which held its sessions on a bench before a small inn, designated by a rubicund portrait of His Majesty George the Third."

Fitz Hugh Lane's still and luminous pictures of the New England coast were in such great

JAMES CLONNEY'S "THE SLEIGH RIDE" (CA. 1845)

WILLIAM SHARP'S "RAILROAD JUBILEE ON BOSTON COMMON" (1851)

demand that he himself founded a lithographic firm to reproduce them. *Owl's Head* now seems extraordinarily like a color photo. Lane's contemporaries, who knew of no such thing, compared it instead to reality, and found it close enough. *Approaching Storm* displays a more romantic temperament. The painter, Martin Johnson Heade, wandered the world searching for unusual effects of light and color. Apparently he never thought of inventing such things; they had to take place before his eyes.

ONE popular artist of the mid-nineteenth century was a far better painter than even his admirers then imagined. William Sidney Mount never let success sway him from simplicity. He well understood that his genius was a daimon of place, a sort of hayseed angel. Accordingly,

Mount stayed close to her green skirts, spending most of his life at Stony Brook, Long Island.

Born at nearby Setauket in 1807, Mount was the youngest son of an affluent innkeeper. He was "very beautiful from his baby-hood," wrote a family friend, "and as tenderly nurtured as one of Queen Victoria's children." In his teens he ventured into Manhattan to study art, but came home again just as soon as he had learned his lessons. Washington Allston admired the young painter and urged him to go abroad to study seventeenth-century Dutch paintings, which his work resembled. Mount turned down all opportunities to follow that advice. "Originality is not confined to one place or country," he observed, "which is very consoling to us Yankees."

Mount toured the lanes around Stony Brook in a mobile studio of his own invention. It was

FITZ HUGH LANE'S "OWL'S HEAD, PENOBSCOT BAY, MAINE" (1862)

horse-drawn and had a stove, a skylight, and a glass window. He would pull up to paint a couple of farmers haggling over a horse, or harvesters sleeping in the noonday shade. At roadside taverns he would stop for beer and merriment. Some of his best pictures are of rustic drinkers and dancers, which prompted a contemporary critic to wish "that such superior talents and skill as are here displayed had been exercised on a subject of a higher grade in the social scale."

A placid country bachelor, Mount painted what he knew, and more ably than anyone had any reason to expect. His life was made up mostly of recreation—hunting, fishing, sailing, dancing, drinking, and playing the violin. "I never paint on a picture," he once wrote with quiet satisfaction, "unless I feel in the right spirit."

Shortly before his death in 1868, he became convinced that a spirit from another world was helping him work. Rembrandt was the fellow's name. Indeed, a letter to Mount, purporting to have been dictated by Rembrandt's ghost, was hailed as a prize bit of evidence for spiritualism. The letter rings weirdly true to the old master's methods—"the mysterious lights and shadows which characterize my productions"—yet also applies to Mount's own best work. The ghost of Rembrandt might have been describing what lay behind the eccentric, happy Long Islander's *Banjo Player*. Mount's relaxed draftsmanship, his instinct for spacious, exquisitely balanced composition, and especially his way of rendering soft sunlight and cool shadow, made him in fact a sort of remote rustic descendant of the master.

MARTIN JOHNSON HEADE'S "APPROACHING STORM; BEACH NEAR NEWPORT" (CA. 1860)

WILLIAM SIDNEY MOUNT'S "THE BANJO PLAYER" (CA. 1855)

THOMAS COLE'S "THE CATSKILL MOUNTAINS" (1833)

THE
HUDSON RIVER SCHOOL

Go forth, under the open sky, and list to Nature's teachings.

—WILLIAM CULLEN BRYANT

THE rise of Jacksonian democracy created a new pride in the American wilderness, and artists began flocking outdoors to record it. Various writers of the period—Cooper, Emerson, Thoreau, Whittier, and Bryant—urged them on. Today it is the amateur painters who rush to nature (or rather to pastoral scenes with red barns and green trees), while the professionals stay at home making abstractions. But a century ago the amateurs were making abstractions, in the form of hooked rugs, patchwork quilts, and

weather vanes, while the professionals scoured the countryside. The best of these, perhaps, was a shy, spry painter named Thomas Cole. "To walk with nature as a poet," Cole wrote, in emulation of his friend Bryant, "is the necessary condition of the perfect artist."

Hoping to be himself "the perfect artist," Cole trudged up along the Hudson River in 1825 to sketch the Catskills. So began the "Hudson River School" of like-minded painters. Cole had reason to know the wilderness better than most of his

COLE'S "THE OXBOW" (1836)

ASHER BROWN DURAND'S "KINDRED SPIRITS" (1849)

friends. Born in 1801, he had emigrated from England to Steubenville, Ohio, and there learned the rudiments of painting from an itinerant portraitist. While he was still in his teens Cole set out himself as a wandering artist, traveling from town to town painting portraits. He lugged along a saddle that he had accepted in payment for one commission, though he owned no horse to ride. Resting on his saddle in the forest between settlements, Cole came to realize that landscapes meant more to him than people.

In his best years as a landscapist, Cole made long walking trips through the Adirondacks, the White Mountains, and the old Northwest Territory. His *Oxbow*, a view of the Connecticut River near Northampton, painted in 1836, looks rather like Arcadia seen through a dusty brass telescope, shining with miles of space and air.

Cole's view of his subject matter was highly emotional and patriotic. "American scenes," he explained, "are not destitute of historical and legendary associations; the great struggle for freedom has sanctified many a spot, and many a mountain stream and rock has its legend, worthy of poet's pen or painter's pencil. . . . And in looking over the *uncultivated* scene, the mind may travel far into futurity. Where the wolf roams, the plow shall glisten; on the gray crag shall rise temple and tower. . . ."

Despite such sentiments, Cole himself made the Grand Tour of Europe as soon as he could, and returned to paint farfetched, neoclassical allegories of minor interest. But before his short life ended in 1848, Cole re-established his connection with the American wilderness, sailing to Maine's Mount Desert Island, where he made some of the finest drawings of his career. He laid his success to his legs as much as to hand or eye. "How I have walked!" he told a friend ecstatically, "day after day, and all alone. . . ."

THE first of Cole's disciples, chronologically and in quality as well, was Asher Brown Durand, a New Jersey-born engraver. When Cole met him, Durand was already a noted artist in his own field. He had assured his reputation with engraved copies of Trumbull's *Declaration of Independence* and Vanderlyn's *Ariadne*, and was making a good living reproducing portraits of the great and engraving bank notes. Encouraging Durand to abandon the copyist's burin for the brush, Cole soon persuaded him to follow his teacher into the woods. "Will you allow me here to say a word or two on landscape?" Cole wrote to Durand in 1832. "It is usual to rank it as a lower branch of the art, below the historical. Why so? Is there a better reason than that the vanity of man makes him delight most in his own image? . . . In landscapes there is a greater variety of objects, textures, phenomena, to imitate. It has expression also, not of passion, to be sure, but of sentiment, whether it be tranquil or spirit-stirring."

Durand soon fell in love with the spreading American landscape, married her, and settled down. "Go not abroad," he soberly advised his colleagues, "in search of material for the exercise of your pencil while the virgin charms of our native land have claims on our deepest affections." His landscapes show the engraver's close attention to detail; every bit of foliage can be identified. By the same token, they are remarkably true to the American scene. No one would mistake the Catskill gorge of Durand's *Kindred Spirits* for a valley in Bavaria or even a passage along the Mississippi. The frock-coated friends in the picture are William Cullen Bryant and Thomas Cole. Bryant had delivered the oration at Cole's funeral, and Durand painted the picture as a gift to the poet. The canvas fairly rustles with impeccable sentiments, and neatly packages the spirit of the Hudson River School.

JOHN Frederick Kensett caught that spirit from Durand himself, in Europe, curiously enough. Despite his own stern warning, Durand had taken Kensett and two other art students abroad in 1840 for study. Kensett stayed on for seven years, but he showed more interest in the landscape than in the art of the Continent, honoring Durand's dictum that one should "go first to Nature . . . and when you shall have learned to imitate her, you may then study the pictures of great artists with benefit."

Kensett painted for a time in England, but seems to have learned nothing from the British landscapists Constable and Turner. He sat musing in the forest of Fontainebleau, walked up the

Rhine, over the Alps, and down into Italy. He returned to roam America more widely and to record what he saw in dry, clear, highly competent pictures. A contemporary critic neatly described Kensett as "the Bryant of our painters, a little sad and monotonous, but sweet, artistic and unaffected." His *River Scene* displays these characteristics at their best.

He was immensely popular. When Kensett died in 1872, the contents of his studio brought a satisfying $137,715 at public auction. But today Kensett's canvases, and those of the Hudson River School in general, are mainly prized as nostalgic memories. Though American schoolboys may still be forced to memorize *Thanatopsis*, their elders seldom read Bryant. And so it is with the painters whom the poets inspired: thoughtful, optimistic, dedicated men whose legacy was a studied hymn to the gentle hills and sweeping rivers of their native countryside.

JOHN FREDERICK KENSETT'S "RIVER SCENE" (1870)

CHAPTER X

JOHN JAMES AUDUBON

Whoso would be a man, must be a nonconformist.

—RALPH WALDO EMERSON

A NONCONFORMIST John James Audubon certainly was, and every inch a man. He was to earn a unique place in American art and folklore as the first great painter of the wildlife he found in his adopted country. Many have since been seized by the same urge to picture the birds and beasts that populate the American fields and skies. None has yet surpassed him.

Audubon for more than half of his sixty-five years seemed destined for nothing in particular. Born in 1785, the illegitimate son of a French sea captain and a Santo Domingo Creole, he grew up in France at a time when Jean Jacques Rousseau's back-to-nature notions were the rage. Sent to America at the age of eighteen to oversee some properties of his father's, young Audubon looked and acted like an absent-minded candidate for the horsy set. He wore fine frilled shirts and black satin breeches, and gallantly courted the women. "I had no vices," he later noted in his journal, "but was thoughtless and pensive, fond of shooting, fishing and riding . . . as active and agile as a buck."

His own phrase, "thoughtless and pensive," well describes Audubon's contradictory nature. Dreamy in a way young ladies found hard to resist, he soon won the heart of sixteen-year-old Lucy Bakewell, who lived in a white-columned Pennsylvania farm mansion called Fatland Ford. One day he painted her portrait in water color, made a mess of it, and then salvaged the picture with an overlay of pastel. This accidentally discovered mixture of mediums was to remain his chief painting technique for the rest of his life.

Audubon married Lucy and bundled her into the Pittsburgh coach. He had heard the call of the frontier. By flatboat, the Audubons went on from Pittsburgh to Louisville. There he opened a general store. He went hunting for sport and for food, and got more and more interested in wildlife for its own sake. He would shoot any new species of bird he saw and carry it home to paint. "If I were jealous," said Lucy, "I should have a bitter time of it, for every bird is my rival."

AUDUBON'S hobby brought in no money at all, and his business suffered from neglect. Finally Audubon and a partner decided on a new start. In 1810 they moved their store to a village called Henderson, 125 miles down the Ohio River. With Lucy and their infant son, Audubon made the journey by skiff. Gone now were his frills and satin; Audubon's habitual costume had become the fringed buckskin of the frontiersman, with leggings, sheath knife, and tomahawk. He was hardly the sober merchant type. When the first river steamboat came to Henderson in 1811, Audubon dove from the wharf to dare the churning paddles, swimming directly under the vessel. In time Audubon's Henderson enterprises collapsed. Lucy went to work as a governess, and he went to jail for debts.

At that dark moment Audubon began to feel his greatness. Released from jail a bankrupt, he

JOHN JAMES AUDUBON'S "WILD TURKEY" (1825)

had only his clothes and his rifle. But he was a vigorous thirty-five, strong as a tree, and clear-eyed as a hawk. He knew the birds of America better than any living man. Then and there he decided to paint hundreds of them just as they looked, and reproduce them in a book. Leaving his family to fend for itself, Audubon soon struck east to find a publisher for the vast project.

The portraitist Sully encouraged the shaggy stranger, but the Philadelphia and New York publishers did not. Audubon boarded ship for England, where he got a better reception. The British welcomed him as a character and bought his pictures for their novelty. He whistled bird songs in elegant drawing rooms, and he sat on the edges of sofas talking about wilderness life. Asked about the bears and wolves, he solemnly confessed that he had never been "troubled by any animals larger than ticks." He kept his hair long and wrote Lucy that his locks "do as much for me as my talent for painting." The eminent critic Sir Walter Besant gave a haughty view of the "longhaired Achaean" in 1837, when Audubon was fifty-two: "Brave is the exhibition of flowing locks; they flow over the ears and over the coat collars; you can smell the bear's grease across the street; and if these amaranthine locks were to be raised you would see the shiny coating of bear's grease upon the velvet collar below."

An anonymous London journalist wrapped up a more inclusive and sympathetic description in one marathon sentence: "The tall and somewhat stooping form, the clothes made not by a West End but by a Far West tailor, the steady, rapid, springing step, the long hair, the aquiline features, and the glowing, angry eyes—the expression of a handsome man conscious of ceasing to be young, and an air and manner which told you that whoever you might be he was John Audubon, will never be forgotten by anyone who knew or saw him." The painter himself wrote to Lucy: "It is Mr. Audubon here and Mr. Audubon there until I am afraid poor Mr. Audubon is in danger of having his head turned."

The splash he made in society helped persuade the publishers Robert Havell & Son to agree to bring out *Birds of America*, a huge edition of 435 Audubon bird paintings in colored engravings. Plate Number One was *Wild Turkey*. Audubon

did full justice to his subject, as if to support Benjamin Franklin's thesis that the turkey and not the bald eagle should have been chosen as the national emblem. The bald eagle, Franklin observed, "is a bird of bad moral character; he does not get his living honestly; you may have seen him perched on some dead tree near the river, where, too lazy to fish for himself, he watches the labor of the fishing-hawk; and, when that diligent bird has at length taken a fish and is bearing it to his nest for the support of his mate and young ones, the bald eagle pursues him and takes it from him. With all this injustice he is never in good case; but, like those among men who live by sharping and robbing, he is generally poor and often very lousy. . . . The turkey is in comparison a much more respectable bird, and withal a true original native of America. . . . He is (though a little vain and silly, it is true, but not the worse emblem for that) a bird of courage, and would not hesitate to attack a grenadier of the British Guards who should presume to invade his farmyard with a red coat on."

Eventually Audubon got 161 patrons from Britain, Europe, and America to subscribe about $1,000 each for the complete set of his *Birds of America*, and returned home in triumph. He had proposed to Lucy, financially independent of him for twenty years, that they share the victory together. Rather reluctantly she agreed, on the grounds that she might be useful in handling his accounts and engagements.

AUDUBON had grown grey as a badger, and was still as tough. He kept traveling and painting, and proudly taught his methods to his two sons, John and Victor. As a base, he bought a pretty estate on the banks of the Hudson River just above Harlem village. There his good friend Samuel F. B. Morse used to visit, tinkering with prototypes for the telegraph. Prosperous by then, and famous, Audubon remarked to Lucy: "I have had an abundance of mortifications and vexations, yet have rather rose above the water."

His last major work, undertaken when he was fifty-four, was a series of 150 paintings of animals, entitled *The Viviparous Quadrupeds of North America*. Victor did the landscape backgrounds for many of the pictures, and young John painted about

AUDUBON'S "BOB-WHITE" (1825)

(WHICH THE ARTIST CALLED VIRGINIAN PARTRIDGE)

half of the animals themselves. The father took the smaller animals for his province; he urged friends to send him specimens preserved in rum.

"No one, I think," Audubon declared, "paints in my method; I, who have never studied but by piecemeal, form my pictures according to my ways of study. For instance, I am now working on a fox; I take one neatly killed, put him up with wires and when satisfied with the truth of the position, I take my palette and work as rapidly as possible; the same with my birds; if practicable I finish a bird at one sitting—often, it is true, of fourteen hours—so that I think they are correct, both in detail and composition."

Ornithologists complain that some of the positions in which Audubon wired his birds were impossible for the creatures to have assumed in real life. But if they were not always correct, his compositions were almost invariably striking. Sometimes, as in his *Bob-White*, he succeeded in showing astonishingly quick, explosive, complex actions with the clarity of spring water. Which bird will the marauding hawk seize? The viewer can never know for sure. Though the fierce flurry that Audubon has stilled and organized for a single instant of time seems about to resume in a fraction of a second, the result remains forever obscured.

Because of their incredible richness of detail, Audubon's pictures were assumed to take weeks to finish. A note which he affixed to one meticulous study of a rooster and hens reads: "These chickens were painted by John James Audubon in one morning before one o'clock lunch, as someone visiting him told him he did not believe such rapid work could be done." Shortly before his death in 1851, Audubon announced the conclusion that his life had been "curious." He added simply that he had enjoyed the world, "a world which, though wicked enough in all conscience, is perhaps as good as worlds unknown."

THE passing decades, which have weathered away the fame of many more artful and more careful men, vastly enhanced Audubon's reputation. His work hangs in scores of museums. He has been the hero of more than a dozen biographies (and of several efforts to prove that he was really the "lost Dauphin" of France, a claim that Audubon himself occasionally advanced). Popular editions of his *Birds of America* have sold thousands of copies. The Audubon Societies have perpetuated his name and imperceptibly transformed the man who once killed hundreds of birds for sport into a sort of scientific St. Francis.

Audubon was at least as much a naturalist as he was an artist; standards set for more imaginative and expressive painting cannot be applied to him. But he did have a strong flair for design, coupled with an almost uncanny feel for the animal kingdom. Audubon's woodpeckers quarrel, his squirrels teeter, chattering, and his wild turkeys gobble and swell. He turned paper into airy space and set creatures free to flourish there.

PART TWO

ERASTUS SALISBURY FIELD'S "HISTORICAL MONUMENT OF THE AMERICAN REPUBLIC" (CA. 1876)

And thou, high-towering One—America!
Thy swarm of offspring towering high—yet higher thee,
*   above all towering.*
With Victory on thy left, and at thy right hand Law;
Thou Union, holding all—fusing, absorbing, tolerating all,
Thee, ever thee, I bring.

—WALT WHITMAN

YEARS
OF
GROWTH

81

CHAPTER I

ARTISTS ON HORSEBACK

Whoo-oop! I'm the original iron-jawed, brass-mounted, copper-bellied corpse-maker from the wilds of Arkansas! Look at me! I'm the man they call Sudden Death and General Desolation! Sired by a hurricane, dam'd by an earthquake, half-brother to the cholera, nearly related to the smallpox on my mother's side! Look at me! I take nineteen alligators and a bar'l of whisky for breakfast when I'm in robust health, and a bushel of rattlesnakes and a dead body when I'm ailing. I split the everlasting rocks with my glance, and I squench the thunder when I speak! Whoo-oop! Stand back and give me room according to my strength! Blood's my natural drink, and the wails of the dying is music to my ears. Cast your eye on me, gentlemen! and lay low and hold your breath....

—MARK TWAIN, in *Life on the Mississippi*

NEVER did painters have a broader, more romantic, varied, wild, and sweeping theme than the winning of the American West. Their canvas was more than a thousand miles square. At its eastern edge rolled the mighty Mississippi, which a contemporary journalist described as "the muddiest, the deepest, the shallowest, the bar-iest, the snaggiest, the sandiest, the catfishiest, the swiftest, the steamboatiest, and the uncertainest river in all the world." South lay the desert and the Gulf of Mexico. On the west the snowy battlements of the Rocky Mountains sparkled against the sky.

In this amphitheater an appropriately vast drama was unfolding. It began with the French *voyageurs* and the roistering flatboatmen out of Cincinnati and Pittsburgh, who opened the Mississippi to settlement and trade. It ascended the Missouri River with the mountain trappers to find green Edens on the slopes of the Rockies. It embraced millions of buffaloes moving across the illimitable prairies, and also their quick finish.

Whole tribes of Indians, now vanished, galloped the land that had been their home, lassoing wild ponies or hopelessly brandishing feathered lances in the face of doom. Like ships in convoy, covered wagons snaked across the New World. The cowboy came with his dusty, bawling cattle. Settlers moored their farms in the oceans of grass. Prospectors panned gold from the salmon streams. Railroad tracks cut across the fading game trails and warpaths. Cities shone clean and raw on the plains. And all in about fifty years.

The men who made it happen were, and had to be, a tough and adventurous breed. The artists who recorded the epic may not have been quite so brass-mounted as Mark Twain's river boatman, but they too needed at least as much pluck as talent. Their works illustrate a unique passage in the unfolding American dream.

GROWING up on the Missouri in the 1820s, George Caleb Bingham was to immortalize the men of the river. His schoolteaching mother had evidently introduced the boy to art in the form of European engravings, but his figures are drawn, clearly, from life. They are arranged in compositions as serenely architectural as those of Poussin, yet the atmosphere of Bingham's canvases comes from nature herself; it has a peculiarly American depth, warmth, and luminosity —the same qualities that Homer and especially Eakins were later to emphasize.

The Wood-Boat shows mid-nineteenth-century settlers waiting to make a sale of corded firewood to a passing steamer. The canvas, long thought lost, was recently rediscovered and hung in the City Art Museum of St. Louis. Seeming to borrow its spirit from the nostalgia of *Huckleberry Finn*, it is a masterpiece of its kind. Though Bingham's *The Concealed Enemy* has more the appearance of a vignette, it does put across the early riverman's haunting knowledge that hostile eyes might be upon him and an ambush waiting around the next bend. By contrast, Daniel Boone leading his family through Cumberland Gap looks comfortably oblivious to all danger.

A small-bodied, high-domed, ailing, touchy, idealistic prodigy, Bingham sold his birthright all too soon for a mess of politics. He became a power in the state of Missouri, serving as state treasurer and adjutant general, and a weakling at his easel. When he died in 1879 his statesmanship was more eulogized than his art, which soon fell into obscurity.

He was as anti-abstract as possible. "I have no hesitation in affirming," he wrote, "that any man who does not regard the imitation of nature as the great essential quality of art will never make an artist." In Fourth of July style he prophesied

GEORGE CALEB BINGHAM'S "THE WOOD-BOAT" (1850)

BINGHAM'S "THE CONCEALED ENEMY" (CA. 1850)

that "this glorious Republic of ours, stretching its liberal sway over a vast continent, will perhaps be best known in the distant ages of the future by the imperishable monuments of art which we may have the taste and genius to erect." Not until the mid-twentieth century did Bingham's own monuments gain their rightful place in the ranks of American painting.

THE first and freshest pictorial record of life among the Western Indians was made by iron-willed George Catlin during the 1830s. A successful miniaturist in Philadelphia, Catlin first felt the lure of the West when he saw an Indian delegation parading through town on its way back from Washington. Catlin resolved that "the history and customs of such a people, preserved by . . . illustrations, are themes worthy of the lifetime of one man, and nothing short of the loss of my life shall prevent me from visiting their country and becoming their historian."

Accordingly, he left his young bride and journeyed to St. Louis, where he enlisted the aid of General William Clark, superintendent of Indian affairs. As part of Clark's entourage Catlin was able to attend treaty-making powwows with the Ioways, Missouris, Omahas, Sacs, and Foxes at Prairie du Chien, and painted the Delawares,

BINGHAM'S "DANIEL BOONE ESCORTING A BAND
OF PIONEERS INTO THE WESTERN COUNTRY" (1851)

GEORGE CATLIN'S "VIEW ON UPPER MISSOURI" (1832)

Kickapoos, Potowatomies, Weahs, Peorias, and Kaskaskias at Cantonment Leavenworth.

When John Jacob Astor's American Fur Company decided to run a steamboat up the Missouri to the Yellowstone, Catlin clambered aboard. He found himself 2,000 miles from his St. Louis base, in the rich, warlike, untouched world of the Crows and Blackfeet. This was a land, he wrote, "where the buffaloes range with the elk and the fleet-bounding antelope; where wolves are white and bears grizzly; where the rivers are yellow . . . the dogs are all wolves, women are slaves, men all lords . . . where the predominant passions of the savage breast are ferocity and honor." Much to his own honor he made the return trip by canoe, painting his ferocious new friends at each village along the way.

Catlin's paintings of the Mandans have particular poignancy, for only five years after he visited them the Mandan tribe was utterly broken by smallpox. His *Mandan Village* seems wonderfully busy and secure, in keeping with Catlin's own opinion that the Indians' lives are "much more happy than ours." Medicine poles guard the place against spiritual ills, and a palisade wards off human foes. On the plain without, "the dead live" (in the Mandan phrase) mummified, on raised platforms.

Old Bear, whom Catlin painted in the full regalia of a medicine man, had given him some concern. Catlin wrote in his journal that while he was painting some other braves, Old Bear "commenced howling and haranguing around my domicile, amongst the throng that was outside, proclaiming that all who were inside and being painted were fools and would soon die; and very materially affecting thereby my popularity." Catlin "called him in the next morning, when I was alone, having only the interpreter with me; telling him that I had had my eye upon him for several days, and had been so well pleased with his looks, that I had taken great pains to find out his history, which had been explained by all as one of a most extraordinary kind, and his

85

CATLIN'S "A BIRD'S EYE VIEW OF THE MANDAN VILLAGE" (1832)

character and standing in his tribe as worthy of my particular notice; and that I had several days since resolved that as soon as I had practiced my hand long enough upon the others, to get the stiffness out of it (after paddling my canoe so far as I had) . . . I would begin on his portrait, which I was then prepared to commence."

This speech, which might well have softened a Yankee banker, fairly melted the savage's heart. Catlin later recorded in his journal that Old Bear's "vanity has been completely gratified . . . he lies for hours together, day after day, in my room, in front of his picture, gazing intensely upon it; lights my pipe for me while I am painting—shakes hands with me a dozen times on each day. . . ."

This typical incident helps explain how Catlin could roam the West alone, fearlessly, with such success. He could portray with steady hand the awesome Osage chief Cler-mont, chatting comfortably as he painted the whacking great war club and the scores of human scalps adorning the chief's leggings. He could cross 500 miles of unmapped prairie with no other companion than a horse named Charley, confident that when he stopped at a tepee to ask directions he would be more likely to receive an invitation for the night than an arrow in the throat.

In eight years Catlin visited forty-eight tribes, amounting (he estimated) to half a million people. He piled up close to 600 paintings of his red friends and their villages, and collected wagonloads of their pipes, weapons, utensils, and finery. Most of the Indians he knew were at the climax of a golden age that began with the introduction of horses from the Spanish in New Mexico. Elegant in their dress and elaborate in their ceremonies, they were happy, free, prosperous, leisured, brave. Knowing the Indians were doomed, as they did not, Catlin painted them with a kind of clean nostalgia. His pictures are like bright dreams that precede an awakening in the dark.

Such an awakening was to come to Catlin himself. He had been inspired by the Peale Museum in Philadelphia to create a similar museum of the American Indian, filled with Indian artifacts as well as his own pictures. To this end he turned from painting to the role of entrepreneur, touring the Eastern Seaboard and later Europe with

CATLIN'S
"MAH-TO-HE-HA, THE OLD BEAR" (1832)

CATLIN'S "CLER-MONT" (1834)

CATLIN'S "BUFFALO HUNT
UNDER THE WOLF-SKIN MASK" (CA. 1830)

88

his collection. Hopefully he wrote in the exhibition catalogue: "[Since] every painting has been made from nature by my own hand—and that too when I have been paddling my canoe or leading my pack horse over and through trackless wilds, at the hazard of my life—the world will surely be kind and indulgent enough to receive and estimate them . . . as true and facsimile traces of individual life and historical fact, and forgive me for their present unfinished and unstudied condition as works of art."

But the world was not so kind. It had been taught to think of Indians either as demigods (by James Fenimore Cooper) or as demihumans (by settlers' accounts), and Catlin's own objective reporting seemed unbelievable. "An Indian is a beggar in Washington City," Catlin had written, "and a white man is almost equally so in the Mandan village. An Indian in Washington is mute, is dumb and embarrassed; and so is a white man (and for the very same reasons) in this place." Now he found himself mute, dumb, and embarrassed before a rising tide of mockery. The majority decided he must be a great old faker. He went bankrupt. His collection passed into the hands of a Philadelphia manufacturer, who stored it in the cellar of a boilerworks.

Catlin's answer, in middle age, was to cap his earlier adventures with more of the same. He

CATLIN'S "SIOUX INDIANS PURSUING A STAG IN THEIR CANOES" (1836)

roamed the Western Hemisphere from Argentina to the Aleutian Islands, painting as he went. He repainted his early pictures from memory, badly, on cardboard, and exhibited them in Manhattan—where he unfortunately ran into competition from P. T. Barnum. Catlin published books in defense of his honor as explorer and artist. Nothing availed; he died in 1872, still under a cloud. But seven years after his death Catlin's original collection found the permanent home he had longed for, at the Smithsonian Institution in Washington.

COMPARED with Catlin, Alfred Jacob Miller was more of an artist and less of a man. The son of a Baltimore grocer, Miller did not hear the call of the wild in his heart, but from the lips of a rich patron, and his service in the Far West was far from arduous. Miller spent only a single summer there. Yet in the space of those few busy months, he managed to lasso immortality. The only painter ever to see a fur caravan on the Overland Trail or a rendezvous of the mountain trappers, he pictured what he saw with zest, a good deal of accuracy, and something of considerably more importance: a passionate sense of the strangeness, the spaciousness, and especially the fleetingness of it all. Where Catlin had been a heroic roamer and recorder of the unknown, Miller was a hired, fired-up romantic in the same region.

Nearly two years' training abroad had made Miller a swift and spirited draftsman, especially of human figures and animals in motion. It had also brought him under the influence of Delacroix, who was imbuing French painters with a romantic attachment to Morocco. The land of the Berbers had many of the same attractions as the land of the red Indians, so Miller's thoughts and style were somewhat prepared for his great adventure. Yet he was not ambitious; after his return to America he modestly set up shop as a journeyman portraitist in New Orleans.

In the spring of 1837, when Miller was twenty-seven, a martial-looking stranger appeared in his studio, looked carefully about, and then left. The visitor was Captain William Drummond Stewart of the British Army, veteran of Waterloo, and heir to Scotland's Murthly Castle and Birnam Wood. Strictly for fun Stewart had spent four summers and a winter adventuring in the Far West. He proposed to go once more, taking in his entourage a painter who would later record the highlights of the trip on the walls of Murthly Castle. Some days after his first visit, Stewart returned to Miller's studio and offered him the job. Only a fool or a coward could have refused, and Miller was neither.

Soon afterwards Stewart's party, of about ten, headed west from Independence, Missouri. They accompanied a caravan of John Jacob Astor's American Fur Company—loaded with blankets, liquor, calico, sugar and salt, tobacco, trinkets, coffee, and ammunition—which was headed for the Wind River country 1,000 miles away. The caravan's course, along the winding Platte, was later to become the first leg of the Overland Trail followed by covered wagons to the Pacific. It led over rolling, treeless land to one of the most beautiful mountain regions on earth. There the beaver trappers and the Indian tribes would forgather for their annual midsummer saturnalia and time of trading, a barbaric fair and mingling of civilization with savagery at the rim of the unknown.

In the course of this adventure Miller got to know many of the heroes of the American West. There was Etienne Provost, who had a "corpus round as a porpoise," according to Miller's notes, and the reputation of an original Old Man of the Rocky Mountains. There were Black Harris, Tom Fitzpatrick, Kit Carson, Bourgeois Walker (discoverer of Yosemite), and the legendary Jim

ALFRED JACOB MILLER'S "FORT LARAMIE" (1837)

MILLER'S "FUR TRAPPERS' RENDEZVOUS" (CA. 1840)

Bridger, to whom Stewart was bringing a suit of medieval armor as a gift. Among the Indians were the mighty Oglala Sioux cutthroat, Bull Bear, and the imperious Flathead, Rabbit-Skin Leggings. Among the half-breeds was Antoine Clement, hardiest of hunters, who used to sing *Dans mon pays je serais content* as he attacked a buffalo, and who was to become Stewart's valet in Scotland.

Miller saw and painted Fort Laramie, the portal to the Rockies, as it originally was. At the Rendezvous he watched 2,000 Snake Indians stage a wild procession in Stewart's honor. He knew "squaw doin's," saw wild horses cavorting in herds, and sat by a campfire drinking wine and eating cheese in country "as fresh and beautiful as if just from the hands of the Creator."

Miller caught the spirit of all this remarkably in his water-color sketches. The work required a civilized sort of concentration, and this occasionally put him in some danger. Miller wrote in his journal that when he was once sketching at Independence Rock, "being completely absorbed, about half an hour transpired when suddenly I found my head violently forced down and held in such a manner that it was impossible to turn right or left. An impression ran immediately through my mind that this was an Indian and that I was lost. In five minutes, however, the hands were removed. It was our Commander. He said: 'Let this be a warning to you or else on some fine day you will be among the missing.' "

In another note Miller describes sketching a buffalo with the help of the half-breed hunter Clement, who "would wound the animal in the flank, bringing him to a standstill. . . . Going as near him as was prudent, holding the sketch-book in one hand and the pencil in the other, it often happened that while absorbed in drawing a ludicrous scene would ensue. The brute would make a charge. Of course, sketch and pencil would be thrown down, the bridle seized, and a retreat made at double-quick time. This would convulse our Indian . . . with merriment, in which state he could not have aided us if he had wished."

By way of taking vacations from vacation, Stewart's party would sometimes leave the main caravan for side trips into still deeper wilderness. They hunted the Rocky Mountain bighorn sheep. They fished for trout "that were unsophisticated and bit immediately we placed the bait

CHARLES WIMAR'S "TURF HOUSE ON THE PLAINS" (CA. 1860)

ALBERT BIERSTADT'S "RAINBOW OVER JENNY LAKE" (CA. 1870)

94

near their mouths in the clear water." Finding a wild mint bed, they got riotously drunk on juleps.

In October the fun was over. Three years later Miller went to Murthly Castle and adorned it with a series of large, brown, dull oils copied from the small, luminous, and spirited sketches on which his fame rests. Thereafter he settled in Baltimore and began a long and undistinguished career painting portraits, an occasional landscape, and copies of his Far West pictures.

CHARLES Wimar of St. Louis and Albert Bierstadt of New Bedford, Massachusetts, were both Germans by birth. They made their way west by a circuitous detour back through their native land, where they learned their trade. The most admired school of European painting was then at Düsseldorf. Standing for romantic realism of the most grandiose sort, it was bound to affect their picturing of that eminently grandiose land, the American West.

Wimar died young, in 1862, but managed first to spend a few summers touring the West and winters painting what he had seen. *Turf House on the Plains* is typical of his stagy style; yet it does convey with startling impact the harsh and lonely life that faced the early plains settlers.

ALBERT Bierstadt was blessed with more skill than Wimar, and he supplemented his training at Düsseldorf with walking-sketching trips through the Alps and the Apennines. Back in the United States in 1857, he soon attached himself to an expedition under General Frederick Lander sent to improve the wagon trail from Fort Laramie through South Pass to the Pacific Coast. His first written impression of the Rockies shows how deeply Bierstadt's vision had been shaped by his European training. The mountains, he noted, "resemble very much the Bernese Alps; they are of granite formation, the same as the Swiss mountains. . . . The grouping of the rocks is charming . . . the color of the mountains is like those of Italy. . . ."

Thereafter Bierstadt took the Rockies for his special province. His Wagnerian interpretations often captured the grandeur, if not the light and air, of the real thing. Examples such as *Rainbow Over Jenny Lake* may seem derivative and stale in an age of color photography; the reverse is the case. Consciously or not, such modern photographers as Ansel Adams echo Bierstadt.

Even in Bierstadt's own day some critics were inclined to frown on his efforts, but collectors reached instinctively for their wallets. Bierstadt's outsize paintings sold for as much as $35,000, more than any American artist before him had been able to command in his lifetime.

BY contrast to Bierstadt, the career of Ralph Albert Blakelock slid rapidly downhill to poverty and despair. It began auspiciously. In 1869, when he was twenty-two, a small, quick young man, emotional in the extreme, Blakelock set bravely out to paint the Great West. Jingling in his pockets the money supplied by affectionate relatives, he moved slowly across the plains to the Rockies, and on to California. Everywhere he sketched the landscape and the Indians, and developed the awed regard for the American wilderness that was to color his entire art. Three years later the adventurer was back in New York, bent on a more difficult mission. He proposed nothing less than to make the primeval forest a part of civilized consciousness.

Blakelock accomplished it without Bierstadt's photographic exactitude and storytelling details. Such darkly glowing canvases as *Moonlight* were drawn from the deep well of memory; yet they reflected not so much what the painter had seen as what he felt. They were the still mirrors of a nature-haunted heart. Being subjective and unfamiliar, his pictures were disdained. He had to peddle them from door to door himself, asking a few dollars each.

Meanwhile Blakelock married, and fathered a swarming, hungry brood. His eldest daughter once recalled that Blakelock's unhappy life was "one continuous struggle to keep his ever-increasing family with a roof over them. We were always moving about (never bettering ourselves), always going down, always having to contrive to do with a little less each time, and my father living on hope that was always being deferred. I am quite positive he inspired all the family with faith in the goodness of the *morrow*."

The morrow proved bad indeed. On the day his ninth and last child was born, according to

95

RALPH ALBERT BLAKELOCK'S "MOONLIGHT" (1889-92)

FREDERIC REMINGTON'S "THE SCOUT, FRIENDS OR ENEMIES?" (CA. 1908)

the most specific account of his troubles, Blakelock desperately offered a painting, years in the making, to a customer for $1,000. He got a counter offer of $500, refused it, and stumbled off to sell the picture elsewhere. Late that day he returned to his first customer and acknowledged defeat. Thereupon the shrewd collector bought the picture for only $300. Blakelock, in a frenzy of frustration and anger, tore up the money. He was seized and found insane.

Years later, in 1916, a Chicago art collector visited Blakelock at a New York State asylum. By then the painter's work was selling for up to $20,000 a canvas, and forgers were busily producing more. Blakelock seemed perfectly sane until the moment when he drew what looked like a roll of bills from his pocket and gave three to his visitor. "Take this back to Chicago," Blakelock soberly advised him. "Don't spend it, but live off the interest." The bills turned out to be

three little landscapes he had painted to resemble paper money. They were done with brushes made by attaching to matchsticks a few hairs from a cat's tail or possibly the artist's own white head. Meanwhile his family was half-freezing and half-starving in a one-room farmhouse far away. One of his daughters had been unwittingly used by the forgers to produce fake Blakelocks, and had also gone insane.

After twenty wasted years, when he was past seventy, sanity returned to Blakelock. He had only a month left to live.

A HEAVY, hearty, and hard-riding man was Frederic Remington, and his life a short charge uphill to glory. He died in 1909, when he was only forty-eight, leaving to the world 2,739 pictures (including illustrations for 142 books, of which eight were his own) and twenty-five sculptures in bronze. This huge body of work records

97

REMINGTON'S "FIGHT FOR THE WATER HOLE" (1908)

the Wild West of cattle wars and Indian uprisings that now lives on mainly in the minds of small boys and Hollywood's horse operas.

Remington's people were moderately wealthy upstate New Yorkers, conservative and doubtless somewhat perturbed by his rough, open, and self-indulgent character. When he was just fifteen they packed him off to a military academy. That same year Remington wrote a letter to a fellow schoolboy: "I don't amount to anything in particular. I can spoil an immense amount of good grub at any time in the day. . . . I go a good man on muscle. My hair is short and stiff, and I am about 5 ft. 8 in. and weigh 180 lbs. There is nothing poetical about me. I don't swear much, although it is my weak point, and I have to look my letters over carefully to see if there is any cussing in them. I never smoke —only when I get treated. . . ."

A year later, at sixteen, Remington entered Yale as one of the university's two art students.

He liked sketching, but he liked football better. Most of all he yearned for adventure. When his father died, leaving him a modest inheritance, Remington quit school and headed west. He was nineteen, a happy wanderer on the Great Plains, with money in his pocket. He worked for fun as a cowboy and ranch cook, and learned to ride like a Comanche. Sometimes, by a campfire under the stars, he heard talk of the railroads that were creeping across the prairie. Their coming meant just one thing to Remington. "I knew the wild riders and the vacant land were about to vanish forever," he later wrote, "and the more I considered the subject, the bigger the *forever* loomed. . . . I began to try to record some facts around me, and the more I looked, the more the panorama unfolded."

After some years Remington returned East with sheaves of drawings, which the illustrated magazines gratefully bought, and Remington settled in New York to make more from memory.

He had a charming Eastern bride, a large studio crammed with cowboy and Indian paraphernalia, and such jovial companions as Theodore Roosevelt, Rudyard Kipling, Owen Wister, and Poultney Bigelow, editor of *Outing* magazine. Summers he would spend in the West, or in Canada or Mexico, collecting new impressions.

One Lieutenant Alvin H. Sydenham, a cavalry officer, has left a vivid account of the mature Remington on the trail. While maneuvering in Cheyenne country on the Tongue River, Sydenham's outfit was joined by the painter. "We first became aware of his existence in camp," the officer wrote, "by the unusual spectacle of a fat citizen dismounting from a tall troop horse at the head of a column of cavalry. The horse was glad to get rid of him, for he could not have trained down to two hundred pounds in less than a month of cross-country riding on a hot trail. Smoothed down over his closely shaven head was a little soft hat rolled up a trifle at the edges. . . . Tending still more to impress the observer with the idea of rotundity and specific gravity was a brown canvas hunting coat whose generous proportions and many swelling pockets extended laterally, with a gentle downward slope to the front and rear, like the protecting expanse of a brown cotton umbrella. And below, in strange contrast with the above, he wore closely fitting black riding breeches of Bedford cord, reinforced with dressed kid, and shapely riding boots of the Prussian pattern, set off by a pair of long-shanked English spurs.

"As he ambled toward camp, there was ample opportunity to study his figure and physiognomy. His gait was an easy, graceful waddle that conveyed a general idea of comfortable indifference to appearances and abundant leisure. But his face, although hidden for the time behind the smoking remainder of an ample cigar, was his most reassuring and fetching feature. Fair complexion, blue eyes, light hair, smooth face . . . a big, good-natured overgrown boy. . . . Mr. Remington shook my hand vigorously: 'Sorry to meet you, Mr. Sydenham. I don't like second lieutenants—never did. Captains are my style of people—they lend me horses.' "

The two became friends, and Sydenham would watch Remington closely to see how the painter worked. But, the officer confessed, "my stock of artistic information was as great when he went away as it was before he arrived. There was no technique, no 'shop,' about anything that he did. No pencils, no notebooks, no 'kodak'—nothing, indeed, but his big blue eyes rolling around at everything and into all sorts of queer places. Now and then an orderly would ride by, or a scout dash up in front of the commanding officer's tent. Then I would see him look intently for a moment with his eyes half-closed—only a moment, and it gave me the impression that perhaps he was a trifle nearsighted."

Remington's drawings from memory of the Tongue River Expedition of 1890 appeared soon afterwards in *Harper's Weekly*. As usual, they were an amazingly accurate rendering of the campaign.

Another summer Bigelow asked his friend Remington to keep him company on a trip abroad. Remington enjoyed the Arabian horses in North Africa and the stud farm of Emperor William II in Germany. Arriving in London, he hurried to Buffalo Bill's Wild West show. He loathed art galleries; yet once he did let himself be dragged to an impressionist exhibition. "Say," he exploded as he left, "I've got two maiden aunts upstate who can *knit* better pictures than those."

Five years after that trip Remington wrote to Bigelow: "No, honey, I should not try Europe again. I am not built right—I hate parks—collars—cuffs—foreign languages—cut and dried stuff. Europe is all right for most everybody but me—I am going to do *America*—it's new, it's to my taste. . . . Have been catching trout and killing deer—feel bully—absolutely on the water wagon, but it don't agree with me. I am at 240 pounds and nothing can stop me but an incurable disease."

Remington never did curb either his feasting or his drinking habits, which involved such barbaric breakfasts as fistfuls of pigs' knuckles, and midmorning shots of whisky at his easel. In another typical letter to Bigelow he wrote: "The latest news is that I haven't had a drink in three weeks and ain't going to have any more till I am about to die, when, after consultation of physicians, I am going to take one martini before I go up the Golden Stairs." He was scared stiff of women (except, curiously enough, his wife). Once, when he was sitting in a first-class compartment of a train in North Africa, contentedly sipping bourbon with Bigelow, a French couple climbed aboard. "Oh hell," Remington cried out, "here comes a damned woman!" and he bolted off to a second-class car crowded with Moors and Kabyles.

In 1898 publisher William Randolph Hearst sent Remington to Cuba to cover the Spanish-American War as an artist-correspondent. When Remington complained that there didn't seem to be any war, Hearst ripped off his famous answering cable: "You furnish the pictures; I'll furnish the war." Eventually Remington got to paint his justly famous *Charge of the Rough Riders at San Juan Hill* with his old friend Teddy Roosevelt in command.

Perhaps the saddest day of Remington's whole life came when, weighing about 300 pounds, he found that horses could no longer carry him. He had ridden every day that he could for all his adult life. He used the Western style, contending that "an Indian or a cowboy would take the average park rider off his horse, scalp him, hang him on a bush and never break a gallop." His studio in the country was built with barn doors so that he could paint horses inside it. To him, every horse was a unique creature, and he pictured each one as such. His quick eye saw that a galloping horse can have all four hoofs off the ground at once, and he painted them that way. Most horsemen scoffed, though high-speed photography proved Remington right. He asked that his epitaph read: HE KNEW THE HORSE. Instead, when he died following an appendectomy, he was laid under a stone at Canton, New York, that reads only: REMINGTON.

To some critics of American art, the name stands merely for illustrations of a certain type, done with dash and skill. But to sharers in the

REMINGTON'S "HOWL OF THE WEATHER" (1906)

HENRY CROSS'S "GERONIMO" (CA. 1900)

CROSS'S
"RED CLOUD AND BURNING HEART" (CA. 1908)

American dream, Remington's name is an honored one. For the dream belongs partly to him, and through him comes part of its definition.

ALONG with Remington and after him, came many less gifted painters to mourn and celebrate the setting of the Wild West's sun. Among them was Henry Cross, a plump New Yorker in rimless spectacles, a chesterfield, and a walrus mustache. Cross was a lot more adventurous than his bland exterior signified. Twice he ran away with circuses as a boy, and at sixteen made his way to Paris, where he studied animal painting under Rosa Bonheur. On his return he joined a circus that was heading west. The first Indians he saw were tame circus spectators. For a time thereafter, Cross painted wild animals on the sides of P. T. Barnum's wagons. Finally the call of uncaged wildness overcame him. He threw up his job with the circus and set forth in search of savages.

Ranging far and wide throughout the Indian uprisings, Cross painted as he went. His talent was for straightforward portraiture of a rather formal sort. He paid careful attention to details of his sitters' dress, posing them as if for a photograph, stern-faced against a background of stormy skies. In the process Cross learned at least one Indian tongue, Sioux, and his portrait of the Sioux chief Red Cloud (who discomfited the U.S. Army time and time again) is one of his best. Before his death in 1918, Cross created a sort of pictorial *Who's Who* of the doomed tribes, together with a gallery of cavalrymen and white

101

scouts. No less an authority than Buffalo Bill once praised his portraits as "striking likenesses . . . having been sketched from life by the greatest painter of Indian portraiture of all times."

CHARLES Marion Russell forsook St. Louis for Montana in 1880 when he was only sixteen. He spent two years as a trapper with an old mountain man before learning to be a cowboy. He was known, naturally enough, as "Kid." Russell "sang to the horses and cattle," as he put it, for eleven years. He also lived for six months in Canada with the Blood Indians, whom he came to love. Purely for amusement in idle hours, the burly, bowlegged young man used to draw and paint a little. His sketches became the wonder of Russell's fellows, who dug into their jeans to pay up to five silver dollars apiece for them. And his paintings were better yet, full of the bright, dry light of the land.

Once a stranger commissioned Russell to paint two pictures. "I thought I'd hit him good and hard," Russell later recalled, "because none of the boys had any money. Grass hadn't even started on the ranges, and our saddles were in soak, so I said, 'fifty dollars,' and I'm a common liar if the fellow didn't dig out a hundred dollars and hand 'em over. He thought I meant fifty dollars apiece, you see. I got crooked as a coyote's hind leg right away. . . . I just bought the fellow a drink and kept the rest. He don't know to this day how bad he beat himself."

In 1896 Russell married a shrewd girl who persuaded him to settle down to art. "Mame's

CHARLES RUSSELL'S "LEWIS AND CLARK MEETING FLATHEAD INDIANS"

the business end," he would say, "an' I jes' paint. . . . She could convince anybody that I was the greatest artist in the world . . . an' yu jes' can't disappoint a person like that." Russell built a log studio in Great Falls, Montana, where a sizable museum stands to his honor today. His pictures brought as much as $10,000 each. "Dead man's prices!" he would exclaim.

Montana adopted him as he had adopted her, and in 1911 the state commissioned him to paint a twenty-six-foot mural for its house of representatives. Russell chose for his subject the fateful first meeting of the Lewis and Clark Expedition with the Flathead Indians. The solidity and the scope of the result, almost inconceivable in a self-taught artist, shows once more that "self-taught" need not mean "primitive." In truth

(A MURAL INSTALLED IN 1912)

Russell was a minor sort of genius; his gift came from above. "To have talent is no credit to its owner," he once wrote of his own achievements, "for what man can't help he should get neither credit nor blame—it's not his fault. I am an illustrator. There are lots better ones, but some worse. Any man that can make a living doing what he likes is lucky, and I'm that. Any time I cash in now, I won."

In age Russell developed a talent for written reminiscence: "Life has never been too serious with me—I lived to play and I'm playing yet. Laughs and good judgment have saved me many a black eye, but I don't laugh at other people's tears. I was a wild young man but age has made me gentle. I drank, but never alone, and when I drank it was no secret."

Asked to address a Montana booster meeting shortly before his death in 1926, the old man was horrified to hear himself introduced as a "pioneer." Misty-eyed, he roared: "In my book, a pioneer is a man who comes to a virgin country, traps off all the fur, kills off all the wild meat, cuts down all the trees, grazes off all the grass, plows the roots up, and strings ten million miles of bob wire. A pioneer destroys things and calls it civilization. I wish to God that this country was just like it was when I first saw it, and that none of you folks were here at all!"

LIKE a bolt of lightning the wily equine flies into the air with volcanic suddenness—with a fantastic violence and rabid spleen that defy description." So William Robinson Leigh described his own painting, *A Lowdown Trick*. Clearly Leigh's view of the artist's role was a self-effacing one. "It's not how a picture is painted that matters," he used to say. "It is what you paint."

The how came first, though, for Leigh. Born in West Virginia in 1866, he got twelve years of stiff training in Munich (which had become the successor to Düsseldorf) under a succession of nature painters named Raupp, Gysis, Von Lindenschmit, and Von Loefftz. Sometimes in old age he would place his fingertips gently together and try to explain the vanished Munich method: "You start with a detailed charcoal drawing and then paint over that—the most distant things first. If there are no clouds, the sky may take no more than a day. The distant figures may be done in a week. It gets more difficult as you approach the foreground—a large canvas may take four to six months altogether—but the most economical way is to finish as you go. At least, that's what *I* was taught."

Leigh always longed to apply this formidable background to the problem of painting the West. But not until 1906, when he was forty, did he get there. He had persuaded the Santa Fe Railroad to give him a free ticket in return for painting the Grand Canyon. The company ordered five more pictures on the strength of the first, and between commissions Leigh roamed the vast, raw, neighboring country on horseback, sketching as he went. He kept on painting the West until his death in 1955, and pictured a vanished era with a chromolithographic exactitude that no man since his day could possibly match.

WILLIAM R. LEIGH'S "A LOWDOWN TRICK" (1948)

CHAPTER II

THE PEOPLE'S CHOICE

I do not need to woo the fickle Muse,
But am her master, justified by thee:
All measures must obey me as I choose,
So long as they are thine, Propriety!

—Bayard Taylor

THE beckoning milestones that marked the opening of the West—Yellowstone, Fort Laramie, Sutter's Mill—fixed America's destiny irrevocably. The balance of political and economic power moved westward with the railroads and wagon trains, old customs and attitudes gave way to the new demands of the expanding frontier, and the pressures of the westward advance added new strains to old conflicts. The question of slavery in the new territories was one rock on which all attempts at compromise foundered.

Yet for all the bloodshed, the bitterness, and the misery of civil war, the meeting at Appomattox Courthouse saw an ideal reaffirmed and a future reassured. In the immense opportunities that lay to westward, that future seemed brighter than ever. As Stephen Douglas had told the Senate some years before: "There is a power in this nation greater than the North or the South—a growing, increasing, swelling power that will be able to speak the law to this nation and to execute the law as spoken. That power is the country known as the Great West. . . ."

Two minor documents of the period were dedicated to the nation's growing sense of its own past. One was the ambitious battle cyclorama at Gettysburg, commissioned by a Chicago businessman and done by a French artist who visited the battlefield in 1881. Now displayed in its own museum, the huge canvas is based on official records and eyewitness accounts, and reconstructs Pickett's Charge in meticulous military detail, coming to a climax with the fighting at Bloody Angle—the high-water mark of the Confederacy. The other historic canvas was the work of a Massachusetts primitive painter named Erastus Salisbury Field. His unique and fantastic *Historical Monument of the American Republic* portrays every major hero and event of the nation's first hundred years. Field included them all as statues and bas-reliefs on his painting of a building that seems to combine Babel and Troy with a prophecy of modern Manhattan—its skyscraping towers connected by railroad bridges.

Yet most contemporary painters, accurately reflecting the popular taste, showed little interest in exploring such heroic themes. During the "brown decades" of convalescence that followed the war came a fabulous economic expansion. By 1890 America had a population of sixty-three million, and its national resources were estimated at sixty-five billion dollars. Opportunity seemed limited only by the vigor and imagination needed to grasp it. The public, in its preoccupation with worldly pursuits, asked of its painters only that they present no problems or surprises. A cross section of the most popular American painters of the day—whether portraitists, landscapists, or still-life artists—shows only one common denominator: a safe and sober mediocrity that could be admired without effort.

THE portraits of George Peter Alexander Healy have long since fallen from critical favor, but during his lifetime their success was complete. Born in Boston in 1813, the son of a Dublin sea captain, Healy began painting as a schoolboy. When Thomas Sully visited Boston and saw Healy's first efforts at portraiture, he said: "My young friend, I advise you to make painting your profession." As Sully predicted, Healy's Yankee grit and Irish charm more than made up for his limitations as an artist.

By painting Boston's wealthy merchants and their wives, Healy got enough money to study in Paris under Baron Gros. The training gave him a cool, firm style, as superficial as it was irreproachable. American tourists gladly posed for their gay, mustachioed countryman, and soon the French and English began following suit. From his twenty-sixth year—when a pretty English girl named Louisa Phipps agreed to marry him, and King Louis Philippe agreed to sit for him—his fortunes soared.

Louis Philippe sent Healy back home to America to paint President Tyler, Daniel Webster, John Quincy Adams, Henry Clay, and the dying Andrew Jackson for the royal collection. Though the French king was sent into exile before the work was done, Healy's international reputation had been assured. Congress voted to commission a series of presidential portraits from Healy, at $1,000 each. He painted Lincoln often, the first time when Abe was a beardless President-elect.

A politician who happened to drop by the senate chamber in Springfield's old Statehouse to watch one of Lincoln's first sittings to Healy has left a close-up description of the occasion. Lincoln "sat to the artist with his right foot on top of the left and both feet turned inward—pigeon fashion—round-shouldered, looking grim as fate, sanguinity in his expression, occasionally breaking into a broad grin. . . . He chatted, told stories, laughed at his own wit—and the humor of others—and in one way or another made a couple of hours pass merrily and never once lost his dignity or committed himself to an opinion."

Healy himself recalled that in the midst of one sitting, Lincoln burst out laughing over a candid letter from a little girl. The President-elect asked him to pass on it: "As a painter, Mr. Healy, you should be a judge between this unknown correspondent and me. She complains of my ugliness. It is allowed to be ugly in the world, but not as ugly as I am. She wishes me to put on false whiskers, to hide my horrible lantern jaws. Will you paint me with false whiskers? No?" Despite his levity at that moment, Lincoln grew whiskers before arriving at the White House; he was never again painted clean-shaven.

Healy entered into a steady career of profitable labor. He traveled constantly, painting Franz Liszt and Pope Pius IX in Rome, Louisa May Alcott in Switzerland, King Charles I in Rumania, Charles Goodyear Sr., the inventor, in Paris, and Henry Wadsworth Longfellow in Cambridge, Massachusetts. In 1892 the old man decided to go back to America and settle down in Chicago. He lived there two years, and then died murmuring: "Happy . . . so happy."

LIKE George Healy, who died "so happy," Eastman Johnson was a fortunate man. The son of a successful Maine politician, he developed as a boy a knack for making flattering likenesses in crayon. Partly because his father smoothed the way, he found himself deluged with portrait commissions. Thus encouraged, he sailed abroad for further study. When he returned in 1855, Johnson was already a highly polished academician. He set himself to painting a series of gentle, domestic scenes, which he imbued with the dignity of great events.

The Old Stage Coach, typical of his mature style, is an elaborate reconstruction of boyhood fun. Such explicitly illustrative art, crammed with contemporary details, must appeal mainly to its own day, and a caustic critic once remarked that Johnson's art ranged "from cute to nice." But he was painting for a public that knew what it liked. The public loved him and made him one of the most honored artists of his day.

STILL-LIFE painters rule a tidy, table-top world, where nothing moves except at their command. Their pictures are peaceful as well as

DETAIL FROM GETTYSBURG CYCLORAMA (1882-84)

GEORGE P. A. HEALY'S "ABRAHAM LINCOLN" (1860)

pleasant, for time is on their side. Many a still-life artist has succeeded by plain patience when genius failed. By careful copying of what is before him, he can create a sort of teasing charm—the charm of candy in a showcase, or a fly in amber.

William Harnett devoted his infinite patience to the narrowest corner of the art: paintings deliberately designed to fool the eye. According to a friend, Harnett himself was "very near-sighted; his glasses were jammed close to the eye socket, through which he seemed to glare from his intense strain to see, but his eyes were micro-scopic." Yet Harnett's art has bemused many a sensible man with 20/20 vision. Looking at his life-size *After the Hunt*, crowds have argued that it is not a painting at all but a cleverly installed and lighted window display of real objects.

A poor, gaunt, and grim-looking Irishman raised in Philadelphia, Harnett long supported himself by engraving silver. He always wanted to be a painter, and devoted practically all his spare time to practicing the art. Still life attracted him particularly because it saved the price of live models and because he could eat many of his subjects after he painted them. When in middle age he began to sell his pictures, Harnett humbly sailed for Europe to improve his technique. His European instructors were quick to condemn his self-taught methods, and he failed to appreciate theirs. Determined "to discover whether the line of work I had been pursuing had or had not artistic merit," he painted *After the Hunt* for the Paris Salon of 1885. It made a hit, and Harnett's fortune, both at home and abroad.

Though the public applauded, Harnett's fel-low painters did not. "In art, true art," painter George Inness objected, "we are not seeking to deceive." Harnett did not mean to fool anyone for long, of course, only to delight them with his deceptions and charm them into buying. His canvases are not lacking in mood; they have an air of quiet sadness, as if the objects he painted were old mementos taken from a forgotten trunk. And his pictures are composed with remarkable skill, as shown by the elaborate ordering, rich in repeated accents, of *After the Hunt*. The diagonal

EASTMAN JOHNSON'S "THE OLD STAGE COACH" (1871)

WILLIAM HARNETT'S "AFTER THE HUNT" (1885)

alpenstock pulls the whole picture together and is also a deception within a deception, for it floats unsupported in mid-air.

Harnett's description of his working methods could hardly be less helpful: "The chief difficulty I have found has not been the grouping of my models but their choice. . . . Take for instance the handle of the old sword [in *After the Hunt*]. Had I chosen a sword with an ivory handle of a different tint, the tone of the picture would have been ruined." Then with stunning inconsistency he added: "In painting from still life, I do not closely imitate nature."

THE Hudson River School spawned a big and adventurous fish in Frederick Edwin Church. Born in Connecticut in 1826, he spent four years under the wing of Thomas Cole at Catskill, New York, learning landscape painting. But Church was not content with bringing into the drawing rooms of his customers scenes that they themselves might find on a Sunday buggy ride. Seeking grander, more distant subjects, he roamed the world and came home to paint the vast canvases that made his reputation.

"Church," declared a contemporary critic, "exhibits the New England mind pictorially developed. His great attribute is skill; he goes to nature, not so much with the tenderness of a lover or the awe of a worshiper as with the determination, the intelligence, the patient intrepidity of a student. He is keenly on the watch for facts and resolute in their transfer to art." *Niagara Falls* shows what the critic meant. Anyone who had visited the spot could see that the seven-foot canvas clearly represented the Horseshoe Falls and American Falls viewed from the Canadian shore near Table Rock, and that it was no more grandiose than the subject. From then on, the public was prepared to agree that Church's *The Heart of the Andes*, *Rainy Season in the Tropics*, and *The Icebergs* were just as true to life—as indeed they were.

Ruskin, the faithful champion of England's proto-impressionist Joseph Turner, was particularly impressed by Church's *Niagara Falls*. He remarked that Church had achieved effects of light on water never before known to art. He also confessed that at first he had not been able to believe that the rainbow seen in the picture was actually painted, but thought it to be a reflection from his window. There can be no question that Church's skill served to stretch the imaginations of his admirers; he brought far places into their

FREDERICK CHURCH'S "NIAGARA FALLS" (1857)

minds accurately and convincingly. Today the movie travelogue and the travel lecturer's slide fulfill much the same function.

HENRY Adams once remarked that American painters "used sex for sentiment, never for force." His point applies to almost all American art, in striking contrast to the French, for example. Adams' own day witnessed the flourishing of a cult of love and beauty—feminine, cloudy, and ephemeral in times that were notably masculine, concrete, and materialistic. The poet Sidney Lanier expressed the cultists' plaintive tone precisely when he wrote:

> "O Trade! O Trade! would thou wert dead!
> The Time needs heart—'tis tired of head:
> We're all for love," the violins said.

Abbott Thayer was high priest of the violin set. Thayer, as the critic James Flexner put it, "specialized in glorifying the American girl. With little wings, she was a fairy; with big wings, an angel; nude, she was the Spirit of the Water Lily; dressed, Virginity."

Born in Boston in 1849, Thayer studied painting in Paris and got a solid academic grounding under Gérôme. He developed a trick of exaggerating lights and shadows to produce a three-dimensional effect without much true modeling. His drawing lacked edge and vigor, but it did have grace, and that suited his unexceptionable female subject matter. He liked to imagine himself a Mantegna, rather than a Yankee, and in fact Thayer's art amounted to a thin echo of the vanished glories of the Italian Renaissance.

The Virgin is a superior example of his talent. The figure looks wrapped in taffy, the composition is symmetrical to the point of rigidity, and the atmosphere fuzzed with sweetness. Yet for those who obey Coleridge's injunction "never to judge of any work of art by its defects," the canvas has quite another air. Done with reverent skill, it can speak softly to the heart.

112

ABBOTT THAYER'S "THE VIRGIN" (1893)

JAMES McNEILL WHISTLER'S "OLD BATTERSEA BRIDGE: NOCTURNE IN BLUE AND GOLD" (CA. 1865)

CHAPTER III

SOPHISTICATES ABROAD

*Art lives upon discussion, upon experiment, upon
curiosity, upon variety of attempt, upon exchange
of views and the comparison of standpoints.*

—Henry James

THE hardy breed that was making factories hum east of the Mississippi and hunting beaver and gold to the west of it had almost nothing in common with the new cosmopolitans of the Eastern Seaboard, who sat stirring tea in real china cups, gazing out at their formal gardens and talking of Mr. Tennyson. This refined race had been born of subtle and prolonged dalliance between New World opportunity and Old World culture. It naturally had trouble deciding which parent meant the more.

For creative men who agreed that "art lives upon discussion," the pull of Europe was especially strong. Three major American painters of the period who felt the call were James McNeill Whistler, John Singer Sargent, and Mary Cassatt. Like West and Copley a century before (and like the less elegant Americans who have populated the Left Bank in Paris ever since), all three longed for the intelligent approval and inspiring example of their European peers. Seeking style rather than subject matter, they brought native genius to their European experience. Soon they were setting stylistic precedents themselves.

WHISTLER'S career began, appropriately enough, with a little explosion. One day in 1854, when Whistler was a cadet at West Point,

the chemistry professor invited him to discuss silicon. The young man obliged: "Silicon is a gas—" Soon afterwards, Whistler was discharged from the Point. He always maintained in later years that "had silicon been a gas, I would have been a major general."

He could explain away almost anything. "I shall be born when and where I want," he used to say, "and I do not choose to be born at Lowell." But Lowell, Massachusetts, was his birthplace, in 1834, and Puritan his upbringing. On Sundays the child's toys were taken away, and a Bible put in his hands. In later years he reflected that "the Bible is a book which, once put down, can never be taken up again." At twenty-one the peppery and unpromising former cadet had left his native shores for good; he was off to Paris to study art.

Gustave Courbet, the French realist master, urged Whistler to paint just what he saw. At the same time he made plain that each man sees things differently from every other, which was good news to so determined an individualist as Whistler. The student learned to visualize precisely. He would turn his back on a scene and describe it in minute detail, with every nuance of color and form. Later, back in his studio, he would rearrange the elements he remembered, making them harmonize anew. He generally preferred to paint things in crepuscular light, without shadows. Sunlight—or any strong light—imposes a definite sense of order because the objects revealed all stand in clear relation to the source of light. Whistler preferred to do his own ordering. "I'll be the sun," he said in effect. By blurring away all clear lights and shadows, he took sole charge of the objects in his pictures. Then he could dispose them to suit himself.

Moving from Paris to London, Whistler set about revealing the River Thames to those who thought they had seen her always. "When the evening mist clothes the riverside with poetry as with a veil," he wrote, "and the poor buildings lose themselves in the dim sky, and the tall chimneys become campanili, and the warehouses are palaces in the night, and the whole city hangs in the heavens, and fairyland is before us, then the wayfarer hastens home. . . . And nature, who, for once, has sung in tune, sings her exquisite song to the artist alone." Those who had the eyes to see were drawn by Whistler's canvases into just such an experience.

Many failed to see. Among the blind was John Ruskin, who had only blue notes to sound for Whistler's art, describing it as "a pot of paint" flung "in the public's face." The exasperated artist sued Ruskin for libel, presenting *Battersea Bridge* at the trial as evidence of his abilities. Looking at the picture, the judge made the mistake of using sarcasm, Whistler's favorite weapon. The following dialogue took place:

His Honor: Are those figures on the top of the bridge intended for people?

Whistler: They are just what you like.

His Honor: That is a barge beneath?

Whistler: Yes. I am very much flattered at your seeing that. . . .

In the end Whistler won his case, plus damages of one farthing. Though Ruskin had the humiliation of hearing the full weight of his scorn assessed at a farthing's worth, Whistler suffered in a more material way. He was fined for half the court costs, which forced him into bankruptcy. Whistler thereupon published a pamphlet that could not have improved his position with the critics, since in attacking Ruskin he scatter-shot them all: "Art, that for ages has hewn its own history in marble, and written its own comments on canvas, shall it suddenly stand still, and stammer, and wait for wisdom from the passer-by? For guidance from the hand that holds neither brush nor chisel? Out upon the shallow conceit! What greater sarcasm can Mr. Ruskin pass upon himself than that he preaches to young men what he cannot perform!"

Even as a polemicist, Whistler had refinement. But the victories of the refined are often Pyrrhic. His individualism made him suspect to the herd, his abilities excited envy and malice, and his wit hurt. For most of his life he had to scrape for funds. He was jostled, scorned, and abused by the many—and worshiped by a few.

The few included George Meredith, Algernon Charles Swinburne, Ellen Terry, Dante Gabriel Rossetti, Walter Sickert, and a dozen lesser lights, who would drop in of a Sunday morning for a breakfast of American buckwheat cakes. Oscar Wilde was inseparable from Whistler for two years after coming down from Oxford, and before they quarreled and broke apart he modeled some of his own personality—including his waspish wit, his habit of ostentatious and distinctive dress, his cult of art for art's sake, and his exalting of art over nature—on the master's.

Unlike Wilde, Whistler was lucky in love. A bouncy, high-stepping, and fast-talking dandy, he would tug at the bit of beard beneath his lip and then paralyze his prey with a quip. He had many beautiful mistresses, two illegitimate children, and, late in his life, an adoring wife. Indeed, he remarked that it is lucky we cannot see ourselves as others see us, for "I know in my case I should grow intolerably conceited."

"One does like to make one's Mummy just as nice as possible," Whistler once confided. His justly famed portrait of his mother took the eye of Thomas Carlyle, who wished to be painted in a similar pose. Carlyle had no notion of what he was in for. Flourishing a three-foot brush like a fencer's foil, Whistler would lunge at the canvas, flick it, stagger back to a far corner of the room, squint, swear and leap to wipe away what he had done. This went on for weeks. The fury of the painter's attack produced an ever more gentle result. Carlyle, who was actually seething with impatience to have the job over and done with,

WHISTLER'S "PORTRAIT OF THOMAS CARLYLE:
ARRANGEMENT IN GREY AND BLACK, NO. 2" (1872)

faded softly into the calm and clouded atmosphere of the canvas, there to stay serene forever.

"One wants the spirit, the aroma, don't you know?" Whistler would explain. "If you paint a young girl, youth should scent the room; if a thinker, thoughts should be in the air; an aroma of the personality . . . and, with all that, it should be a picture, a pattern, an arrangement, a harmony, such as only a painter could conceive."

"What are we to do," asked one sour critic, "who find ourselves in disagreement with Mr. Whistler's principles?" Imperturbably the master replied: "Do, my dear Sir? Why, die!"

Whistler's own death came in 1903 after much suffering and greater joy. For, as he maintained,

"Art and joy go together." His style had long since become milk-thin compared to his teacher Courbet's robustness. Whistler's weakness was weakness. His strengths were subtlety, mystery, glistening suppleness. He worked with mist and magic in about equal parts.

JOHN Singer Sargent, America's most brilliant virtuoso of the brush, seems curiously bound to his own era. His very name whispers of the gilt frames, plush draperies, chandeliers, fringed bellpulls, spats, bowler hats, and potted palms that furnished the Victorian and Edwardian ages. Yet he was much more interested in people than in props and backgrounds.

117

JOHN SINGER SARGENT'S "DAUGHTERS OF EDWARD D. BOIT" (1882)

Born abroad, and born elegant, Sargent was the son of a Philadelphia doctor who had retired to Europe. Traipsing from spa to spa with his parents and sisters, he grew up to be a tall, portly, rubicund fellow with bulging blue eyes and a high collar under his full beard. He lived in a wondrously complacent world, where no gentleman ever had to make his own bed. Sargent developed just one passion—painting. Choosing for his ideal the sort of portraiture practiced long before by Frans Hals and Velásquez, he learned his lessons from those masters brilliantly and in an amazingly short time.

It was in Paris, at a scant twenty-seven, that Sargent proved himself a painter of felicity and not just flair. His *Daughters of Edward D. Boit* found a place in the Salon of 1883 and in public esteem. While one critic dismissed the picture as "four corners and a void," others were more discerning. "The naturalness of the composition," wrote Henry James, "the loveliness of the complete effect, the light, free security of the execution, the sense it gives us of assimilated secrets and of instinct and knowledge playing together —all this makes the picture . . . astonishing." But, James added prophetically, "May not this breed an irresponsibility . . . on the part of the youthful genius who has, as it were, all his fortune in his pocket? . . . It may be better for an artist to have a certain part of his property invested in unsolved difficulties."

The canvas that so impressed James echoes Velásquez' masterpiece, *The Maids of Honor*, which Sargent had studied at the Prado. As Sargent himself well understood, he was by no means a second Velásquez. Where the Spaniard firmly persuades the eye to believe in the painted image, Sargent only beguiles it into a momentary suspension of disbelief. Velásquez' reverent handling of the way light caresses objects becomes mere virtuosity in Sargent. And the arbitrary manner in which Sargent causes the light to pick the flower-like figures out of the gloom smacks more of the theater than of life. Yet no painter alive today could carry off half so well what Sargent set out to do.

A year after his triumph with the Boit children, Sargent sent to the Salon another painting, with the cautious title *Portrait de Mme.* . . . . His subject happened to be the reigning beauty of the hour, except in Sargent's eyes. He confided to a friend that Madame was "a uniform lavender or blotting-paper color all over," although he justly added that she did possess "the most beautiful lines." He had painted her with the accent on her low neckline, which produced a *succès de scandale*. Paris, that always astonishing jade, found the picture immodest, and Madame herself was embarrassed. She refused the canvas (which

TAFT MUSEUM, CINCINNATI

SARGENT'S
"ROBERT LOUIS STEVENSON" (1884-87)

Sargent later sold to Manhattan's Metropolitan Museum). In the furor few Parisians noticed that the picture combined bare flesh and black satin, starkness and stylishness, in a single unforgettable image. The portrait has the rare quality of standing whole and clear in the mind's eye—a sure sign of mature style.

Deciding to put the English Channel between himself and his detractors, Sargent moved to London and took an ornate studio on Tite Street. Soon the rush of business forced him to take another studio next door, and hire two maids to help his valet. A blunt bachelor, he kept a rubber stamp in his correspondence desk that printed the single word "Damn." He installed his mother and an unmarried sister in a flat around the corner, and spent much of his spare time there. Robert Louis Stevenson, who sat to Sargent for his portrait in 1884, described him as "a person with a kind of exhibition manner and English

119

SARGENT'S "MADAME X" (1884)

accent, who proves, on examination, simple, bashful, honest, enthusiastic, and rude. . . ."

Society delighted in Sargent's society and worshiped his talent. To be "done by Sargent," at prices of $5,000 and up, became the thing. Celebrities flocked to his studio. But instead of immortalizing, Sargent rather paralyzed most of them, turning them into clotheshorses, handsome or beautiful as the case might be, with elegant gestures and bored, sleepy expressions. Arranging to be portrayed, Joseph Pulitzer asked whether the artist did not wish to begin by studying him, "by talking, conversing, and generally summing up my character." Sargent smiled: "No, I paint what I see. Sometimes it makes a good portrait; so much the better for the sitter. Sometimes it does not; so much the worse for both of us. But I don't dig beneath the surface for things that don't appear before my eyes."

The fleshly envelope was enough for Sargent. "I do not judge," he would explain. "I only chronicle." But without judges there can be no justice, and Sargent was unconsciously unjust to his sitters when he treated them as mere objects. President Woodrow Wilson, he once remarked coldly, "has not a very paintable brow." Theodore Roosevelt made him feel "like a rabbit in the presence of a boa constrictor," but he made no effort to paint the big-stick side of Roosevelt's character, presenting him rather as a plump Boy Scout master at a temperance meeting.

Like all portraitists, Sargent had to put up with endless complaints from dissatisfied sitters. He once defined a portrait as "a painting with a little something wrong about the mouth." In one case the problem of the mouth became so acute that Sargent said to his sitter: "Well, Madame, perhaps we had better leave it out altogether." Another time it was the painting of her nose that a lady disagreed with. "Oh, you can alter a little thing like that," said Sargent, quickly handing her the portrait, "when you get it home." He would not agree to paint John D. Rockefeller until he got a guarantee that no alterations in the portrait would be suggested.

Once in a great while a particularly appealing subject would lift Sargent from his apathetic—almost scornful—capability to glorious heights. In *Mademoiselle Suzanne Poirson* and *Egyptian*

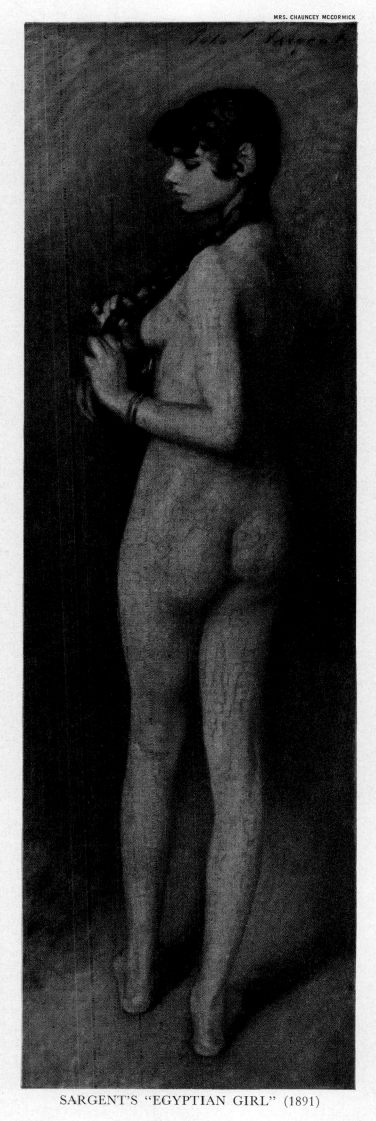

SARGENT'S "EGYPTIAN GIRL" (1891)

SARGENT'S "MADEMOISELLE SUZANNE POIRSON" (1884)

SARGENT'S "EL JALEO" (1882)

122

Girl, for example, he forgot himself and painted for pure love of beauty. Then the dullness of his everyday work would burst upon him, and the well-fed, well-bred giant would burst out that portraiture is "a pimp's profession." Once, in a momentary triumph over practical considerations, he wrote to a friend exultantly: "No more *paughtraits!* I abhor and abjure them, and hope never to do another, especially of the Upper Classes." At such times he would drop everything for a while and take a trip. His travels resulted in reams of limp, glistening water colors, and a few strong genre pieces in oils such as his early *El Jaleo*. He visited America often, and refused a

knighthood in Great Britain rather than give up his American citizenship. In Boston he put great effort into a series of allegorical murals for the public library and art museum, which he vainly hoped would be pleasing to the ages.

Since his death in 1925, Sargent's reputation has descended rapidly from its Edwardian peak. His friend Sir Edmund Gosse gives part of the reason. Sargent, he says, "thought that the artist ought to know nothing whatever about the nature of the object before him . . . but should concentrate all his powers on a representation of its appearance. The picture was to be a consistent vision, a reproduction of the area filled by the

MARY CASSATT'S "A CUP OF TEA" (CA. 1880)

eye. Hence, in a very curious way, the aspect of a substance became much more real to him than the substance itself." In short, Sargent was a painter of appearances. Nothing could be more foreign to the modern analytical temper, which keeps denying that appearances count for much.

WOMAN'S vocation in life," Mary Cassatt once said, "is to bear children." She herself produced hundreds of children, and their mothers, too—but all on canvas. Never married herself, Cassatt painted her chosen theme with an intimacy that only a woman could command, with an honesty that put off almost everyone but her fellow artists, and with a discipline to match her own strenuously exacting taste. She was America's first great woman painter, and, to this day, the nation's best.

A tall, taut Philadelphia society girl, Cassatt insisted on going to Europe to study art. Her banker father declared he would almost rather see her dead. Nevertheless, in 1866, Cassatt went. She was then only twenty-two; she had assurance of wealth to last a lifetime, ambition enough for several, and a courageous, discriminating mind. After traveling extensively throughout Europe, studying and copying the old masters in Holland, France, Italy, and Spain, she finally settled down in Paris and gave herself over to the influence of that exacting, woman-hating modern master, Edgar Degas. On first seeing her work, Degas exclaimed: "I would not have admitted that a woman could draw as well as that."

As a close friend (no one knows just how close), Degas transmitted much of his almost cruelly precise draftsmanship to Cassatt. The impressionists—Manet, Monet, *et al.*—followed his lead in charming the prim, determined creature into their sunlit circle. From them she learned to subordinate form, space, and texture to the pure

124

CASSATT'S "LA LOGE" (1879)

play of light, and to give her pictures their characteristic air of calm and gracious ease.

She made a habit of painting plain people in unconsciously beautiful poses, and with the same care that earlier artists lavished on saints and goddesses. Coolheaded and warmhearted, gentle yet austere, her art maintains a constant balance within her modest range. *A Cup of Tea* shows how at home she could be with her own Victorian background, while *La Loge* hints at submerged sensuousness. *Mother and Child* goes deeper. The baby's burgeoning life is subsiding to bedtime weariness; relaxed and perfectly possessive, the child clasps its mother's chin. The mother is just as peaceful, though stiff in her tight bodice and careful to hold her baby securely until it sleeps.

From the start, French critics noted her rather puritanical simplicity. "She remains exclusively of her people," said one. "Hers is a direct and significant expression of the American character." But America failed to realize the fact; she had no native fame until after her death. On a visit home in 1899, at the height of her powers, the Philadelphia *Public Ledger* commented in a brief social note: "Mary Cassatt, sister of Mr. Cassatt, president of the Pennsylvania Railroad, returned from Europe yesterday. She has been studying painting in France, and owns the smallest Pekingese dog in the world."

Understandably, Mary Cassatt felt more at home in Paris. For decades she rarely left her studio, painting from eight in the morning until the light failed, and then turning to her drawings and etchings. During World War I the light failed in her eyes. Blind, she lived on for another decade, feeling her way about with an umbrella, and snapping her large and bony fingers as she recalled the great days of impressionism.

CASSATT'S "MOTHER AND CHILD" (CA. 1890)

CHAPTER IV

MASTERS AT HOME

I shall be telling this with a sigh
Somewhere ages and ages hence:
Two roads diverged in a wood, and I—
I took the one less traveled by,
And that has made all the difference.

—ROBERT FROST

WHILE the American expatriates flared like comets abroad, a glow that was to become an enduring light flickered and burst into flame at home. In George Inness, Winslow Homer, Thomas Eakins, and Albert Pinkham Ryder, American painting had found its masters.

The making of a masterpiece is a lonely thing. It requires solitude first of all—to see, to feel, and to accumulate. Not many men can endure such intense visions or the pain of their solitary bodying forth. These four drew strength from their very solitude as well as from the land about them. They were re-creative realists; the truths they met and re-created on their own terms were like lightning flashes from native skies.

Each of the four took strikingly opposed views of their common world. To Inness reality meant a mingling of nature with his own emotions. The classic definition of art as being "nature seen through a temperament" applies perfectly to his canvases. Winslow Homer had a colder eye: he saw reality as a struggle in which the great forces of nature stood to win. Thomas Eakins looked into the hearts of men, and to him the deepest reality consisted of their valiant strivings. Albert Pinkham Ryder gazed into his own heart, finding reality in the form of visions bedded there.

Among them, the four quadrangulate the American spirit: romantic and realistic by turns, deeply engaged in life, yet deeply visionary.

THE true use of art," wrote George Inness, "is, first, to cultivate the artist's own spiritual nature, and, second, to enter as a factor in general civilization. . . . Every artist who . . . aims truly to represent the ideas and emotions which come to him when he is in the presence of nature is in process of his own spiritual development and is a benefactor of his race. Of course, no man's motive can be absolutely pure and single. . . . But the true artistic impulse is divine."

Those cool words, within which passions race like atoms in a cloud chamber, are typical of the man. Like Van Gogh, he was an epileptic with only a frail hold on earthly life, and he had the same ravenous desire to see through nature's veil, to discern and depict the eternal truths hidden in the temporal.

Born in 1825, Inness was raised in what was then the neat, green, and quiet town of Newark, New Jersey. At fourteen he was given a grocery store by his merchant father, who thought that business cares might awaken the boy from the dream world in which he lived. Young George

128

GEORGE INNESS' "JUNE" (1882)

set up an easel behind his counter and painted happily every day, taking time out only to hide himself when would-be customers wandered in. A little girl finally destroyed this idyl by standing too long in the store to which her mother had sent her. George at last popped from his hiding place and yelled: "What in the name of all the devils do you want?" The child rushed into the street terrified, screaming: "Candles! Candles! Candles!"

So young Inness was deprived of his business and set to studying art. The Hudson River School painters impressed him at first sight; he at once resolved to surpass them all. It did not take long. Admiring friends sent him abroad at mid-century to study, and he soon absorbed the lessons to be had from the landscapes of Constable and Turner, Théodore Rousseau and Corot. As a painter of intimate, sensitive, "civilized" landscapes in the European manner, young Inness had no American rivals, though Bierstadt and Church far outdid him in producing grand theatrical effects. Since grandeur makes the more immediate appeal to an unsophisticated audience, Americans were slow to sense how good Inness really was. Still fame and fortune gradually came to him.

Inness cared nothing for that. All he wanted was the happiness of his family, and freedom to paint. The trappings of prosperity simply chafed him. When his wife insisted on buying him a new suit, he would go to bed for days with a volume of Swedenborg to postpone wearing it. The everyday world of people and things was like a foreign country to him. Once, when asked how many children he had (there were six altogether), the painter replied with a frown: "I don't know." Then he brightened, remembering that his wife was somewhere about: "Lizzie will be here soon. She knows."

The sort of landscapes that Inness liked best surrounded his successive homes in Brooklyn, Medfield, Massachusetts, and Eagleswood and Montclair, New Jersey—all set in similarly gentle, rolling country, marked by quiet groves and meadows. When sketching in the fields, Inness would be as quiet and composed as the world about him. But painting in his studio, he was quite another person. "He painted," his son has

130

INNESS' "THE DELAWARE WATER GAP" (1859)

recalled, "at white heat. Passionate, dynamic in his force, I have seen him sometimes like a madman, stripped to the waist, perspiration rolling like a millrace from his face, with some tremendous idea struggling for expression. After a picture was complete it lost all value for him. He had no more interest in it. What was his masterpiece one day would be 'dishwater' and 'twaddle' the next. He would take a canvas before the paint was really dry, and, being seized with another inspiration, would paint over it. I have known him to paint as many as half a dozen or more pictures on a single canvas."

Inness' urge to paint over canvases did not confine itself to his own work in progress. "He was no respecter of persons or pictures," wrote his son, "and it made no difference who painted the original, who was the owner. . . . I believe he would far rather have painted on a picture than on a clean canvas." One lucky customer

INNESS' "THE COMING STORM" (1880)

132

who bought a fine seascape from Inness found it changed into a far better apple orchard when he went to see it at an exhibition.

The purest kind of artist, Inness was willing to sacrifice his entire labor at any moment for a more immediate vision. Recognizing, as he had written, that "the true artistic impulse is divine," Inness asked only to serve the inspiration that now and again possessed him. A scrawny fellow with straggly hair and steel-rimmed glasses, he

served his inspiration faithfully until his death in 1894. Though he sometimes mired down in swamps of sentiment, he also trod the heights.

Yet in a sense his painting could not be more down to earth. *June*, *The Delaware Water Gap*, and *The Coming Storm* are all faithful to nature, though never slavishly so. In each, Inness subordinated the details to general effect and the general effect to his mood of the moment. Far apart in mood, the three canvases show the wide range of emotions Inness could conjure up. He considered emotions as "spiritual" as morals. He argued, with the simplicity that was perhaps his chief strength, that the aim of art is "not to instruct, not to edify, but to awaken an emotion."

IN 1875 the almost painfully civilized Henry James described Winslow Homer as "almost barbarously simple." Homer, James went on, "has chosen the least pictorial features of the least pictorial range of scenery and civilization: he has resolutely treated them as if they . . . were every inch as good as Capri or Tangiers; and, to reward his audacity, he has incontestably succeeded. It makes one feel the value of consistency; it is a proof that if you will only be doggedly literal, though you may often be unpleasing, you will at least have a stamp of your own." The painter was then thirty-nine, with a successful illustrating career behind him, and lonely grandeur waiting in the years ahead.

Such paintings as *Snap the Whip* and *Prisoners from the Front* bear an uncomfortable resemblance to magazine illustrations reworked on canvas; yet these trial flights already showed Homer's love for ordinary people and things, and his broad, simple, direct way of describing them. Clearly he would never be either a virtuoso or a visionary; neither his techniques nor his ideas were the sort to astonish the world. But, as James saw, Homer had a "stamp" of his own. He had integrity, the foundation of greatness.

Homer's father was a Boston hardware merchant, his mother a flower painter. (Two years before she died the old lady bound her flower studies into a book so that, as she explained in the inscription: "When beneath the daisies these fingers are at rest, these flowers might yield of her joyous life a fragrant memory.") At nineteen

133

WINSLOW HOMER'S "PRISONERS FROM THE FRONT" (1866)

Homer was apprenticed to a commercial lithographer. He spent two years copying pictures for sheet music, cards, and posters, and hated the long hours—eight to six—which left him only the early summer mornings for fishing. The work itself distressed him, as he explained to a fellow apprentice, because "if a man wants to be an artist he should never look at pictures." Homer was already determined to be an artist.

All artists try to paint what they see, but some look at others' pictures, some look inside themselves, and some look out. Homer was one who looked out. His huntsman's eyes, above the hairy battlement of his mustache, saw the world his contemporaries saw, only much more sharply. "When I have selected the thing carefully," he liked to say, "I paint it exactly as it appears." At twenty-one he was already exact enough to make a living as a free-lance illustrator. Two years later Homer moved to a Manhattan boardinghouse. *Harper's Weekly* commissioned him to cover Lincoln's inauguration, and later assigned him as an artist-correspondent to the Army of the Potomac. Characteristically, he concentrated on everyday camp life, avoiding heroic or spectacular scenes. In his thirties he had begun to sell an occasional oil (at about $200 as against $20,000 for a big Bierstadt or a Church). Presumably because of their fresh, clean quality and absence of niggling detail, his canvases were criticized for lack of "finish."

Homer developed into a rather prickly person: straight, slim, small, and silent, dressed in a black cutaway and razor-creased steel-grey trousers. He had put a sign reading COAL BIN on his studio door to throw would-be visitors off the track. His favorite expression was "certainly not," and his chief joy leaving town on hunting and fishing trips. Homer's brief escapes led to a lasting one; they inspired his water colors. With characteristic firmness, he mastered the water-color medium absolutely, to create crystal-clear reminders of his own vacations. Reminding others of theirs, the water colors sold readily at about seventy-five dollars each. Homer now had a small but steady source of income, and could

HOMER'S "SNAP THE WHIP" (1872)

135

HOMER'S "PALM TREE, NASSAU" (1898)

136

HOMER'S "EIGHT BELLS" (1886)

give up illustrating. Perhaps he was still too poor to marry. In any case Homer remained a bachelor. A friend recorded that he "had the usual number of love affairs," but unfortunately neglected to explain exactly what he meant by "love affairs," or what "the usual number" might be. Homer, as was to be expected, smilingly kept his own counsel.

At forty-eight Homer turned his narrow back on the world, retiring to Prout's Neck, a hamlet along the Maine coast, where his father and brothers had bought property. In the summers the place was gay with children, clambakes, and fishing excursions. Winters, he stayed on alone, painting and meditating in his storm-battered, snowbound little house. Homer wryly allowed that his retirement from the world of people was to avoid jury duty. He walked the beach constantly, and built an open-ended shack from which to observe the sea in rough weather. He did his own cooking, which he relished. Winter evenings, he would amuse himself with his small

collection of coins and firearms. He fished and hunted, refusing to paint any faster than his pictures sold, but painting better all the time. "The Sun will not rise or set," he wrote, "without my notice, and thanks."

Homer's thanks took the forms of fathoms-deep seascapes, such as *A Summer Squall* and the classic *Eight Bells*. They have little poetry, but the weight, poise, and clarity of perfect prose. They are products of intense and reverent looking, carried on not for hours or days but for years. They show a contemplative mind and firm hand, both subservient to the magnificence of nature flooding in through the eyes.

In his old age Homer explored the Caribbean, and spent some winters there. One result was his terrifying *Gulf Stream*, in which a healthy young Negro waits for inevitable death. Because of its subject the picture long failed to find a customer. With grim humor the old painter told his dealer to inform two prospective buyers that "the unfortunate Negro who now is so dazed and parboiled

137

HOMER'S "A SUMMER SQUALL" (1904)

will be rescued and returned to his friends and home, and ever after live happily." Homer died in 1910 himself, at the age of seventy-four, cheerfully aloof from the world to the last.

THOMAS Eakins' father, known as "Master Benjamin," taught elegant handwriting to the sons of Philadelphia's first families. He was devoted to his son, whose own devotion to art was fed in about equal parts by training at the Pennsylvania Academy of the Fine Arts and by courses at Jefferson Medical College, where he got a knowledge of anatomy approaching that of most physicians. By scrimping, Master Benjamin was able to send young Tom to Paris in 1866 to further his studies.

"The big artists," Tom Eakins wrote home, "were the most timid of themselves and had the greatest confidence in nature.... I love sunlight and children and beautiful women and

men, their heads and hands, and most everything I see, and some day I expect to paint them as I see them." That defined precisely the philosophy that was to govern Eakins' whole life. It seemed peaceful indeed; yet the shabby, clear-eyed, and intense young Philadelphian in Paris had choppy weather ahead. After three years of study he wrote again: "What I have arrived to I have not gained without hard, plodding work. My studies and worries have made me thin. For a long time I did not hardly sleep at nights, but dreamed all the time about color and forms. . . . My worst troubles are over; I know perfectly well what I am doing. . . . I can finish as far as I can see."

Eakins meant not merely that he could finish what he set out to do, but that he had learned to paint what he saw "without polishing or hiding or sneaking it away to the end." He later explained: "There is no intermediate between

138

the highest finish and a start." In other words a job worth doing is worth doing superbly.

Returning to a loyal and established family and good friends in a stable, prosperous community, Eakins was a handsome man of twenty-six—physically powerful, brilliant, persevering, brimful of vitality, and fully trained in his chosen profession. Only his greatest virtue, honesty, counted against him. By a prompt demonstration of that virtue, Eakins set himself apart from the public he had hoped to serve. The trouble arose, first, from his absorbing interest in anatomy. Eakins had kept on with his anatomical studies in medical college after coming home; he chose a surgical demonstration as the subject of his first major canvas. Called the *Gross Clinic*, it struck Philadelphia as being gross indeed. It was not just the scene's "unpleasantness" that

people objected to, but also Eakins' unblinking attention to facts—for instance, the blood on the surgeon's hand. "The more we study it," a critic complained, "the more our wonder grows that it was ever painted in the first place, and that it was ever exhibited in the second."

Eakins and his father remained very close. Tom lived at home, painting in a studio on the top floor. The old man's moderate income from fortunate investments in real estate kept them going. At forty Eakins brought home a wife. They had no children, but the house was filled on holidays with nieces and nephews. A few friends and admirers—mostly sportsmen, scientists, teachers, and musicians—helped keep things lively for the family. Public interest there was almost none, until Eakins' father was long dead and Eakins himself a weary old man. The total of the artist's

HOMER'S "THE GULF STREAM" (1899)

earnings from a lifetime of devoted labor came to less than $15,000—the price of a single minor Eakins canvas today.

This lack of worldly success stemmed not from his being ahead of his time, as with so many unappreciated painters, but behind it. Eakins' whole delight came from doing what he called "solid, heavy work," as Gérôme had taught him in Paris. His contemporary, John Singer Sargent, was setting a new fashion for painting of just the opposite sort: virtuoso brushwork that put the emphasis on style instead of solidity, and that strove to impress the beholder instead of convincing him. Eakins deliberately hid his powers, as he had been taught. His pictures were always solid and convincing, but they never appeared "masterful" in the misunderstood sense of slick, or dashing, or chic.

Many of his pictures he simply gave away. *Max Schmitt in a Single Scull*, for example, went to his friend Schmitt, with whom Eakins often went boating on the Schuylkill River. (The artist painted himself sculling in the middle distance.) The preparation for that picture gives some hint of Eakins' infinitely painstaking methods. He began with mechanical drawings, done to scale, of the boats, oars, and bridges. Then, by a process of his own devising, based on trigonometry, he placed them in proper perspective and proportion. Transferring the perspective drawing to canvas, he lightly sketched in the landscape and figures. Next he made rag models of the figures and built a model scull from a cigar box to study in the sunshine. At last he was ready to paint, using thick pigment for the near lights and transparent glazes for the distant shadows, slowly building up the picture's almost hallucinatory illusion of sunlit reality.

But the end result, a magical rendering of figures in space, is more than illusion. As with

THOMAS EAKINS' "MAX SCHMITT IN A SINGLE SCULL" (1871)

all Eakins' masterpieces, *Max Schmitt* communicates the painter's passion, intense and searching, for visual truth.

Eakins' passion for truth is most evident in his paintings of people. It precluded all flattery, all soft generalizing, so naturally he got few portrait commissions. But his portraits of friends, such as *The Concert Singer*, have an immortal warmth. Eakins seldom painted people in repose; he showed them at the top of their best efforts, when he could. The singer had to be actually singing while Eakins painted her, though she posed off and on for two long years. The hand with the baton in the lower left-hand corner was posed by her conductor, in action.

Similarly, Eakins' painted professors are really lecturing, his oarsmen are breathing deep and regular with the stroke, his musicians lovingly bow their instruments, his thinkers think hard, and his dreamers dream deep. If they almost all seem sad it is because, like repose, the greatest effort also has something sad about it. Eakins saw life as a solemn commitment to do the best possible under very difficult circumstances. He knew the best is never good enough. And with his usual honesty he made that plain, too. There are no saints or heroes among his portrayals, no apotheoses, only good courageous failures—that is, good courageous people.

Some of the less courageous were thoroughly annoyed by Eakins' honesty. "How beautiful an old woman's skin is!" he once exclaimed. "All those wrinkles!" But the women who posed for him could happily have done without them. They blushed to hear their daughters explaining to visitors that "mother was sick when this was painted." One eminent doctor among the disappointed sitters wrote Eakins asking that his portrait be altered. "I presume my position in art," Eakins patiently explained, "is not second to your own in medicine, and I can hardly imagine myself writing to you a letter like this: 'Dear Doctor: the concurrent testimony of the newspapers and of friends is that your treatment of my case has not been one of your successes. I therefore suggest that you treat me with Mrs. Brown's Metaphysical Discovery.' "

Being his own man, active in body and mind, Eakins could not help raising a good deal of

EAKINS' "CONCERT SINGER" (1892)

EAKINS' "WILLIAM RUSH CARVING HIS ALLEGORICAL FIGURE OF THE SCHUYLKILL RIVER" (1877)

dust locally. He got a reputation for eccentricity that was not entirely unmerited. He painted in his undershirt. When angry, he just whistled. He kept a blackboard by him in the dining room to diagram topics of conversation. He told dirty jokes to decent folks. He read books on mathematics, as well as Latin, Italian, and French, for pleasure. He kept a dozen pets at a time, including a monkey. He once rode through Philadelphia on horseback in Western regalia.

Where his own generation saw oddity, the next one saw character, and Eakins was blessed with youthful believers. One girlish enthusiast recalled that he once remarked on the beauty of her back, and asked if she would pose for him in the nude. "His manner was so simple, so honest, that I said, 'Well, I shall ask my mother and see.' My mother did not forbid it, but said it would be better not to on the whole, and that Tom Eakins was somewhat hipped on nudes." The story—especially the stuffy, victorious figure of the mother—has an aura of eternity.

Eakins celebrated one instance in which the story turned out differently. Back in 1809 a Philadelphia sculptor had been commissioned to carve a symbolic representation of the Schuylkill River. Despite the scandal involved, the sculptor had managed to persuade a lithe and courageous society girl to pose, naked, as the Schuylkill. *William Rush Carving His Allegorical Figure of the Schuylkill River* is Eakins' reconstruction of the event. Innocent, hearty, graceful, the girl spirals like a candle flame in the shadowy studio. Her clothes are piled in the foreground; a chaperon quietly knits close by; Rush plies his mallet. The scene could not be more workaday. It is also momentous; the strong, shining girl is both happy sacrifice and pioneer.

In his late thirties Eakins took over the Pennsylvania Academy and completely remodeled its curriculum—switching it away from the study of antique casts to the live model, and from line drawing to oil painting. Perspective and anatomy, of course, were thoroughly taught. The students took part in dissections. Elaborate electric and gymnastic devices were used to demonstrate the actions of the body. Indeed, there were times, one student recalled, "when a skeleton, a stiff, a model and the Negro janitor Henry all

jerked and jumped when the battery was turned on." Dissection, Eakins confessed, "is work, and hard work, disagreeable work." But he believed it as essential to art as to medicine. He could not abide short cuts any more than he could sloppy generalizing. "Get the character of things," he would insist. "If a man's fat, make him fat; if a man's thin, make him thin. Don't copy. Feel the forms. Respectability in art is appalling."

Respectable Philadelphia was indeed appalled when Eakins, demonstrating the action of the pelvis, removed a male model's loincloth. Some lady pupils protested, and though nine-tenths of the student body stood back of him, Eakins was finally forced to choose between restraint and retirement. In 1886, after ten years of inspired teaching, he decided to quit the Academy.

The Swimming Hole demonstrates Eakins' continuing interest in the nude, and his urge to paint it under the most difficult conditions of arrested motion and reflected light. For the diving figure he constructed a wax model suspended from strings. Being an enthusiastic swimmer, he put himself in the right foreground. His red setter Harry is the center of action. The picture has something of the heat of summer and the gleam of flesh against green foliage—transposed, as in all Eakins canvases, to a slightly darker register than nature's—but it is perhaps overelaborate. Eakins could not paint relaxation in a relaxed way. Nor did he ever relax his own arduous attention to detail. When a civil engineer named Fairman Rogers commissioned him to paint the family coach-and-four with eight people aboard, Eakins began by making two sculptures of one of the lead horses, the first flayed and the second whole. He naturally took similar pains throughout the picture. His price was a modest $500.

Eakins kept up his own scientific researches. At one point he assisted Eadweard Muybridge, the photographer, who was putting the motions of the human body on film. Eakins invented and built a single camera to replace Muybridge's battery of cameras. It was equipped with two revolving disks, through the holes of which the subject could be photographed as a series of overlapping images on the same plate. He contributed a paper on "The Differential Action of Certain Muscles Passing More Than One Joint" to the Academy of Natural Sciences of Philadelphia. His thesis was that a muscle should be considered "not only with reference to the levers to which it is attached, but with relation to the whole movement of the animal. Then it will be seen that many muscles rated in the book as antagonistic are no more so than are two parts of the same muscle. . . . The least action anywhere is carried through the whole animal."

Eakins' point was something well known to all great draftsmen, but not to scientists. He himself had learned it partly from his enthusiasm for spectator sports, prize fighting especially. For a time so many boxers frequented his studio that it seemed like a gym. *Between Rounds* shows a hard-bodied, chalk-white fighter named Billy

Smith determinedly resting up for the kill. The canvas, austere though it is, sings, in Whitman's phrase, of "the body electric."

As he aged, Eakins grew heavy, bearish, and rather sad. Honors began coming to him too late. When the Pennsylvania Academy awarded its teacher emeritus a gold medal, he showed up at the ceremony wearing bicycling togs. There he announced in his high, gentle voice that the Academy, which had failed to support him as a teacher, had "a heap of impudence to give him a medal." Immediately afterwards, he bicycled on to the mint and turned in the gold medal for seventy-five dollars cash.

Eakins tasted one moment of fame when Dr. Albert C. Barnes, the temperamental champion

EAKINS' "THE SWIMMING HOLE" (1883)

EAKINS' "BETWEEN ROUNDS" (1899)

of advance-guard painting, bought one of his oils in 1914 for a reputed $5,000. Reporters hurried to interview the seventy-year-old painter, who seized the chance to strike a blow for what he called "a great and distinctly American art." His remarks went crisply to the point: "If young art students wish to assume a place in the history of the art of their country, their first desire should be to remain in America, to peer deeper into the heart of American life, rather than to spend their time abroad obtaining a superficial view of the art of the Old World. In the days when I studied abroad, conditions were entirely different. The facilities for study in this country were meager. There were even no life classes." Eakins told the reporters that he considered Winslow Homer the best American painter of his time. He added thoughtfully that Whistler,

too, "was unquestionably a great painter, but there are many of his works for which I do not care." Few dreamed of placing Eakins himself in such exalted company. When he died soon afterwards in 1916, he was still largely unknown to the world.

Among the few to grasp his importance was Walt Whitman, who sat to him at the age of sixty-eight. "I never knew of but one artist, and that's Tom Eakins," Whitman said, "who could resist the temptation to see what they thought ought to be rather than what is." To criticism of his own portrait Whitman retorted: "It is likely to be only the unusual person who can enjoy such a picture—only here and there one who can weigh and measure it according to its own philosophy. Eakins would not be appreciated by . . . professional elects; the people who

EAKINS' "THE FAIRMAN ROGERS FOUR-IN-HAND" (1879)

EAKINS' "WALT WHITMAN" (1887)

like Eakins best are the people who have no prejudices to interpose." And he concluded: "Eakins is not a painter; he is a force."

Whitman's appraisal holds up. Though still disdained by some "professional elects," Eakins has come to be recognized as perhaps the strongest painter in American history. He made art the servant of honesty. He chose showing over showiness, and thereby earned the lasting gratitude of all men who place the true even higher than they do the beautiful.

AS do many creative men, Albert Pinkham Ryder found himself partly as a result of illness. And like his peers he possessed a deep vitality that illness only triggered, like a match set to fireworks. But among artists Ryder was unusual in that his illness was of the eyes. When he was a boy, an infection following a vaccination damaged his sight. Bright light bothered him, and sorting out the small details of the visual world was a strain. Reading came especially hard to the boy; as a result, he got no farther than grammar school.

The elder Ryder, a fuel dealer on the New Bedford, Massachusetts, water front, must have wondered what would become of his dreamy son.

One day he brought home some paints to amuse the boy. "When my father placed a box of colors and brushes in my hands," Ryder afterwards recalled, "and I stood before my easel with its square of stretched canvas, I realized that I had in my possession the wherewith to create a masterpiece that would live throughout the coming ages. The great masters had no more."

Young Ryder went into the fields to paint naturalistically. But, as he wrote, "in my desire to be accurate I became lost in a maze of detail. Try as I would, my colors were not those of nature. My leaves were infinitely below the standard of a leaf. . . ." Then one memorable day "the old scene presented itself . . . before my eyes framed in an opening between two trees. It stood out like a painted canvas . . . three solid masses of form and color—sky, foliage and earth—the whole bathed in an atmosphere of golden luminosity. I threw my brushes aside; they were too small for the work in hand. I squeezed out big chunks of pure, moist color, and, taking my palette knife, I laid on blue, green, white, and brown in great sweeping strokes. As I worked, I saw that it was good and clean and strong. I saw nature springing into life upon my dead canvas. . . . Exultantly I painted until the sun

ALBERT PINKHAM RYDER'S "GRAZING HORSE" (CA. 1880)

148

sank below the horizon. Then I raced around the fields like a colt let loose and literally bellowed for joy."

Well he might. Ryder had leaped to maturity as a painter. And in doing so, he had created a new kind of painting, all his own, precisely fitted both to the weakness of his eyes and to the power of his reverence for the seen world. His early *Grazing Horse* is an example of that triumph. By themselves, such canvases—both solid and tender, both simple and mysterious—would have won him a sure place in art history.

They earned him a little esteem even in his own day. One of Ryder's three elder brothers had become a successful restaurant owner in New York. So Ryder and his parents moved to the city to be near him. There the young man's paintings began to attract attention. In 1873, when he was twenty-six, he exhibited at the National Academy. In his early thirties he was able to leave his family and live quietly in Greenwich Village on the proceeds of his paintings, which fetched up to $500 each.

All seemed well in a small way. But as the years went by, people began to whisper of his strange ways. He roamed the streets interminably and alone. On a moonlit midnight he would stroll down to the Battery to sit for hours gazing at the water. Large, heavy, bearded, and childlike, he would sit in the park writing execrable poems, which the wind blew away. He would show as a great treasure a yellowed photograph of a girl from a tooth-paste ad. Once a friend found him staring straight up into the summer afternoon sky from the curb of a crowded street. "I watched him for quite a while," the friend reported later, "and when at last I stepped up and greeted him, he said, as a sort of apology, 'Kind of beautiful skies this time of year,' and continued his observation."

Such profound and prolonged observation as Ryder gave the summer sky and moonlight on the bay had less and less to do with exactitude. He was not weighing and recording, but rather projecting into deep and glistening spaces the visions of his mind. He was, in fact, remaking himself as an artist.

An artist, as Ryder explained simply, "should strive to express his thought and not the surface of it. What avails a storm cloud accurate in form and color if the storm is not therein?" From about forty on he painted the world of imagination, not that of nature. He would test his canvases not by comparing them with what the real world looked like, but by asking himself whether or not they seemed spiritually true. The black, pursuing menace in the sky of *Under a Cloud* seems hardly like a real cloud at all; yet the storm is unmistakably therein.

The Race Track lies in a light that is not of this world. Ryder was once asked to settle a dispute as to whether it represented night or daylight, and replied with courteous ambiguity that he "had not given it much thought." He gave endless thought, but none to what people would think. Inspiration, he said, "is no more than a seed that must be planted and nourished. It gives growth as it grows to the artist, only as he watches and waits with his highest effort."

The hidden strains of that effort were costing Ryder dear. He suffered from gout and kidney trouble. His eyes were often inflamed. He took to describing his long walks as "nerve cures." Once, apparently, he rushed to propose to a girl he had never met, a singer whose voice had moved him. Shortly after this, a sea-captain friend took him to England for a change of air. Ryder paced the bridge at night, watching the water. By day he lay on the floor of his cabin, painting. In England he stayed with the captain and played games with the neighborhood children for a couple of weeks, which steadied him so that he came home cured for a time and ready for more hard looking and hard work.

Toilers of the Sea points man's vessel toward the moon, as if to a compelling vision of eternal life. *Siegfried and the Rhine Maidens* echoes precisely, with its richly writhing shapes and shadows, the fierce enchantment of Wagner's music. Thus to transpose music into art requires a deep sense of the rhythms inherent in nature. Oriental painters elaborately cultivate that sense; Occidentals seldom do. Ryder possessed the gift to a supreme degree. Line, light, form, even his brooding color are all made to dance in the rhythmic structure of his best work.

The critics could be particularly hard on his best. One grittily advised a course in "the hard,

RYDER'S
"UNDER A CLOUD" (AFTER 1880)

RYDER'S "THE RACE TRACK" (1895-1910)

grinding, sweaty toil of academic drawing and accurate anatomy." Another admonished him to "show what you can do in the glare of day! See whether your poetry is strong enough, healthy enough to stand the wear and tear of life!" Ryder never seemed to notice such taunts. Actually he himself was not apt to appreciate the art of others. Of European painting he remarked off-handedly that "we all like our own songs the best." Discussing a noted American painter who had just died, he said, "Yes, he painted very well, but he was not an artist."

Technically, Ryder did not paint at all well. He never mastered his medium, only wrestled it into obedience. This took a fantastic amount of work on each canvas, lasting sometimes for years.

He used alcohol, candle wax, and varnish as well as oil, mixing them indiscriminately. He changed some compositions scores of times, moving the center of interest all about the canvas. In the evening he would put a thin layer of quick-drying glaze over his day's work, and next morning paint on top of that, locking in the wet under-surface, which consequently took years to dry. As a result, almost his entire production (about 150 canvases) has already cracked, yellowed, or blackened horribly. Were it not for color repro-ductions, later generations might look curiously at the ruins of his work and wonder why anyone ever admired it.

A painter friend once praised a canvas he saw in Ryder's studio and was gratified to be offered

152

it as a present. "But after [Ryder] had washed the picture's face in a basin of very dirty water and dried it with a dirty towel, he stood gazing at it with a faraway look in his eyes, a look of fondest love. He had forgotten that I was there. When I gently recalled him to earth, he turned to me and, with the simplicity of a child, said kindly and regretfully: 'Come again next year and I think you can have it, if I find I can do what more it needs. I have only worked on it a little more than ten years.' "

There is tragicomedy in Ryder's drive for perfection, forever reworking his canvases, polishing and changing, scrubbing, rubbing, scraping, loading, and coaxing them to a perfect pitch of surface until the colors glowed like banked fires. Ryder was building destruction in along with beauty. He knew it, too, to some extent, and his excuse was feeble indeed. "When a thing has the elements of beauty from the beginning," he would argue, "it cannot be destroyed. Take [the *Venus de Milo*]—ages and men have ravaged

it, its arms and nose have been knocked off, but still it remains a thing of beauty. . . ."

Perhaps it was not his pictures that really interested Ryder, but the experience of painting. Perhaps his reason for keeping them and reworking them year after year was not to bring them to a perfect and ephemeral pitch, but simply to have the fullest possible experience of them. In a famous letter he wrote: "Have you ever seen an inchworm crawl up a leaf or a twig, and then, clinging to the very end, revolve in the air, feeling for something to reach something? That's like me. I am trying to find something out there beyond the place on which I have a footing."

At the turn of the century Ryder was fifty-three, and his powers were already fading. But connoisseurs were beginning to appreciate his genius. Forgers were busily heaping up the present store of false Ryders, and his reputation had begun building toward its present peak.

Because he was famous by then and because of public taste for the macabre, Ryder is best

RYDER'S "TOILERS OF THE SEA" (BEFORE 1884)

known for the eccentricities of his last years. He had paid for his childlike virtues—never welcome in the adult world—with an increasing childishness. Now he lived in wretched squalor, hoarding every scrap of old newspaper, every cheese rind or apple core from his table. When callers came, it took him a quarter of an hour to clear a path to his door. Dead mice lay all about in the traps that had caught them, and live ones scampered near the ancient stew that simmered year in and year out on his stove. He slept on a window shade on the floor to avoid bedbugs. Fat and shambling, he puttered mainly with his old pictures, as often as not doing them more harm than good. Pictures, reading matter, junk, food, nothing would he let go. Everything must be saved and kept, a wealth of useless treasure that closed in around him at the end with the weight of tombstones.

It was a sad last chapter for the youth who had pranced bellowing about a field on a summer evening and for the man who said: "The artist needs but a roof, a crust of bread, and his easel, and all the rest God gives him in abundance."

Ryder remains the greatest lyrical painter that America has produced. It has been said that his genius was for putting what all men feel about such things as moonlight and storm winds into recognizable form. Yet he does far more than project a collective unconscious: he enriches individual consciousness from the depths. It is not the shock of recognition that his painting evokes, but the feeling little children have of being lost and found again in a strange, God-filled world.

RYDER'S "SIEGFRIED AND THE RHINE MAIDENS" (BEFORE 1891)

CHAPTER V

THE SUMMER SIDE

All the beautiful changes and chances
Through which the landscape flits and glances—
Till now, you dreamed not what could be done
With a bit of rock and a ray of sun.

—JAMES RUSSELL LOWELL

COLOR is a sometime thing. A man need not have a highly developed color sense in order to get about, though he must see shapes accurately. Hence his color impressions tend to be dim, vague, and intermittent, and to reproduce badly in the mind's eye. This helps explain why the impressionist painters of the late nineteenth century struck their contemporaries for a time as madmen. In subordinating form to color, they seemed to do violence to nature. And in picturing the sunny dazzle of daytime outdoors, they seemed to be exploring a strident, eye-hurting never-never land.

Such adventurous French painters as Claude Monet and Pierre Auguste Renoir nevertheless persisted in following the evidence of their eyes rather than the accepted, dun-colored mode of seeing. Though they lost their first battles to a color-blind public, they could not lose the war, since optical truth was with them. The truth spread slowly. Towards the close of the century, it inspired a minor but ingratiating impressionist group in America. They opened new windows to fresh air and sunlight, producing a clear and cheerful view of America's summer side.

DWIGHT W. Tryon was among the first and subtlest of the American impressionists. A stocky Yankee, brown and wrinkled as a walnut, he specialized in tender and crepuscular views of his native New England countryside. They brought him a sizable fortune, so that he himself was able to collect pictures as well as paint them, and to endow a museum at Smith College. Tryon saw nature as a prim Salome, wrapped in all her seven veils. Deftly, delicately, with more tact than passion, he painted her veiled in atmosphere. *Springtime* looks not like paint on canvas but like a diffusion of colors in misty space. No one will ever say of a Tryon that This Is It. But art need not always be final, bold, or grand.

CHILDE Hassam was a doubly fortunate man. He was a painter, and a painter was what he yearned to be. He was also prosperous from the start. The son of a Boston businessman, he learned magazine illustration at an early age and made a good living at it. Three years of study in Paris opened his eyes to impressionism, and by the time he returned to the American scene, his countrymen were ready to accept the results. Hassam painted pictures that were pretty and at the same time robust, like a small brass band playing in the park.

Refusing to use the name Childe, his friends took to calling Hassam "Muley" as a tribute to his stubbornness. He studied the light on the church at Old Lyme, Connecticut, as stubbornly, and almost as often as Monet had studied the rosier light on Rouen Cathedral. Yet no one

155

DWIGHT TRYON'S "SPRINGTIME" (1897)

CHILDE HASSAM'S "CHURCH AT OLD LYME" (1906)

would compare the invariably pleasant Hassam with the trail-blazing Monet. Where Monet had created new problems to solve, Hassam skillfully ducked old ones. For example, the clock faces in his *Church at Old Lyme* could not have been painted in sharp focus without violating his soft-focus view of the building, nor could they have been done in soft focus without frustrating man's natural urge to read clocks—so he simply hid them behind the leaves.

MAURICE Prendergast was one of the most timid revolutionaries in the whole history of American painting. A poor Bostonian, apprenticed early to a painter of show cards for stores,

he labored and dreamed of becoming an artist until he was twenty-seven. By then he had saved $1,000, with which he planned to go to Paris and study painting. But at the last moment Prendergast's confidence faltered. Unsure of his talent, he showed some of his sketches to a minister's wife and put the case to her: Should he go to Paris? "I certainly should!" she said, with proper Bostonian briskness. So he did.

The $1,000 lasted Prendergast for more than three years, during which time he learned and unlearned much. Impressionism impressed him chiefly as a technique. What he took from it was the use of pure colors laid side by side in tiny strokes, like mosaic. This happened to accord

157

well with a way of seeing the world of nature that was peculiarly his own: gentle, dreamy, naive, and perhaps a trifle astigmatic.

Prendergast painted the world as a tapestry of nice people having fun amidst soft airs. His rich command of color and design gave dignity to a vision that might otherwise have seemed schoolgirlish. However, his pictures looked queer indeed to his contemporaries. Home again and penniless, Prendergast found that he could sell almost nothing. He went back to lettering store cards, and lived frugally with his brother, a fellow artist and frame maker, in a Boston suburb. Sundays he would spend painting the girls in bright dresses at Revere Beach. But Prendergast always kept his distance from them, and quoted Kipling's lines in explanation of his caution:

If a man would be successful in his art,
   art, art,
He must keep the girls away from his heart,
   heart, heart.

In 1914, when his brother's frames began to be profitable, the two left Massachusetts and settled down in Manhattan's Washington Square. There Prendergast did finally gain the appreciation of a small circle of admirers; towards the end of his life he even had some exhibitions. Very quietly, he had made a unique contribution to American painting. On the back of one of his sketches, a collector found this message from Prendergast the devoted artist to Prendergast the neglected man: "The love you liberate in your work is the only love you keep."

MAURICE PRENDERGAST'S "SUNSET AND SEA FOG" (1915)

CHAPTER VI

THE ASHCAN SCHOOL

Far below and around lay the city like a
ragged purple dream, the wonderful, cruel,
enchanting, bewildering, fatal, great city.

—O. HENRY

SOON after the beginning of the twentieth century five passionate young painters bunched together like the fingers and thumb of a fist, struck a mighty blow for artistic freedom of worship, and pushed American art into the quickened tempo of the modern age. The oldest, and acknowledged leader of the group, was a tall, slant-eyed, loud, and fiery philosopher of art named Robert Henri. The other four had all been illustrators for the Philadelphia *Press*. Henri gave them dignity and a mission by teaching that their news pictures—terse, hurried, and immediate—carried the seeds of great art. "What we need," he argued, "is more sense of the wonder of life, and less of this business of picturemaking." The true painter, Henri maintained, is a sort of sidewalk superintendent of his times, a spectator with strong ideas and even stronger feelings about what he sees, who relishes the real life around him and paints it swiftly, sharply, tenderly—and darkly.

The prevailing darkness of the pictures the five artists painted earned them a scornful nickname, "the Revolutionary Black Gang"—which was, much later, to become known as "the Ashcan School." Their lavish use of black actually was a conservative throwback to Rembrandt, Frans Hals, and Goya. But their choice of subject matter was as new as the twentieth century.

The dream of a rural democracy and of a nation of white towns in green valleys had long since died. Now, at the center of the American scene, arose that splendid, steel-boned monster, the modern metropolis. Vast and clangorous, it presented a challenge to painters that Henri and his friends accepted with delight.

THE son of a successful faro player out of the Wild West, Robert Henri had studied art for eleven years in Europe. During the 1890s he formed his circle of disciples in Philadelphia, apostrophizing them over punch and rarebit in his studio each Thursday night. Everett Shinn, George Luks, William Glackens, and John Sloan formed the inner circle. On the *Press* the artists covered the fires, suicides, wrecks, speeches, holdups, and parades that news photographers cover today. Necessity taught them to work fast and accurately and to tell a story by means of a few carefully chosen details. Henri's chief talent happened to be portraiture, but his feeling for a sitter was just as dashingly direct as the approach of his colleagues to a fire. As *Old Model and Her Daughter* demonstrates, Henri cared much less for anatomy than for personality, less for human flesh than for human drama. His canvas creates little illusion of light, air, or solid forms. It is, compared with Eakins, for example, hasty and

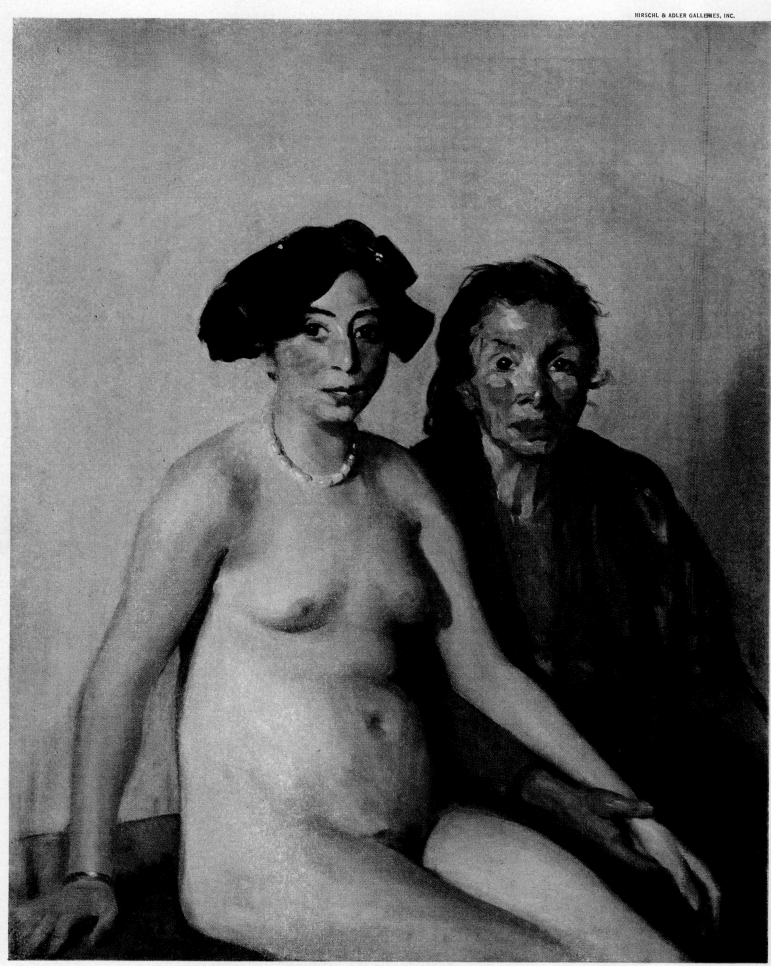

ROBERT HENRI'S "OLD MODEL AND HER DAUGHTER" (1912)

overdramatic painting. But for all its faults the picture has one compelling quality that sets it apart; it has the breath of life.

One by one Henri, Luks, Shinn, Glackens, and Sloan moved to New York and set up shop as painters and art teachers. They were laughed at, but they were also listened to. Henri soon proved himself a great teacher; Luks and Sloan were not far behind. All three urged their students to "plunge into life," which could mean a number of things. To different students it meant reading Whitman and Dostoevsky, watching Isadora Duncan dance, attending prize fights, spending a night in Central Park, roaming the Bowery, playing baseball, or haunting dance halls. All this took time from painting, yet pumped needed life into it. As Everett Shinn later explained, that was the purpose, for "when Diamond Jim Brady was the towering pinnacle of vulgar glitter . . . and Lillian Russell heaved her eternal voluptuousness against the hungry jackal gleam in the tired businessman's eye . . . art in America . . . was merely an adjunct of plush and cut glass. . . . Its heart pumped only anemia."

In 1908 the fiery five ripped the plush and rattled the cut glass with a historic exhibition. They took over a Manhattan gallery and filled it with a show formed in uneasy alliance with Maurice Prendergast, the impressionist Ernest Lawson, and a painter of misty nudes named Arthur B. Davies. "The Eight," as they came to be known, shocked the city—and drew some 300 visitors an hour. What, for instance, were decent folk to make of George Luks?

LUSTY, that tent of a word, fits Luks exactly. *The Spielers* shows his love of life and joy as well as the underlying sadness of the deeply sensual. It is both promising and vaguely forbidding, as if to say: "These children, too, will age and soon will die. Meanwhile, enjoy their dance." But if Luks's paintings seem to murmur, he himself crowed with boisterous vigor. Knowing the niceties of beer and cheese better than those of art, he would shout: "Art, my slats! I can paint with a shoestring dipped in pitch and lard! It's in you, or it isn't. Who taught Shakespeare technique? Or Rembrandt? Or George Luks? Guts! Guts! Life! Life! That's *my* technique!"

EVERETT Shinn was the most cosmopolitan and for a time the most successful member of the group. His pictures found readier acceptance than those of his friends because Shinn chose to paint the world of theater and fashion instead of Greenwich Village. Shinn's best works, such as *Trapeze, Winter Garden, New York*, have a fragile glamour, like momentary reflections in a black marble bar.

Love of the theater made Shinn into an amateur acrobat and professional playwright as well as a painter. His *Hazel Weston, or, More Sinned Against than Usual* played in seven languages for a quarter of a century. He did less well with *Lucy Moore, the Prune-Hater's Daughter*, in spite of a memorable last line: "Oh, you prune, you've been my ruin!" Clearly, life was something of a cocktail for Shinn—dizzying, exhilarating, and eagerly sipped. "I was often accused of being a social snob," he recalled in old age. "Not at all —it's just that the uptown life with all its glitter was more good-looking. . . . Ah, the clothes then—the movement, the satins, women's skirts and men's coats and the sweep of furs and swish of wild boas, oh Lord!"

OF the whole group, William Glackens probably found it hardest to follow Henri's lead. He was a born black and white illustrator, not a painter. His drawings were relaxed and exact, his painting comparatively tense and blurred. For all its bold simplicity of conception and execution, his *Park on the River* fails to achieve the cheerful picnic spirit that Glackens was striving for. The colors are not only gloomy but completely unconvincing.

Glackens would break his long silences with questions such as: "How do you paint a hand?" or, "When do you know that your picture looks like the sitter?" At about forty he began questioning the dark, limited palette that Henri favored. Finally he abandoned it to follow the rainbow of sun-warmed colors that the French impressionists had brought to painting. In technique, *Nude with Apple* is a homage to Renoir. Beyond that, it is also a homage to the pretty model, an expression of Glackens' own quietly appreciative character, and a convincing demonstration of the fact that some painters are made, not born.

GEORGE LUKS'S "THE SPIELERS" (1905)

A GOOD picture should tell you some of the things a blind man knows about the world." That single observation shows how much deeper John Sloan went than his friends of the Ashcan School. He painted no mere appearances flashing upon the retina, but implosions of reality upon the mind itself. Like Henri and the rest, Sloan considered himself to be a spectator, but he was a highly speculative one. The camera, he liked to point out, "is mentally blind." He argued that cameras cannot see form, for example, since "we don't even learn form through the eyes; we learn it from the sense of touch." Sloan painted what he thought and felt about things he had seen. Memory sifted out the extraneous details, and mulling over strengthened what was left. *Wake of the Ferry* is a triumph of Sloan's method, and a high point in American painting. It says so much with so little and proves that what the eyes receive in a single glance can fill the whole being.

Sloan was born poor and, he liked to pretend, without talent ("My sisters and I all drew equally well"). One thing he did have on his side was the illusion of being Irish, which gave him courage

EVERETT SHINN'S "TRAPEZE, WINTER GARDEN, NEW YORK" (1903)

to display, and therefore to develop, a certain degree of temperament. Another was his predominantly Scots blood, which gave him the toughness to withstand hard times. In his teens he made a living designing calendars and valentines; in his twenties he illustrated newspapers; in his thirties he began teaching art; in his forties he sold his first canvases—six in ten years. "The only reason I am in the profession," he could say with conviction, "is because it is fun."

He did have fun. Sloan loved Greenwich Village, and once, standing on top of Washington Square arch, he proclaimed it an independent republic. Gaunt, peppery, bespectacled, he came to enjoy talking almost as much as painting. "My New York pictures are no more 'realism' than a poem is," he remarked in old age, puffing his pipe for punctuation. "You young people don't realize how sweet—sweet and sad—New York was before Prohibition. But now, who'd want to paint a street strewn with automobiles? The skyline? It's like a comb in the restroom of a filling station. A tooth here and there missing, and all filled with dirt. Unfortunately, we're the dirt."

When asked about the innovations that had changed Manhattan's art even more than its

WILLIAM GLACKENS' "PARK ON THE RIVER" (1905)

GLACKENS' "NUDE WITH APPLE" (1910)

165

JOHN SLOAN'S "WAKE OF THE FERRY" (1907)

skyline, he would shrug elaborately: "The ultra-modern movement was wonderful medicine for adults. But since then the kids have raided the medicine cabinet—and for them, it's drugs." The question whether Sloan himself succumbed to foreign drugs is still wide open. Like Glackens, he came under Renoir's spell in middle age and began working full time from the model. *The Lafayette*, painted in 1928, is naive poetry; *Model in Dressing Room*, done five years later, is studious prose. Sloan finally got a habit of adding hundreds of red pin stripes to the flesh of his nudes. They "clinch the form," he explained, but for most people they spoiled the picture.

Pioneering kept him poor. In 1933 Sloan sent the following letter to some sixty American museums: Sloan "will die some time in the next few years (he is now sixty-two). In the event of his passing, is it likely that the trustees of your museum would consider it desirable to acquire one of his pictures? . . . After a painter of repute dies, the prices of his works are at once more than doubled. John Sloan is alive and hereby offers

SLOAN'S
"MODEL IN DRESSING ROOM" (1933)

SLOAN'S "PIGEONS" (1910)

167

these works at *one-half* the prices asked during the last five years. . . ." The letter drew one lone customer when the Boston Museum bought his 1910 work, *Pigeons*.

While Sloan's independence held the world at a distance, his wit and warmth kept friends close. He was always fighting the powerful and pretentious, whether with cartoons (such as that of a prostitute on trial, captioned: "Before her makers and her judge") or with verbal darts. He attacked the National Academy as being "no more national than the National Biscuit Company." When he was praised for painting "the American scene," he laughed: "As though you didn't see the American scene whenever you open your eyes! I am not for the American scene; I am for mental realization. If you are American and work, your work will be American." Sloan's own work was clearly in the American grain, as was his tough, warm nature.

SLOAN'S "THE LAFAYETTE" (1928)

PART THREE

GEORGIA O'KEEFFE'S "FROM THE PLAINS NO. 1" (1953)

THE WORLD A STAGE

And we move on: we move down:
With the first light we push forward:
We descend from the past as a wandering people
 from mountains.
We cross into the day to be discovered.

—ARCHIBALD MACLEISH

JOSEPH STELLA'S "THE BRIDGE" (1922)

CHAPTER I

THE BRIDGE BUILDERS

Macadam, gun-grey as a tunny's belt,
Leaps from Far Rockaway to Golden Gate . . .
Keep hold of that nickel for car-change, Rip,—
Have you got your "Times"—?
And hurry along, Van Winkle—it's getting late!

—Hart Crane

THE eve of World War I found America, an ever-growing industrial power, moving on inevitably to a commanding position on the world stage. Yet it was a bleak and sterile time for American artists. The Ashcan School still held a beleaguered beachhead in Greenwich Village. Here and there an isolated maverick painter fired off a few defiant shots. But the rest of the nation was thoroughly occupied by the forces of the academicians. They decreed what painters should be shown, naturally favoring the slick, pompous artists of their own sort, men whose very names have long since been forgotten. With each official show, the leaders moved that they were just as good as their colleagues of the Paris Salon. Eagerly, the critics seconded the motion.

What the academicians and their supporters failed to realize was the fact that the Salon no longer mattered in School of Paris painting. The art of Europe was undergoing a deep and far-reaching revolution, and from that revolution were to come the reinforcements for an assault on the entrenched positions of the academicians in America. The attack was led by a band of twenty-five American artists having nothing in common beyond a healthy interest in the new. Some of them had been abroad, and returned to report that great things were happening there. To capture the new spirit, the group resolved to stage a mammoth exhibition of contemporary European art. The show, which was held at Manhattan's 69th Infantry Regiment Armory, from mid-February to mid-March, 1913, was the most important ever staged in America.

The Armory Show, best remembered in popular history for Marcel Duchamp's startling *Nude Descending a Staircase*, was an enormous display of no fewer than 1,600 works. Parading along the burlap-covered walls were canvases by Cézanne, Van Gogh, Gauguin, Picasso, Braque, Matisse, Derain, Rouault, Bonnard, Duchamp, Dufy, Léger—the entire School of Paris in all its fantastic array. There was also a sampling of American art, looking wan and wistful by comparison. "The American artists exhibiting here," the exhibition catalogue bravely declared, "consider the exhibition as of equal importance for themselves as for the public. The less they find their work showing signs of the developments indicated in the Europeans', the more reason they will have to consider whether or not painters and sculptors here have fallen behind. . . ."

Behind what? That was the question that the public, chuckling, and faintly embarrassed, kept wondering. The critics tried to answer and they failed. Wrote the young Duncan Phillips (who has since dedicated his brilliant Phillips Collection in Washington to modern art): "The bond which holds together the motley army of iconoclasts is the common desire to overthrow the established standards taught in the schools and respected in the homes." Frank Jewett Mather Jr. compared the exhibition to "a lunatic asylum. The inmates might well seem more vivid and fascinating than the every-day companions of home and office." Royal Cortissoz spluttered against the "gospel of stupid license and self-assertion. . . . When the stuff is rebuked, as it should be, the post-impressionist impresarios and fuglemen insolently proffer us a farrago of super-subtle rhetoric. The farce will end. . . ."

There was nothing really farcical in what the artists were doing, though they themselves could find a certain bitter humor in their isolation from the rest of the world. Rebuffed by a tradition-bound academy and a timid public, the French impressionists and post-impressionists of the late nineteenth century had made loneliness a virtue, and concentrated on art for art's sake. Beginning with the idea that a picture should not be judged by who wants or likes it, a few painters broke through to a truly revolutionary theory. A picture, they decided, should be judged by itself alone, and not as a reference to anything at all outside itself, whether in man or nature. A painting is an independent object, they proclaimed, take it leave it.

This aim, taken literally, is obviously far too extreme for all but a few painters; yet it remains the magnetic pole of modern art. The moderns all point, however waveringly, in the direction of complete independence. They may be on shaky ground intellectually, but they know what they don't like: they don't like interference and they don't like messages. They are as truculent and carefree—at the top of their bent—as the mountain trappers of the old Wild West, or research physicists working on a university grant.

In fact, the strengths and weaknesses of modern art closely parallel those of the contemporary phenomenon, pure science. Medieval alchemists maintained that only a good man could transmute base metal into gold. Pure science cuts away such moral considerations to concentrate on finding new truths. The same goes for modern art, which tends to rule out human values in order to create brand-new pictorial values.

The experiments of the moderns were nowhere near as chaotic as they seemed. Each required a rigidly defined field, or canvas, a number of elements, shapes, and colors, and finally some rules of procedure. Instead of reflecting nature as she is, the moderns were bent on prodding her into new positions. This required a new set of techniques bearing a certain resemblance to the Mock Turtle's arithmetic: "Ambition, Distraction, Uglification, and Derision." Mainly the moderns called into play the forces of abstraction and distortion. This instantly made shapes and colors more important than what they represented. It set off a debate about the relative importance of form and content that has split American painting down the middle ever since.

The Americans who first came down on the side of form felt with John Sloan that what the School of Paris had to teach was "wonderful medicine," and they were soon translating their European inspiration into American idioms. But since content has a way of shouldering into even the coolest and most formal sort of art, the American moderns shortly found the face of the nation shining through their abstractions and distortions. One group set itself the task of applying French cubism to American subject matter.

Cubism, the invention of Picasso and Georges Braque, was essentially a walk-around art. It cut the world into blocks and then tilted and twisted the blocks independently of one another. Thus whole objects were partly dissected and viewed from various angles simultaneously. The French had applied the cubist technique chiefly to pipe-smoking poets, absinthe bottles, and guitars. The Americans expanded this Bohemian material to include the hard and fast aspects of modern life: asphalt, stop lights, speedways, jazz, elevators, locomotives, punch presses, and molten steel.

ONE pioneer American modern, an Italian immigrant named Joseph Stella, had seen the artistic possibilities of this new subject matter even before the Armory Show. Arriving in America in 1896 when he was nineteen, Stella started

172

CHARLES DEMUTH'S "MY EGYPT" (1927)

out as a magazine illustrator, depicting mainly the peasant types he remembered from his native Italy. But in 1908 a magazine sent him out to Pittsburgh with instructions to sketch the boom city as it really looked. Stella came away inspired by "the unceasing volcanic explosions of the steel mills, the yellow Allegheny River, cutting its tortuous, snakelike course through fog and smoke." Then a return trip to Europe brought him into contact with the cubists and also with the Italian futurists, who painted objects as if in motion, seen in several different positions at once. Back in Manhattan at the time of the Armory Show, Stella resolved to build a bridge between European painting and American experience.

One canvas, appropriately named *The Bridge*, fulfilled Stella's ambition. Beyond that, it keynoted a distinctly American school of modern painting that still persists. Relating in spirit, not detail, to Brooklyn Bridge, the picture soars and sparkles like a daydreamer's—or night driver's—vision. The bridge itself seems to be in motion, as if it could actually lift the observer up and into space. Following the sweeping, steel-cable lines inward is like a headlong plunge into blue night.

ANOTHER of the pioneer bridge builders was Charles Demuth, who also had learned cubism in Paris before the Armory Show. For generations the Demuths had been tobacconists in Lancaster, Pennsylvania. Young Charles came home from studying art in Paris to become the town's chief mystifier instead, painting oddly prismatic reflections of the world about him. He confessed to having drawn out his inspiration "with a teaspoon, but I never spilled a drop."

The cubists had taught Demuth to shatter shapes; he proceeded to crack the very skies as

STUART DAVIS' "EGGBEATER NO. 3" (1928)

174

LYONEL FEININGER'S "GELMERODA NO. 4" (1915)

LEE GATCH'S "INDUSTRIAL NIGHT" (1948)

well. He painted Pennsylvania factories and Provincetown houses impaled, piecemeal, on diagonal panes and slivers of blue, grey, and white light. To underline the fact that his subject matter could be as monumental as his art was lapidarian, he titled his painting of grain elevators *My Egypt*.

SHORTLY before Lyonel Feininger's death in 1956, he was asked what artist had influenced him most. Came the instant reply: Johann Sebastian Bach. Bach's music, the painter explained, "is incomparably terse, and that is one of the reasons it is so mighty."

Feininger left Manhattan for Germany at sixteen, and did not return until he was past sixty; yet his work relates more to Stella and Demuth than it does to German expressionism. Tall, still, lantern-jawed, Feininger needed no violence to express his personality. In youth he painted fanciful comic strips for children, full of the tricks that clouds, chance rays of light, and odd perspectives can play with a playful imagination. In middle age he slowly froze and crystallized the fancy that had animated his vision, learning to see all things as parts of a single harmony. *Gelmeroda No. 4* happens to represent a German

village, with its church, but the painting might just as well have been inspired by the ships and searchlights of New York Bay. From the music of Bach to Gothic architecture to broken rays of light to canvases as scrupulously put together as racing engines, was no great journey for Feininger. "The whole world," he once explained, "is nothing but order."

STUART Davis brought a jackhammer jazziness to the bridge-building school. Squat, bigjawed, jolly, and combative, he changed the laboratory coolness of Stella, Demuth, and Feininger into a rough kind of frenzy. Trained by Robert Henri, Davis exhibited some Ashcan School water colors at the Armory Show. He even sold one, but the European part of the exhibition made it impossible for him ever again to paint as he had been taught. Gazing at the rhythmic distortions of Van Gogh, Gauguin, Matisse, and the other European masters, Davis recalls, he "sensed an objective order in these works which I felt was lacking in my own. It gave me the same kind of emotional excitement I got from the numerical precisions of the Negro piano players in the Newark saloons. I decided that I would quite definitely have to become a 'modern'

176

RICHARD FLORSHEIM'S "NIGHT CITY" (1956)

CHARLES SHEELER'S "THE ARTIST LOOKS AT NATURE" (1943)

artist. It took an awful long time. I soon learned to think of color more or less objectively, so that I could paint a green tree red without batting an eye. Purple or green faces didn't bother me at all, and I even learned to sew buttons and glue excelsior on the canvas without feeling any sense of guilt."

What did trouble him was a haunting conviction that trees, red or green, should bear leaves and grow out of the ground. Not until 1927 did he stop worrying about what his pictures represented. In that year he nailed an egg beater, a rubber glove, and an electric fan to a table, and painted them over and over. "Through this concentration," he explains, "I focused on the logical elements. The result was the elimination of a number of particularized optical truths which I had formerly concerned myself with." By the time he got to *Eggbeater No. 3*, Davis had freed himself pretty well. The picture still hinted at some "optical truths"—the red of the glove, and the crossed blades of the fan for example— but nobody could possibly imagine beating an egg with anything in his picture. Davis had beaten the beater, and gone on to invent the blunt, bright, surprising, and highly personal brand of abstraction that has distinguished the painting he has done ever since.

For most of his life, Davis has lived and taught in Greenwich Village, where they still play the Dixieland music he loves best. Methodically downing glass after glass of water in out-of-the-way night clubs, he sits scowling happily, listening to the beat. His own paintings are as hot and abstract as the music, but to say they have no subject matter strikes Davis as ridiculous. It is "equivalent to saying that life has no subject matter. . . . Some of the things that have made me want to paint, outside of other paintings, are . . . the brilliant colors on gasoline stations, chain-store fronts, and taxicabs . . . fast travel by train, auto, and airplane, which brought new and multiple perspectives; electric signs; the landscape and boats of Gloucester, Massachusetts; five- and ten-cent-store kitchen utensils; movies and radio; Earl Hines's piano. . . ." In other words Davis, like the other pioneer American moderns, makes a science of organizing and simplifying what he sees and feels. He reduces his environment to designs that are rhythmic and electric enough to compare favorably with those of France's Fernand Léger—or even with Earl Hines's piano.

EXAMPLES of the continuing struggle to paint the New World's new worlds are *Industrial Night*, by Lee Gatch, and *Night City*, by Richard Florsheim. "Of course," says Gatch of his picture, "it's a steel mill in operation at night. You see curved tracks, loaded cars, and an industrial lake with a reflection of the nail paring of the moon. The upper part, where the mill is operating, becomes ornamental shapes rather than descriptive shapes—off-focus." The picture also has a remarkable sense of motion, conveyed by its diagonal curves, as if the scene were glimpsed from a speeding train. Painted with Gatch's peculiar sense of color, it seems compounded of smog, crystal, gas jets, chemical dyes, and moonlight.

Richard Florsheim pictures the city as a vast and lofty shadow-hive humming with lights and movements. It is perhaps a City of Dreadful Night, but it is also true. And the particular truths about American cities expressed by Florsheim were never before confined to canvas.

OF all the American artists who have reduced modern life to cool, hard, clean designs, Charles Sheeler is the most accomplished. He came roundabout to his machine-tooled style, studying flamboyant portraiture in Philadelphia, admiring the French moderns in Paris, and then passing on and back to the geometrical rigors of Italian Renaissance art. For most of his life he made his living from photography, which taught him that "light is the great designer." Like Piero della Francesca, he came to believe that "a picture could have incorporated in it the structural design implied in abstraction, and be presented in a wholly realistic manner." Sheeler paints what he sees, with the emphasis on its abstract composition.

The Artist Looks at Nature is unquestionably Sheeler's most personal picture. In it he sits alone, turned from the viewer, a pale, spindly fellow in a lyre-back chair. As with most long-time painters, his neck cranes from hunched

179

shoulders. Having the blinkered oblivion necessary to painstaking art, he works at an American interior before the walled town of Carcassonne, in France. But the landscape is the sort he prefers: smooth-shaven, without litter, serene, and mastered by man's works. The whole has a two-sided humor—self-deprecatory, yet dignified.

Now in his seventies, Sheeler lives with his Russian-born wife in a small stone house filled with Shaker furniture, up the Hudson River from New York. Sheeler will not refuse a walk in the sun, or a sociable Martini, but his apparent serenity has a honed edge, and his mind is on his work. He came away from a trip to California reassured by the towering redwood trees. "They never changed their minds," he observed. His own standards are set as high as a redwood. Holbein and Rembrandt meet his personal test; in their pictures "the object is accounted for in all its three hundred and sixty degrees of reality rather than the hundred and eighty degrees which the physical eye usually takes in. Both have viewed their subjects with the physical eye plus the eye of the mind." Sheeler gives less credit to his own immediate predecessors, Homer, Eakins, and Ryder, though he has been known to praise Raphaelle Peale's still life, *After the Bath*, as "the finest nude I ever saw."

Sheeler never makes a show of the problems of painting, and asks no sympathy for his efforts. He builds each new picture as meticulously as an engineer builds a prototype machine, keeping it by him until all the bugs are out. "I favor," he says, "a picture which arrives at its destination without the evidence of a trying journey rather than the one which shows the marks of battle. An efficient army buries its dead." This attitude makes for something chill, even forbidding, in Sheeler's art, which does not bother him at all: "I like for people to wipe their feet before entering my house."

Herman Melville once remarked that Benjamin Franklin was "everything except a poet." The same criticism might be applied to Sheeler, who admires Franklin enormously. Like Franklin, he could be accused of concerning himself with mind and matter more than spirit; his pictures are intellectualizations of a man-built world. And yet, again like Franklin, Sheeler can tug at intuitions far below the surface of the mind. *Golden Gate*, which he painted at seventy-two, seems to be saying that life is much more serious and glorious than at first appears. The canvas does not so much abstract some physical aspects of twentieth-century life as it refines them, to the point of utmost power. It proves once again that art needs no gestures, that it can be precise and silent as a frozen pond, and still fully alive. Once, looking at the picture, the old man murmured that he felt it to be "a gateway, a beckoning into the new." The same can be said for Sheeler's art as a whole.

SHEELER'S "GOLDEN GATE" (1955)

MAX WEBER'S "LATEST NEWS" (CA. 1940)

THE WINDING PATH

They said, "You have a blue guitar,
You do not play things as they are."

The man replied, "Things as they are,
Are changed upon the blue guitar."

—WALLACE STEVENS

FOR every American who uses the new techniques of modern art to interpret modern life, there are two who use them to reflect the kingdom of nature. The two worlds interpenetrate, naturally, and many artists portray some of both. But in general, where Sheeler paints a bridge, John Marin paints a tree, and where Davis paints an egg beater, Karl Knaths paints the ocean. With a few exceptions, those pioneer moderns in America who cared most for nature found cubism too cold and cutting an instrument. Instead, they adopted the arbitrary colors and rhythmic distortions of the Paris *Fauves*—the "Wild Beasts"—Matisse, Rouault, Derain, and Dufy. Fauvism was not so much a technique as an attitude, the expression of abandonment. It meant putting heart over mind and striving to duplicate the vivid candor of a child.

In trying to reflect nature in paint, the moderns show it in odd, broken ways, as if through elaborate crystals. Their work is much more personal and diverse than that of children, but it shares a child's strong natural drift towards abstraction. Starting with nature, the moderns often become fascinated with mere paint itself. They stop reflecting and start playing—that is, painting abstractions. Then, often as not, something recalls them to their original intention, and they introduce the subject once again. This vacillation was typical of the pioneer American moderns. At worst, it resulted in considerable confusion. At best, it gave something like the best of both worlds.

"In part," said Aristotle, "art completes what nature cannot elaborate; and in part, it imitates nature." Though agreeing that both design and representation have a share in art, he would doubtless have been amazed to see how carelessly, or with what fine freedom, the pioneer moderns mingle the two. Theirs has been a winding path, haphazard, and laced with surprises.

AMONG the first Americans to follow the winding path of modern painting was Max Weber, the mild little son of a Brooklyn tailor. By the time he was twenty-four, Weber had earned enough money teaching art and carpentry to make an instinctive trip to Paris. The year was 1905; Picasso and Matisse were just coming into their own. Weber got to know them, along with the other shabby young men of Montmartre who had paint under their fingernails and the light of the future in their eyes. A particular friend of his was the great Paris primitive, Henri Rousseau, whose spirit was as gentle as Weber's own. Weber learned from them all, and three years later he came home to spread their message. As with most of Weber's paintings, *Latest News* derives its multiple perspectives from cubism and its touches of surprising color from the *Fauves*. The picture shows India-rubber workers wrestling with albatross-like newspapers during their lunch hour. Its strengths are sensibility and sophistication.

These also happened to be the strengths of a bushy-browed photographer named Alfred Stieglitz, to whom Weber imparted what he had learned in Europe. Stieglitz had already discovered on his own that photographs can symbolize an extraordinary range of thoughts and feelings. Discussing School of Paris art with him, Weber showed Stieglitz that paintings can do the same. Stieglitz, who had a small income to implement his great and immediate enthusiasm, used the art gallery he had opened to introduce Cézanne, Toulouse-Lautrec, Rodin, and Matisse to the American public. But until the Armory Show jolted it into awareness, the public in general ignored Stieglitz' gallery. Undaunted, he was meanwhile forming a brilliant circle of young American painters. Along with Charles Demuth and Weber, it included Arthur Dove, Marsden Hartley, Georgia O'Keeffe, and John Marin.

ARTHUR Dove was the first "pure" abstractionist, in America or abroad. The son of a Geneva, New York, brickmaker, he began his career as a magazine illustrator. A trip to Paris in 1907 delighted him and diverted him from mere representation. Home again, he naturally gravitated into Stieglitz' group. The friends were certain that their art mattered, but in the years before the Armory Show nobody else suspected as much. That made things exciting, as well-kept secrets can be, and altogether unprofitable. Dove met his financial problem by retiring to a Connecticut farm, where living was cheap, and he could fish for his own dinner. Landscape, he decided, was just the subject for his brush. With pantheistic fervor he poured his feelings about nature into half-recognizable abstractions, trying always to dissolve what he saw into what he felt.

In the course of this lonely effort Dove gradually eliminated all direct reference to the scenes before his eyes. In 1910 he thus crossed a new frontier of art just a year ahead of Wassily Kandinsky, who was to tread the same path independently in Germany. Dove's *Abstraction No. 2* is a distillation of nature; few representational landscapes carry more sense of sun and shade, stone and tree. And he kept on mingling nature with abstraction. When paint failed to convey his feelings he made pictures by pasting objects together in a frame. His portrait of his grandmother is a bit of her needle point, a page from her Bible, and some pressed flowers against a

ARTHUR DOVE'S "ABSTRACTION NO. 2" (1910)

background of weathered shingles. To represent weeping willows in the rain, he mounted twigs, flecked with gelatin, on glass. Wild and precise at once, he would try anything, and always with exquisite craftsmanship. Sometimes, when his refinement compensated for his lack of force, Dove's art could be as poignant and haunting as the cry of a distant bird.

MARSDEN Hartley was a craggy, stubborn, profoundly earnest man who made his whole painting career a matter of experiment. Even in old age he seems to have considered himself a promising youth, and in one sense that remained true. But though he never got a sure grasp of art, he could on occasion demonstrate that he had a tremendous grip.

He liked to be known as "the painter from Maine"; yet he traveled considerably in Europe and appraised its art with a shrewd Yankee eye. Almost the first American to appreciate German expressionism, he adapted the explosive palette of Wassily Kandinsky and Franz Marc to his own blunt ends. *Portrait of a German Officer*, done on the eve of World War I, is a handsome back of the hand to Prussian pomp and circumstance. Curiously, it also points ahead to the abstract expressionism practiced at mid-century.

Hartley himself renounced expressionist art long before it became fashionable to embrace it. In 1928 he wrote that he had spent half his life as an artist obeying William Blake's injunction to "put off intellect and put on imagination; the imagination is the man." In a prose style as awkward, reaching, and resonant as his paintings, Hartley continued: "From this doctrinal assertion evolved the theoretical axiom that you don't see a thing until you look away from it—which was an excellent truism as long as the principles of imaginative life were believed in and followed. I no longer believe in the imagination. I rose one certain day—and the whole thing had become changed. I had changed old clothes for new ones, and I couldn't bear the sight of the old garments. And when a painting is evolved from imaginative principles I am strongly inclined to turn away because I have greater faith that intellectual clarity is better and more entertaining

184

MARSDEN HARTLEY'S "PORTRAIT OF A GERMAN OFFICER" (1914)

HARTLEY'S "ROBIN HOOD COVE, GEORGETOWN, MAINE" (1938-39)

than imaginative wisdom or emotional richness. . . . I would rather be sure that I had placed two colors in true relationship to each other than to have exposed a wealth of emotionalism gone wrong in the name of richness of personal expression."

Towards the end of his life Hartley settled once more in Maine; and instead of trying to express his own personality, he devoted himself to the stern beauty of the native landscape. The results were more personal than before. The bluntness and impatience with detail that distinguished his early abstractions were even more marked in his late landscapes. And *Robin Hood Cove* has a quality of self-containment that was lacking in the overloud abstractions.

With *Flowers from Claire Spencer's Garden*, he almost succeeds in speaking the language of love. It is perhaps as close as the puritanical bachelor came to tenderness. A year before his death in 1943 he remarked: "Everyone's been in love, but I could never afford to get married. As

HARTLEY'S "FLOWERS FROM CLAIRE SPENCER'S GARDEN" (1939-40)

187

O'KEEFFE'S
"NEW YORK NIGHT" (1929)

a matter of fact I don't know what kind of husband I'd have made. I know I make a good friend. But a husband—"

In his flower picture, the wheeling, black-bordered, white, red, and yellow blossoms echo Hartley's early *Portrait of a German Officer*, but it is as if the echo came from a distant and happier hillside. "We are subjects of our nativeness," he wrote. "And so I say to my native continent of Maine, be patient and forgiving, I will soon put my cheek to your cheek, expecting the welcome of the prodigal, and be glad of it, listening all the while to the slow, rich, solemn music of the Androscoggin, as it flows along."

WHEN Alfred Stieglitz first saw Georgia O'Keeffe's abstract drawings one day in 1916, he said: "Finally a woman on paper." He wrote to her, and got back a letter from South Carolina that must have reinforced his impression: "Mr. Stieglitz—I like what you write me— maybe I don't get exactly your meaning—but I like mine—like you liked your interpretation of my drawings. It was such a surprise to me that you saw them—and I am so glad they surprised you—that they gave you joy. . . . I can't tell you how sorry I am that I can't talk to you—what I've been thinking surprises me so—has been such fun—at times has hurt too—that it would be great to tell you. Some of the fields are green —very very green—almost unbelievably green against the dark of the pine woods—and it's warm—the air feels warm and soft—and lovely."

She was twenty-nine, a lonely, thin-lipped, rawboned art teacher with straight black hair done up in a bun. The next year Stieglitz put her drawings on exhibition. O'Keeffe, who happened to be in Manhattan, stormed into the gallery to stop the show. Her abstractions, she explained, were a private matter which the public would find incomprehensible. Gently, Stieglitz asked whether she herself knew what they meant. O'Keeffe turned her dark, level gaze on him: "Do you think I'm an idiot?" She established herself as a member of Stieglitz' group, and eight years later they were married.

Next to Mary Cassatt, O'Keeffe is the best woman painter America has yet produced. Her style, based on clean colors, sharp edges, and

JOHN MARIN'S "SEA PIECE—BOAT FANTASY" (1951)

THE DOWNTOWN GALLERY

MARIN'S "SUN, ISLES AND SEA" (1921)

strong patterns, remains constant, though her subject matter is extremely diverse. "Singing," she once said, "has always seemed to me the most perfect means of expression. Since I cannot sing, I paint." Somewhat shrill and thin her painting can be at times, but it always does have the spontaneity of music, with line and color counting for much more than the bones, blossoms, barns, skyscrapers, clouds, crosses, and canyon walls she uses for lyrics.

No American ever painted a pelvis or a skull more cleanly than O'Keeffe. Her brush, like a surgical knife, pares and sculptures them paper-white against the ice-blue skies of her beloved New Mexico, where she now lives. She brought to flower painting the photographic discovery of the closeup, exploring the innermost recesses of calla lilies, irises, and hollyhocks. Cityscapes, such as *New York Night*, convey much the same sense of fragrant invitation as do her flowers.

In her late sixties, O'Keeffe has gone back more and more to the straight abstractions that had first intrigued Stieglitz forty years before. *From the Plains No. 1* goes yet farther back for

inspiration. O'Keeffe herself was brought up in Sun Prairie, Wisconsin. The painting demonstrates both her American earthiness and her contrasting streak of Puritanism, also American, which wants everything sharp and bare.

JOHN Marin was the best of Stieglitz' circle, and in the first rank of American painting. A spindly, sharp-beaked, draggle-feathered crow of a man, Marin was as pithy and angular in speech and gesture as in his paintings. "I guess," he once wrote Stieglitz, "a picture is good when it just don't irritate the eye. Poetry, imagination, intellect, temperament, oh they can come in on a later train."

Marin's methods of not irritating the viewer's eye were very much his own. The work of many landscape painters looks as if it had been laboriously traced on a pane of glass set between the artist and the scene. Marin broke the glass and let daylight and fresh air flood in. The straight lines that swing through his paintings like guide wires keep the eye shifting from the flat surface of the picture to tilting transparent planes inside

190

it. The curving, calligraphic lines follow the rhythms rather than the contours of what was actually before him, re-creating the contradictory pulls and thrusts of sea, tide, wind, boats, trees, and mountains.

Marin spent most summers on the coast of Maine, and most of his art has the sparkle and lilt of a sunlit sea after a storm. Except for Winslow Homer, no other water-colorist in American history comes close to matching Marin's naturalness in transcribing nature. Some of his paintings look as if they were dashed off in a couple of minutes, and perhaps they were. "It's like golf," he once explained. "The fewer strokes I can take, the better the picture." At times he would paint with a brush in each hand, his hands seeming to fight each other over the paper. "See that blue spot out there?" he would ask a visitor, pointing his dripping brush seaward. "You can't put that on paper—so you just put down a color that the paper will like, a color that looks all right in itself." While working, he would turn the picture on its side, or even upside down, testing the composition: "Think of the wonderful balance of squirrels; they scratch themselves equally well with hind-paws or fore-paws without losing their balance. I like my pictures to have that kind of balance."

The very doing of it, Marin believed, is part of what painting is about. Therefore he would stop working on a picture while it still had the excitement of a work in progress, inviting the viewer to relive his own joy not only in nature but in painting itself. His joys were as great as the man. In old age he wrote from Maine: "The Hurricane has just hit—the Seas are Glorious—Magnificent—Tremendous—God be praised that I have yet the vision to see these things."

He led a retiring yet on the whole triumphant life. One of his few disappointments was that the

MARIN'S "SEASCAPE FANTASY, MAINE" (1944)

MARIN'S "SPRING NO. 1" (1953)

oils he began painting in his later years never pleased people as much as his water colors. Compared with the water colors, *Sun, Isles and Sea* and *Sea Piece—Boat Fantasy*, the oils, *Seascape Fantasy* and *Spring No. 1*, are certainly less flowing but they have more solidity. *Spring No. 1* was painted in 1953, the year Marin died. It aptly illustrates his most eloquent statement of faith: "Seems to me the true artist must perforce go from time to time to the elemental big forms— Sky, Sea, Mountain, Plain—and those things pertaining thereto, to sort of re-true himself up, to recharge the battery. For these big forms have everything. But to express these, you have to love these, to be part of these in sympathy. One doesn't get very far without this love, this love to enfold too the relatively little things that grow on the mountain's back. Which, if you don't recognize, you don't recognize the mountain."

By the practice of re-truing himself to nature, Marin succeeded in avoiding the last pitfall of great artists, the sin of pride. He was even humble enough to admit that he was not humble enough in his self-judgments. He once remarked on having been so pleased with one of his own pictures that his head "swelled enormously— came near killing me." Self-expression, as an ideal, was always anathema to him: "An idiot surely puts himself into what he does." Not self-expression but self-immolation was what he practiced: "The high priest of art don't give a damn who did it."

Like most artists, Marin worshiped this world. He hated to leave it. A few days before his death, his biographer visited Marin and tried to comfort him in his pain, saying: "Think what it mounts up to to have been painting past eighty and getting better and better." In reply, the friend reported, Marin only "shook his head slowly. 'Nurse,' he said after a moment, 'please bring me some whisky.'"

STIEGLITZ' stable of painters exerted an enormous influence on the next generation. From their example, rather than the School of Paris, derive such modern American painters of nature as Karl Knaths, Milton Avery, Balcomb Greene, William Kienbusch, William Thon, and Theodoros Stamos. If none of the six has yet

KARL KNATHS' "HORSE MACKEREL" (1947)

193

MILTON AVERY'S "CLEAR CUT LANDSCAPE" (1951)

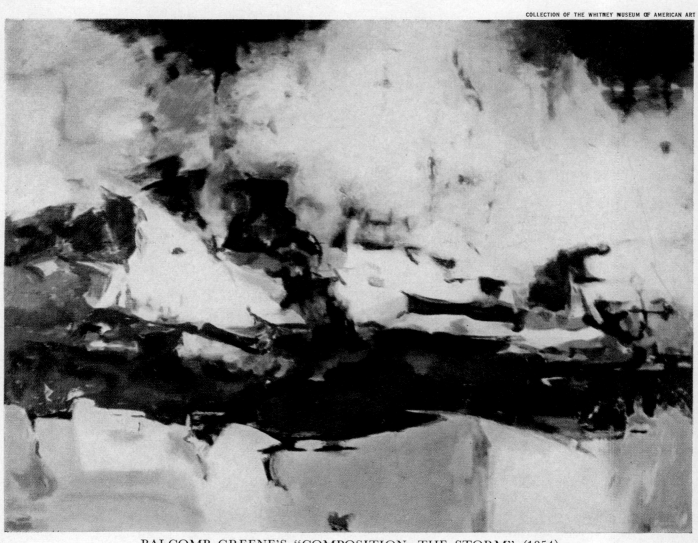

BALCOMB GREENE'S "COMPOSITION: THE STORM" (1954)

proved himself a major artist, each of them does provide a fresh, distinctive view of the world.

The fish in Karl Knaths' *Horse Mackerel* can be vaguely made out; it hangs head down from a boom on a fishing pier. The glistening Atlantic Ocean comes through much clearer than the giant tuna, and indeed some of it seems to show through the tuna's body. Then again, the waves resemble scales, as if the whole scene were perhaps a reflection in the flank of a far larger fish. Such are the ambiguities Knaths finds in the waters around his Cape Cod home, and expresses in superbly disciplined designs.

Clear Cut Landscape is also strong in design, but its principal concern is with color, Black is a lion among colors, always tending to dominate and to destroy the illusion of space. The fact that Milton Avery can make his black lie down peacefully and at a distance amidst lamblike moonlit hues shows the consummate skill he possesses as a colorist.

Balcomb Greene's *Composition: The Storm* took its inspiration from a hurricane that battered his house on Montauk Point, the eastern tip of Long Island. But under those breakers rolls a nude. Greene had been making a series of pictures of a woman lying nude before a window with the light flowing over her like foam. A few obscuring strokes and smudges, stormily applied, brought the waves in too.

William Kienbusch, whose art reflects both Hartley and Marin, followed his masters' footsteps to Maine. There he discovered "the world of many things I love—islands, trees, the sea, fences, gong buoys, churches, roses, mountains." Instead of describing such things in paint, he interprets them with a very free hand, feeling that "I betray nature if I copy." *The Weir and the Island* shows a fish weir of burnt spruce set in a tideway. The boughs of spruce, Kienbusch recalls, "stood up out of the water like wild orange branches in a blue field. The three bars represent low tide, and then the island. It's a kind of wild picture."

Landlubbers speak of "lighthouses," mariners of "lights." William Thon, another city painter

WILLIAM THON'S "LIGHT IN AUTUMN" (1953)

195

WILLIAM KIENBUSCH'S "THE WEIR AND THE ISLAND" (1955)

who went to Maine and stayed there, was using sailor's language when he called his canvas *Light in Autumn*. Thon has built a house on the Maine coast, like a single cozy room in the rock-hewn, sky-ceilinged mansion of his surroundings. His self-appointed task is to translate those surroundings into a few square feet of painted canvas —to bring the outdoors indoors and hang it on a wall. *Light in Autumn* has the flawed-crystal complexity, the hint of cubism applied to the open air, that is his trademark. Thon builds each composition on a lattice of smudgy rectangles, laid in partly with a putty knife, and laces his sharp, delicate outlines well into the lattice. An extraordinary richness of texture is the result. More important, Thon's technique stretches and changes the viewer's own vision. In his pictures air has a peculiar sparkle and density, and the things it encloses look fragile to the point of evanescence.

Heart of Norway Spruce looks much more like a Chinese calligraph than a tree, but it represents a tree nonetheless. Theodoros Stamos, who was born in New York of Greek immigrant parents, says stoutly that all of his pictures "are painted from nature. I consider myself a realist." With him, the winding path doubles all the way back to Arthur Dove, who also painted his full-out abstractions "from nature."

THEODOROS STAMOS'
"HEART OF NORWAY SPRUCE" (1952)

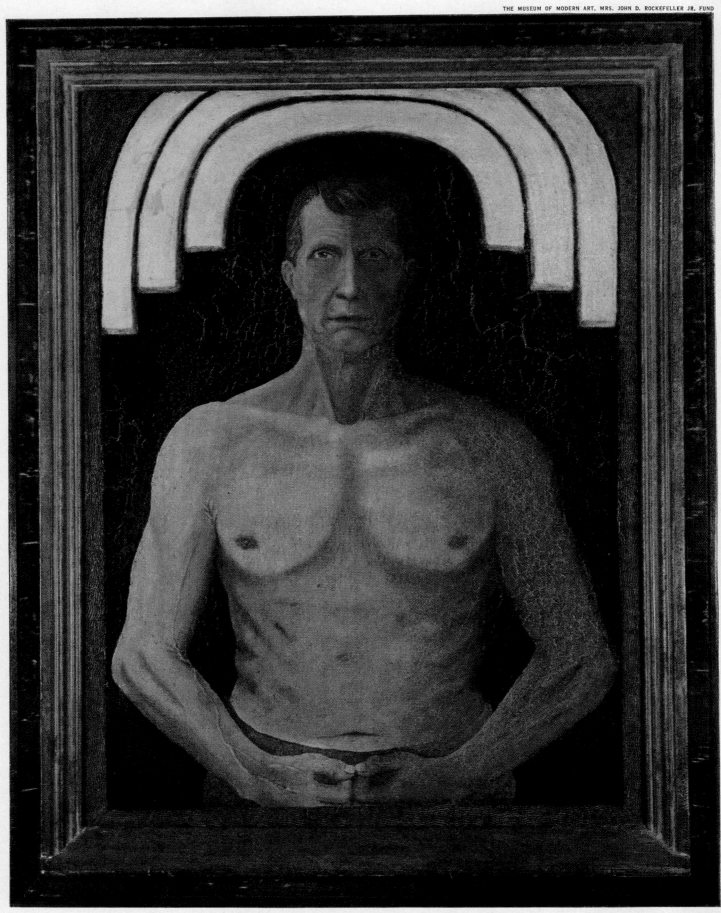

JOHN KANE'S "SELF-PORTRAIT" (1929)

CHAPTER III

THE INNOCENTS

*In any field of endeavor your true and authentic
amateur is a man who plays a game gleefully.*

—HEYWOOD BROUN

MOST great pictures are painted, of course, by artists who dedicate their whole lives to their work. But that does not prevent a host of eager amateurs from trying to recapture on canvas the world they see about them. Every Sunday thousands of paintings are lovingly coaxed along by men and women who drive trucks, sell shoes, or direct large corporations during the week. Although only one in a hundred might please a critical observer, ninety-nine in a hundred are beautiful to those who made them. They record days of happy experience.

Occasionally, out of this great and growing army of amateurs, a painter emerges who graduates to professional status while retaining the innocent freshness that is the envy of the true professionals. John Kane, Horace Pippin, and Grandma Moses all started painting late in life. Unschooled, simple, with only the most rudimentary grasp of their craft, all three show that enthusiasm, determination, and reverence for life can overcome a lack of technical skill.

ONE of John Kane's first memories was that of being soundly whacked by a teacher for drawing in school. He never drew during school again, and for decades thereafter he would have seemed a most unlikely candidate for painting fame. Born in 1860 of poor Irish parents in Scotland, he had to forswear the sunshine at the age of nine and start work in the coal mines.

At nineteen Kane moved to America. A big, brash, pious youth, he reveled in his strength.

And, like hundreds of thousands of fellow immigrants, he played a sweaty, cheerful role in the making of his adopted country. Indeed, he was later to boast in his autobiography of having "done almost every kind of work a laboring man can do." After mining, he took up "gandy dancing" (tamping down the gravel between railroad ties) and steelmaking. On Sundays he might pick up an extra five dollars prize fighting, bare-fisted, in a saloon. Once he held Gentleman Jim Corbett, who was still an unknown, to a five-round draw: "It was only a friendly bout. . . . I knew I could do away with him if I wanted to."

Sundays also meant the Roman Catholic Mass to Kane. Because his seven-day week interfered with church, he gave up a good blast-furnace job and went on to street paving, which was harder work. Kane believed that he might have become "the best block paver in the whole Pittsburgh district, perhaps, except it was at this time I met with my accident and had to give up paving." He was run over by a railroad locomotive, which sheared off his left leg below the knee. Kane was thirty-one. The accident, he said, "had the effect of steadying me. It showed me life wasn't all for good times."

By way of compensation, the railroad signed Kane on as a watchman at thirty-five dollars a month. After eight years of that, he graduated to painting railroad cars. The job recalled him to his childhood love of drawing, and during his lunch hour he would paint landscapes on the sides of the cars. Getting back to work in the afternoon, he would put a flat coat of paint over his pictures, blotting them out forever.

"I believe generally God finds a way to help those inclined to art," Kane wrote, "and so it was in my case." The first art work he did for a living was coloring photographs. He would go from door to door offering his services, at three dollars and up, depending on the size. Most of the photographs he got to color were of dead loved ones, and he listened to thousands of stories of bereavement. Meanwhile, he married and begot three children. The third, his first boy, died in infancy while Kane was out looking for a priest to baptize him. This tragic experience so unnerved him that he left his home and began twenty-five years of wandering, drinking, and working intermittently, unable to rest.

He learned and practiced two new trades, carpentry and house painting. A habit of painting pictures for pleasure, on scraps of beaverboard, helped comfort him, and finally brought him the calm he sought. His pictures were mostly stiff but vivid transcriptions of sights he liked—a stone church with every stone outlined, or a green Pennsylvania hillside with every tree in place. Art collectors still knew nothing of him or his work ("Rich people are in a class by themselves," as he put it), but workingmen began paying from five to twenty-five dollars for his pictures. He took to carrying a painting kit wherever he went, in hopes of seeing something paintable. "We get imagination out of the fields and hills and all besides," he explained. "We can learn something from nature each time we go out, each time we hear the robin say, 'Paint me, John. Paint me.'"

His only natural enemies were ants and small boys. He defeated the ants by tying his trouser cuffs about his socks. The boys were more difficult: "I have always loved boys. But I cannot abide their jeers and comical suggestions. They think they are being very funny at the expense of a poor old man like myself who tries to concentrate on the beauty that takes his very soul."

In 1927, when he was sixty-seven, Kane first had a picture accepted for exhibition, at the Carnegie Institute's Pittsburgh International. "When you walk the way of life all your days with the poor, as I have," he wrote, "one honor the more, one rebuff the less, is nothing." Yet honors began coming to him. He gave up house painting at the age of seventy and settled down in the Pittsburgh slums. There, after a quarter of a century spent apart, his wife rejoined him. And there it was that he painted his finest picture, the *Self-Portrait*.

Looming against a background as dark as the mouth of a cave, under a Byzantine arch, the subject gazes out upon the world with unshakable earnestness. The artist stands stripped to the waist as if for a chest X ray (he was actually to die of tuberculosis at seventy-four), bringing his strong, work-worn hands together in a gesture of resignation. It is as if he were consenting to give up laboring and be just himself alone. The face is deathly calm, and yet alert. It seems as if the thin mouth would never speak again, and as if the eyes were awaiting a sign from heaven.

LIKE John Kane, Horace Pippin came to art naturally as a child, and had it whipped out of him fast. A Pennsylvania Negro boy, born in 1888, he attended a rural one-room school. "When I was seven," he once recalled, "I began to get into trouble. It happened this way. In spelling, if the word was dog, stove, dishpan or something like that, I had a sketch of the article at the end of the word. And the results were, I would have to stay in after school and finish my lesson the right way. This happened frequently and I just couldn't help it. The worse part of it was, I would get a beating . . . for coming home late, regardless of what I were kept in for."

At fourteen, freed at last from the complexities of school, he went off on his own as a farm laborer. Later he worked as a hotel porter, iron molder, and furniture packer. Volunteering for military service in World War I, he fought on the Western Front. "To see those shells bursting in the night was a pretty sight," he remembered, "but the gas, dust and smoke was terrible." A sniper's bullet partially paralyzed his right arm.

Marrying a motherly widow named Ora Jennie Featherstone Wade, Pippin settled down in West Chester, Pennsylvania. He had no need to work; they lived on his disability pension combined with what she made as a laundress. But it was not a happy time. The shock of his war experience had left him a brooding, saddened man.

Then one day Pippin took a brush in his crippled right hand. Supporting his right wrist with his left hand, he proceeded to exorcise his memories of war with a powerful primitive oil called *End of the War: Starting Home*. This he followed with scenes from the Bible and pictures of Negro family life, done with increasing gaiety and ease. At fifty he began to be taken seriously as an artist. Before his death at fifty-eight, Pippin was being acclaimed as the best Negro painter anywhere. Only his wife refused to believe in his success. For security's sake she continued to take in washing, which clouded their last years together.

One of Pippin's most compelling canvases is *John Brown Going to His Hanging*. "Almost any reading Negro," the poet Vachel Lindsay wrote,

"is bound to remember *Uncle Tom's Cabin* with gratitude, and John Brown as well. He is bound to have an infinite variety of thoughts about them, grave and gay." Pippin's somber-toned, elaborately patterned canvas is itself both grave and gay. The bare boughs seem to jig against the frigid sky. The picture expresses just the spirit of Brown's own words when, sitting bound on his coffin, he approached the field of execution: "This *is* a beautiful country. I never had the pleasure of seeing it before."

FOR Grandma Moses, life seems to have been very happy on the whole, and as with most primitive painters her life is inseparable from her art. She was born in 1860, far enough back

HORACE PIPPIN'S "JOHN BROWN GOING TO HIS HANGING" (1942)

GRANDMA MOSES' "OUT FOR THE CHRISTMAS TREE" (1946)

to have had a great-grandfather in the American Revolution. In fact there is a powder horn with an inscription to prove conclusively that one of them was:

Hezekiah King.
Ticonderoga, Feb. 24th, 1777.
Steal not this horn for fear of shame
For on it is the owner's name.

Grandma says that her ancestry was "Scotch, Irish, English, French, and Indian, and that's a good combination, isn't it?" She was one of ten children born to a frugal couple, "back in the green meadows and wild woods on a farm in Washington County," near the town of Greenwich in upper New York State. Her earliest artistic efforts were turned to painting paper dolls. She used her mother's laundry bluing for the eyes

and grape juice for the lips, and after they were finished she made them dresses of colored paper.

One winter her father fell ill, and passed his convalescence painting a landscape around the walls of a room. Little Anna Mary "got into" the paints. She remembers making "some 'very pretty lambscapes,' as my brothers said I called them," on small scraps of slate, wood, and glass. "Father would say, 'Oh, not so bad.' But Mother was more practical, thought that I could spend my time other ways."

Among the other ways were ordinary farm-yard and household chores, plus the making of soap, candles, and dresses. "Little girls did not go to school much in the winter," she says, "owing to the cold and not warm enough clothing." Therefore she got only "through the Sixth Reader." But neither cold nor chores could stay the children from their appointed rounds of fun:

"Wintertime! When zero stands at twenty-five or thirty, when we cannot deny the pleasure of skating till we have bumped heads and bleedy noses, and the ice is like glass. Oh, what joy and pleasure as we slide down the hill, who can re-build what we see on that Christmas tree. Oh, those days of childhood!"

The words strike precisely the same happy and melodious note as does *Out for the Christmas Tree*, which was painted some seventy years after Grandma's childhood. "I like to paint old-timey things," she once said. "Something real pretty."

Grandma's preference for the pretty and the nostalgic, together with her obvious debt to the Currier & Ives prints popular in her childhood, have blinded many critics to the merit of her best work. *Out for the Christmas Tree* makes a subtle harmony of many opposites. It is greyish yet radiant, busy yet spacious, exuberant yet serene. The picture takes one by the hand and leads one through a merry, weaving kind of folk dance, up snowy hills and down again, over fences, along the delicately waving treetops, and into warm houses. All flows naturally, for the painting is brilliantly controlled.

Even as a little girl playing with her brothers, Grandma made a habit of excelling: "If they'd climb up a tree, I'd climb higher. If they'd climb to the eaves of a house, I'd climb to the ridge-pole." She took on larger challenges when she was twelve, going off "to earn my own living as what was then called a hired girl. This was a grand education for me, in cooking, housekeeping, in moralizing and mingling with the outside world." After fifteen years of this education, she met and married a farm hand named Thomas Salmon Moses. She remembers, with the certainty of true love, that he was "a wonderful man, much better than I am." But admiration did not prevent her from regarding herself right from the start as a full partner in his enterprises: "I had to do as much as my husband did, not like some girls, they sit down, and then somebody has to throw sugar at them."

The young couple headed south with their nest egg of $600, and rented a farm near Staunton in the Shenandoah Valley of Virginia. There Anna Mary was to bear ten children, just as her mother had, and raise the five that survived infancy. There, too, she was to supplement the family income by making butter and also potato chips, a novelty in those days, for sale to the neighbors. After eighteen years in the South, the family moved north again to Eagle Bridge, New York, and bought a dairy farm there. The children grew up and married. In 1927 Grandma's husband died.

Two of her sons had nearby farms of their own. The youngest stayed on with her. The grandchildren, and later on the great-grandchildren, gave her increasing pleasure. She occupied herself in her leisure hours with making worsted pictures (of yarn, drawn through netting) until arthritis made handling the needle too difficult. "I used to wrap my hands up in scarves," she recalls, "and lay them on a chair beside the bed at night. I couldn't sleep on account of the aching, just like a toothache. Then one night I got desperate, so I got up and hunted the doctor book, the 'Family Adviser, Philosophy of Diseases.' The best recipe was: three cups of sweet milk every day, and from three to five drops of turpentine in it. I took it for about three months, and all of a sudden there were no pains any more, but the hardness of the joints stayed."

Her sister Celestia had suggested that painting might be fun for her, and Grandma found it was. "I painted for pleasure, to keep busy, and to pass the time away, but I thought of it no more than doing fancy work." When she was persuaded to send some pictures to a country fair, along with canned fruits and jam, her preserves won prizes and her paintings none. But not long afterwards, in 1938, a druggist in the nearby town of Hoosick Falls put some of her pictures in the window for sale. There they were noticed by a Manhattan connoisseur, and word of the unknown primitive's abilities spread fast. Within two years Grandma's fame and fortune were made. She was then seventy-nine.

Grandma still paints in her own precise way. She lays her pictures flat on a table so she can rest her elbows while working. Old coffee cans hold her brushes; at her feet is a gallon can of flat white paint for sizing the pieces of sawed Masonite she paints on. She does her pictures in batches, like cookies, simply to save paint. "I'll use this blue for the sky in all of them, and then

I'll take this green for all the trees. That way your paints don't dry up on you. Let's see, I can start a batch of five on Monday and have them finished off on a Saturday. It's according to how I feel, and my callers." Selling at up to $3,500 a picture, Grandma's "batches" earn very well. "I will say," she says, "that I have did remarkable for one of my years and experience."

She calls her paintings "daydreams, as it were. I look out the window sometimes to see the color of the shadows and the different greens in the trees, but when I get ready to paint I just close my eyes and imagine a scene." *Christmas at Home* is a glowing memory of the country Christmases she knew as a girl. Hog killing came just before Christmas, and that meant big, juicy spareribs and fresh sausage cakes. "We used to tell people,

'Come and see us during the Christmas.' Why, we'd keep the table set with plates, ready for anybody to come in and eat, until New Year's. Christmas is not just one day."

Hospitality is perhaps the key to Grandma. Certainly her great and utterly unexpected fame, coming toward the close of such a long and useful life, pleases her mainly for the personal contacts it brings, and bothers her only because it brings too many. A "Do Not Disturb" sign from a hotel room hangs outside the front door of her farmhouse to ward off the thousands of tourists who besiege her sunny old age. Yet those who get past that printed plea find that Grandma's principal interest is still people. A visitor, asking what she was proudest of having done in life, got a grandmotherly answer: "I've helped some people."

MOSES' "CHRISTMAS AT HOME" (1946)

CHAPTER IV

PAINTERS OF PEOPLE

*Painting is the intermediate somewhat
between a thought and a thing.*

—SAMUEL TAYLOR COLERIDGE

LIKE painting, man himself is a subtle merging of mind and matter. The portraitist's task is to express both at the same time. By minimizing the discrepancies and magnifying the similarities between the inner and outer selves, the best portraitists make an image that shows the two parts merged in harmony. Such an image can reveal the whole man far more clearly than his actual presence would.

Since the days of Copley and Stuart, the problems of a revealing portraiture have been a major preoccupation of American art. The twentieth century has produced perhaps a hundred workmanlike portraitists in America—and a handful of brilliant painters who also do portraits. They share in common the urge to reach past man to the workings of his mind.

THINGS are really there," Charles Hopkinson says, with a diffident wave of his hand, "so why shouldn't one try to capture the there-ness of them?" To the dean of American portrait painters, Justice Holmes's craggy nature and crackling thoughts were just as much "there" as his physical envelope. They are clearly there on Hopkinson's canvas too.

"What interests me," Hopkinson says, "are the finer things that one sees in the character. That is very old-fashioned, I know. But just as on the stage it is easier to act a drunken man than a fine

character, it is easier to draw a caricature than to paint a face that denotes fine character. I've always tried to find the fine things rather than to make a sneering comment." Hopkinson, at eighty-eight, has discovered and painted the fine things about a long cavalcade of outstanding men. Poets, philosophers, statesmen, a brace of bishops, and a score of college presidents have all come under his sympathetically searching eye and accomplished brush.

Looking for the fine things in reticent fellow Yankees can be frustrating, Hopkinson admits. Once, while painting Calvin Coolidge, he asked a question he hoped would change the President's tight-buttoned expression into one of farsightedness and courage. What, he demanded suddenly, had been Coolidge's first thought on learning of President Harding's death? "I thought I could swing it," Coolidge twanged, without the least change of expression.

EUGENE Speicher made his first mark at Manhattan's Art Students League back in 1907, when his portrait of Georgia O'Keeffe, a fellow student, took a prize. At the Armory Show six years later, Speicher was chagrined to find how much he still had to learn about drawing and color, especially from Renoir. His portrait of Mrs. Ogden Phipps, done in 1941, shows how thoroughly he learned his new lessons.

205

"Man's legitimate preoccupation," as George Moore said, "is woman." And female sitters have always brought out the best in Speicher. "When I begin painting," he remarked, "the model is alive and the blank canvas is dead. Once I've started and got the idea on canvas, the canvas becomes imbued with life, and the model is not dead but something to refer to." He referred to Mrs. Phipps with proper enthusiasm, creating an image as firm, serene, and sunny as a ripe peach on a window ledge.

JAMES Chapin's *Ruby Green Singing* is on a different level altogether. The painter was attempting nothing less than to express "the beauty of Negro music and the Negro people." Grand themes seldom require grandiose means, and Chapin let a lone singer of spirituals carry on her young shoulders the entire weight of what he had to say.

"The symbol of the human gesture interests me a lot," Chapin says. "Not the gesture of hands or feet so much as the carriage of the human body and the human head." Ruby Green's own

CHARLES HOPKINSON'S
"OLIVER WENDELL HOLMES" (1931)

EUGENE SPEICHER'S
"MRS. OGDEN PHIPPS" (1941)

JAMES CHAPIN'S "RUBY GREEN SINGING" (1928)

FRANKLIN WATKINS' "SOLITAIRE" (1937)

carriage is like a flower growing toward the sun. Music rises in her like sap. She might almost be singing William Blake's lines:

Look on the rising sun: There God does live,
And gives his light, and gives his heat away;
And flowers and trees and beasts and men receive
Comfort in morning, joy in the noonday.

And we are put on earth a little space,
That we may learn to bear the beams of love;
And these black bodies and this sunburnt face
Is but a cloud, and like a shady grove.

THE people in Franklin Watkins' pictures are apt to be agitated around the edges, dancing to the jumpy lines he borrowed in part from Toulouse-Lautrec. Watkins used two different models for *Solitaire*, and says he would no longer recognize either one. But the black, white, and red of the cards against green felt, he recalls, gave him "an electric excitement of disproportionate emphasis." The props and settings that Watkins provides are likely to be striking, and very nearly clashing, in color. He has the reputation of a "witty" and "theatrical" sort of artist, but Watkins' wit turns inward: "I feel portrait painting is a sort of screening of yourself as much as a study of the person sitting in front of you. *Solitaire* was the illustration of a mood of query." In other words, instead of trying to merge the inner and outer natures of the character portrayed in this picture, Watkins has made the experiment of identifying his own feelings with how his subject looks. The pale player who questions his beautifully colored cards with so little apparent hope is mostly a reflection of Watkins himself and his own feelings as he painted.

208

LOUIS BOUCHE'S "MURAL ASSISTANT" (1937)

WATKINS' wit and mood are well matched in Louis Bouché's *Mural Assistant*. The subject was actually Bouché's brother-in-law, who dropped by one day when Bouché was painting a mural, and fell naturally into such an intriguing pose that the artist decided to paint him instead. Bouché has made his living painting "miles and miles of murals." His easel paintings are far better, though too sketchy and intimate to attract the attention they deserve.

Mural Assistant pokes gentle fun at a little man perched in front of a wall by picturing him as the enthroned monarch of a vast, imaginary, painted world. This painting-within-a-painting also puts Bouché's mural and easel painting in proper perspective. It shows that his more pretentious and better-paid work can be compressed into less space with no loss.

An Edwardian sort of gentleman with sixty happy years of work and play under his ample waistcoat, Bouché loves painting "because art is just love, that's all. If you love, you're so immersed in it you must float. I get very excited when I paint. My blood pressure goes up like the devil. Drawing doesn't excite me so much because I don't draw as well. But when it comes to messing paint around, I have more confidence. What I like best besides subject matter is the pastry quality, the paint itself."

THERE is no hint of "pastry quality" in Peter Hurd's painstaking portraits, though he does them in egg tempera. Hurd uses transparent paints on wooden panels coated with shining white. The resulting luminosity accords well with the clean air, cold shadows, and blazing sun of his native New Mexico. More important, his meticulous technique suits his reverence for reality. "What motivates me," he says, "is a constant wonder. My wonder never ceases about the miracle of life on this planet, and here where I was born is one of the earth's most dramatic presentations in enormous contrasts of color, light, weather, geology, plant and animal life. It is hard to tell anyone just how painting can be a religious experience, but it is with me."

José Herrera is the artist's polo-playing friend and foreman of his ranch. Part Mexican and part Apache Indian, he stands in the foreground of Hurd's picture as a part and symbol of the land both men love. The portrait describes not just a person, but a world and a way of life.

PETER HURD'S "PORTRAIT OF JOSE HERRERA" (1938)

THOMAS HART BENTON'S "JULY HAY" (1943)

CHAPTER V

FROM THE HEARTLAND

*It is the place of autumnal moons hung low and orange at the
frosty edges of the pines; it is the place of frost and silence;
of the clean dry shocks and the opulence of enormous pumpkins
that yellow on hard clotted earth; it is the place of the stir
and feathery stumble of the hens upon their roost, the frosty,
broken barking of the dogs, the great barnshapes and solid
shadows in the running sweep of the moon-whited countryside,
the wailing whistle of the fast express.*

—THOMAS WOLFE

THOMAS Cole and his followers of the Hudson River School, the men who recorded the opening of the Far West, and the Ashcan artists of the metropolis, all described specific times and places in American history. So, in the 1930s, did three champions of the American Middle West —Thomas Hart Benton, John Steuart Curry, and Grant Wood. They captured the public imagination and almost succeeded in shifting the center of American painting from Manhattan to the Midwestern heartland. All three made a point of bypassing the connoisseurs to go straight to the people with pictures anyone could understand. They asked not to be judged but enjoyed, and enjoyed they were. Beyond that, their art said things about the nation that had never been expressed before. But the movement was doomed to collapse within a decade and the painters themselves slipped from popular favor.

In explaining the spectacular rise of the Midwestern School, Benton himself suggests a reason for its fall: "Because of the breakdown of our economic society in 1929 and the early 1930s, the effort to come out of the Depression occasioned a terrific concentration on America—what

it meant, what it was composed of, why it was the way it was—by Americans. Frankly, Wood, Curry, and I profited from this concentration."

But by the end of the thirties, America was beginning to look outward again to Europe and to Asia, and to the threats of war abroad. When the country turned once more to the three Midwesterners, the fashionable thing was to wonder what anyone had ever seen in them. Vastly overrated in their days of triumph, they have been underrated ever since.

THOMAS Benton's contributions to American art have been very much a part of his own full and adventurous life, which began in Neosho, Missouri, in 1889. His father, Congressman Maecenas Eason Benton, had arrived in southwestern Missouri from Tennessee soon after the Civil War, "riding a horse and knocking the snakes out of his path with a long stick." Young Benton's pleasures were those of a backwoods boy—hoedowns, turkey shoots, possum hunts, and hay rides. The talk he heard at table was almost all politics, which instilled a dangerous delight in rhetoric. But painting attracted Benton

213

even more than politics, leading him far from home to study in Chicago and afterwards Paris.

Years afterwards, Benton decided that Paris had meant merely "a girl friend to take care of you and run you . . . a lot of talk and an escape into the world of pretense and theory. I wallowed in every cockeyed ism that came along, and it took me ten years to get all that modernist dirt out of my system. I was merely a roughneck with a talent for fighting, perhaps, but not for painting. . . ." He came home to work in the Norfolk Navy Yard during World War I, and later knocked about the nation for a dusty, delightful ten years or so. On his travels he finally came to realize what it was he wanted to paint—his homeland, seen fresh and in detail.

July Hay is a thoroughly Bentonian achievement with all the energy of line, richness of textures, and, above all, enthusiasm for subject that made him famous. It is also airless and spaceless, bulging like a bas-relief—faults which derive directly from a peculiar and laborious technique of Benton's own invention. Confronted with the artist's age-old choice of whether to paint from nature, from memory, or from imagination, he rejects all three. Instead, he makes a painted clay model of his subject and then pictures that. Not just the faults, of course, but also the remarkable individuality of his art stem from this technique.

What made Benton himself such an instructive example of pride and prejudice, high riding and hard falling? Partly it was the self-centered nature of the project that he had envisioned. Other American painters had their own ideas of how to interpret America, and to Benton's outspoken anger most of them refused to follow obediently in his wake. It was this truculent exclusiveness that distorted and eventually stultified the message of the "regionalists" as a whole. By 1940 Benton in particular had become a mossback isolationist in art, blaming his own reverses and the success of his rivals on a conspiracy of museum directors and thus declaring the art world's most unnecessary war. When he went on to say that Pablo Picasso's *Guernica* (now at the Museum of Modern Art in Manhattan) had been copied from an old batik, and that no good painting had "come out of France since 1890," dust and

JOHN STEUART CURRY'S "WISCONSIN LANDSCAPE" (1938-39)

CURRY'S "HOGS KILLING A RATTLESNAKE" (1930)

din obscured the battle. Then, somehow, Benton had surrounded old Rembrandt van Rijn: "You can see by his face in his portraits that he isn't as bright as you are, and so you hate to have to admit that a dumb Dutchman could paint better than you can." Like Alexander at the River Oxus, Benton poised wistfully on the banks of the Renaissance: "I would like to have an old master some time—a Titian from the National Gallery, say—to take apart layer by layer and destroy. Then I could learn their lost technical art and paint as well as them."

But when not bragging and arguing, Benton worked hard in solitude before his easel, wrestling, as all dedicated artists do, with an invisible angel. Meanwhile, the art experts sternly reappraised Benton's own pictures, and stacked them away in the dark of museum cellars.

JOHN Steuart Curry was born in 1897 to a Kansas stock farmer who prided himself in producing cattle so fat that "the rain set in the middle of their backs." The boy grew up agile and powerful, and got a large part of his education on football fields. He went on to become a moderately successful magazine illustrator, but editors kept complaining that he tried to make serious paintings out of his illustrations. Taking this warning for encouragement, Curry in his late twenties set himself the problem of painting what he called "museum pictures."

These, he soon discovered, struck most connoisseurs as being far too illustrational. Curry's wide-angled *Wisconsin Landscape*, for example, might well be used for a brochure advertising the state's rural riches. Fondly embracing a great green chunk of countryside, the canvas celebrates Curry's tenure as art professor at the University of Wisconsin. He held that post from 1936 until his death a decade later, and used it to promote not just regional painting but the individualism that lies at the root of all fine art. One of his lectures that has been preserved stands among the most sensible, inspiring statements of its kind:

"Some of us look forward to a great and alive American art. We look forward to a great and alive art in the Middle West, but be reminded of this—the great art is within yourself—within your own heart is the secret of the power that will attract your fellow men. Bring this power

215

GRANT WOOD'S "MIDNIGHT RIDE OF PAUL REVERE" (1931)

forth and with it you bring life to the despised and long-neglected subject. With this power you give a brilliant radiance to the old and hackneyed idea. . . . Your greatness will not be found in Europe or in New York, or in the Middle West, or in Wisconsin, but within yourself; and realize now that for the sincere artist there is no bandwagon that goes the whole way, no borrowed coat of perfect fit, and no comforter on whose breast to lay your curly head."

John Curry, a man as thin-skinned as he was thick-muscled, suffered from his own sense of isolation. His only real comfort lay in producing a handful of near masterpieces, among them *Hogs Killing a Rattlesnake*. Taken from childhood experience, the canvas adopts a boy's perspective —low, close up, and awe-struck. The earth, the apple tree, and the sky are peaceful, represented with all the economy and rhythmic unity of an Albert Pinkham Ryder. In this placid setting the fat, fast, furious swine make a writhing composition that converges like fate upon the wildly writhing snake. An electric current coils through the whole picture, becoming almost palpable as it leaps the gap between the snake's head and the snout of the rearing hog. Here is nature dark, immediate, and inscrutable—a wilderness in the barnyard. The subject could not be less attractive; yet the viewer cannot help entering into the action. He is drawn as if by centripetal force to feel with the victorious hogs and the doomed serpent both.

GRANT Wood made himself known to the American art world with all the suddenness and shock of an apparition. It happened in 1930, when Wood's *American Gothic* won a bronze medal at a Chicago Art Institute show. It was not the award that mattered, of course, but the extraordinary freshness and bite of the picture itself. The meticulously painted panel combined many old ideas to create a contemporary archetype, the Midwestern farmer, and fix him for all time. As usually happens to close and brilliant observers of character, Wood was first upbraided as unfair, and later—when the truth of his observations began to dawn—hailed as a genius.

Being no genius, he was never able to repeat his first triumph. But the qualities of inspiration Wood lacked were partly compensated for by a high degree of craftsmanship and sophistication. Technically, *American Gothic* derives from the so-called Flemish primitives, whose paintings of the fifteenth and sixteenth centuries had such astonishing richness of pattern, finish, and detail. Wood reflects those qualities in his fascinated attention to such humdrum material as the rickrack braid bordering the woman's apron, the seams of the man's scrupulously clean denim, and the roof shingles. But the pose of Wood's couple (they were actually his sister and dentist) derives from twentieth-century snapshots. It is head-on, purposefully unimaginative. The man gazes fixedly into the camera eye. The woman's eyes have wandered; she has something on the stove inside. Neither smiles, which is unusual in a snapshot, and this helps create the vague sense of paradox that gives the picture life. The Gothic window, which relates in shape to the woman's hairdo and the man's brows, seems to imply that these people come out of the Middle Ages, yet makes it plain that they are very far indeed from the high-colored richness of the Gothic world. And the pitchfork, thrust abruptly forward like Poseidon's trident, brings to mind how far from salt water these people live.

Wood was thirty-eight when he painted *American Gothic*. He had made a long and painful detour to find his subject matter and his personal method. He was born into a poor farming family in Anamosa, Iowa, and from the time he was ten, when his father died, young Wood had to scratch hard for a living. The boy raised sweet corn and tomatoes to sell from door to door, and milked the cows of his more prosperous neighbors. At the lowest point he bought a vacant lot in Cedar Rapids for a dollar down and a dollar a month, built a ten-by-sixteen-foot shack, and lived there with his mother and sister for two years. When times eased, Wood would wander, taking odd jobs and art courses where he found them. The courses led to teaching in public schools, from which he finally saved enough to visit Europe.

In Paris, Wood grew a pinkish beard, parted in the middle. He wore a Basque beret as well, but nothing seemed to help his painting. Concluding at last that all his best ideas "came while milking a cow," he went home to Iowa, shaved off his whiskers, and traded in his beret for a pair of overalls. Then in 1928 the American Legion commissioned him to design a stained-glass window for the Cedar Rapids Memorial Coliseum, and staked him to a trip to Munich to learn the necessary techniques. In Munich Wood got his first long look at the Flemish primitives and saw his destiny clear. He came home determined to become the Memling of the Midwest.

"At first," Wood said later, "I felt I had to search for old things to paint—something soft and mellow. But now I have discovered a decorative quality in American newness." That quality is almost too apparent in the *Midnight Ride of Paul Revere*, which looks rather like a neat, sand-table model of the action. Wood might just as well have used pillows and a quilted coverlet for the landscape, a broad silk ribbon for the road, and dollhouses for the village. He did use a rocking horse for Revere's horse. Still, the painting tells its story lightly, clearly, and unforgettably. It suggests that Wood might have made a fine illustrator of children's books.

Scarcely a dozen years after the enormous success of *American Gothic* and eleven years after *Paul Revere's Ride*, Wood died of cancer. He was one of the bland, cherubic sort that conceals his tears in a twinkle and his hungers in humorous asides, but the collapse of regional art had affected him deeply. Thomas Benton, who visited him in his last days at the hospital, had a touching report to make later: Wood "told me that when he got well he was going to change his name, go where nobody knew him, and start all over again with a new style of painting."

BENTON had a similar story to tell of John Steuart Curry, who died in 1946: " 'John,' I ventured, 'you must feel pretty good now, after all your struggles, to know that you have come to a permanent place in American art. . . .' 'I don't know about that,' he replied. 'Maybe I'd have done better to stay on the farm.' "

Of the once-famed triumvirate only Benton now remains, standing like a gnarled and blocky stump in deep center field of American art. The pyrotechnics of the abstract expressionists give the old Missourian almost as much puzzlement as pain. "The art of today," he exclaims, "is the art of the 1920s, which we repudiated!"

WOOD'S "AMERICAN GOTHIC" (1930)

219

CHAPTER VI

TRAVELING MEN

I never heard a mocking bird in Kentucky
Spilling its heart in the morning.

I never saw the snow on Chimborazo.
It's a high white Mexican hat, I hear.

I never had supper with Abe Lincoln.
Nor a dish of soup with Jim Hill.

But I've been around.

—CARL SANDBURG

ALONG with the artists of the heartland, hundreds of other twentieth-century Americans have found their inspiration in specific places, near or far, bringing to their chosen locales a corresponding diversity of temperaments and techniques. Loren MacIver and Ogden Pleissner crossed the sea to explore Europe; Leon Kroll, Maurice Sterne, Samuel Green, and Waldo Peirce each captured a separate facet of New England; Walter Stuempfig has conducted a passionate affair with Pennsylvania; John Koch has shown the sleek side of New York and Reginald Marsh the rough. The finest painter of the lot, Charles Burchfield, has moved from dreary industrial suburbs out into the open countryside of Ohio and New York.

BORN in Brooklyn in 1905, Ogden Pleissner seems born to the tweed. He has the cool eyes and calm hands of a sportsman, and puffs a pipe as if it were part of himself. Four years of portrait and figure painting at Manhattan's Art Students League made Pleissner feel painfully cooped up

as a youth, and he has been painting outdoor water colors ever since. "I get a big kick out of nature," he says simply, "the moods and changes of the year and weather. And I like the transparency of water color, the way the light hits the white paper and then bounces back at you through the paint."

The Tower, Avallon demonstrates Pleissner's feeling for both weather and water color. Less sensitive hands would have turned the subject, a tourist landmark, into a sort of postcard. Instead of painting a quaint stop on a French tour, he created an old stone reality under a new dawn.

LOREN MacIver's *Street* looks like one made to tiptoe down. Any trampling would shake the scene apart, or dissolve it into mist. The artist, whose proper habitat is Greenwich Village, painted it from her memories of a trip to Paris. "You can't call the street by any one name," she says, "and you can't look for it."

Married to the poet Lloyd Frankenberg, she creates a twilit world halfway between poetry

220

and painting. What she lacks in clarity and force she more than makes up for in subtlety and charm. Among her first memories is painting a picture of a derby hat, which filled her with awe "because it was so black." Her wonderment at the look of everyday things persisted through adolescence, and still motivates her art. She is that rare artist in whom childlikeness and sophistication balance. There is no American painter quite like her, and of recent European artists only France's Odilon Redon had a similar approach to art. MacIver has built her own private nest in the tree of American painting, filled with Easter eggs and decorated with the tinsel, chalk, oil smears, blossoms, and bits of colored glass she salvages out of the everyday world.

LEON Kroll is filled with an abiding interest in human flesh and humanized landscape. People as he paints them are smooth and still as statues, and his landscapes are not only tilled and pruned but even dusted. Kroll's best work is done at Cape Ann, Massachusetts, a place he has made his own through his art.

After twenty-three years of showing at the International Exhibitions organized by the Carnegie Institute, Kroll took the top award in 1936 with a Cape Ann canvas called *The Road from the Cove*. The rather operatic scene, centering on a man seemingly felled by sunstroke, was painted from nature, but with a bit of tidy rearranging. "I just combine different things that have the character of the Cape," explains Kroll. "My pictures are based on abstract design. All the elements are worked in, and they are not photographic representations." Kroll's smooth way with design has earned him as many honors as any other living American painter.

FOR many years," Maurice Sterne wrote in his sixties, "I tried to paint as *well* as I knew how. I stopped trying when I realized that one

OGDEN PLEISSNER'S "THE TOWER, AVALLON" (1953)

must paint *better* than one knows how." It was an adventurous and hugely successful career which brought him to that realization.

Born in Latvia, Sterne came to New York City in 1889, when he was eleven. Supporting himself with what jobs he could get, he read Walt Whitman and studied art in his off hours. For a time he was a bartender on Third Avenue, and his first painting commission was for a picture of a foaming stein labeled "5 Cents." He studied anatomy under Thomas Eakins, and then returned to Europe on a traveling scholarship. Sterne had his first big show in Berlin. From there he drifted to Greece—where he spent a year in a monastery—and then to Bali, where he painted the cool yet busty pictures that made both himself and the island famous.

After eleven years abroad, Sterne came home to marry the heiress Mabel Dodge, and settled down with her in Taos, New Mexico. She divorced him for a Taos Indian named Tony, explaining in her breezy way that Sterne "seemed old and

CORNELIUS KROLL

LEON KROLL'S
"THE ROAD FROM THE COVE" (1936)

LOREN MacIVER'S "THE STREET" (1956)

spent and tragic, while Tony was whole and young in the cells of his body." At forty-five, Sterne still felt young enough to marry a honey-haired, seventeen-year-old dancer named Vera Segal, of Isadora Duncan's group. They took a forty-eight room castle in the Sabine hills northeast of Rome, and lived well on private and American government commissions. Sterne's great charm, combined with his reticent, crafts-manlike way of painting, made him a major figure in art, but he longed to develop himself further. Writing in his emphatic style to a friend in 1940, he said: "I know only that painting being an expression and interpretation of a *point of view*, there *can't* be just one right way, but innumerable ways." Sterne was then on the verge of changing entirely his own approach to art. It happened during World War II, when he had come home again and moved into a summer cottage in Provincetown, Massachusetts.

"I was too ill to work and was admiring the view from my porch," he afterwards wrote. "The incoming tide, the crimson and orange and gold of the sunset, the delicate nuances . . . when suddenly, nature ceased to be nature and became a wet painting. This sensation was so real that when a seagull suddenly soared across my vision, I exclaimed, 'The fool! Its lovely white wings will be smeared with paint.' " *After the Rain* documents such a moment. It is one of many splendid canvases in which the artist has confounded art and nature to create a new reality where oils mix with water, and brushstrokes flicker with the wind. "Here in America," Sterne explained, shortly before his death at seventy-nine, "our great contribution to art is in our response to the moment. I try to do in painting what is quick and spontaneous—what happened. It's like building a campfire on a rainy day. Very difficult; the wood is sodden and you are down on your knees in the wet. . . . Suddenly the white flame blazes up, and there it is." This spontaneous combustion, beyond mere craft, is what he meant by painting "*better* than one knows how."

MAURICE STERNE'S "AFTER THE RAIN" (1948)

SAMUEL Green, the head of Wesleyan University's art department, makes no effort to capture any single moment. Experienced mainly in etching, he delicately details what he sees, bit by bit and day after day. "I painted *Woodshed Interior* in the back shed of my house," Green recalls. "I'd had a bad attack of summer grippe, and I couldn't go any place, so I sat there and painted." His water color has the quietude of a convalescence. There is something comforting about the well-worn tools; the fact that they have been used over and over and will be used many times again conveys a sense of permanence.

Although Green's painting carries neither the conviction nor the nostalgic overtones of William Harnett, it does hark back to the nineteenth-century master. For Green, like Harnett, has made a handful of inanimate objects describe a whole way of life.

PAINT ain't work." That remark just about sums up Waldo Peirce's approach to art. His canvases are the careless overflow of a brimful spirit. Though they are not great, they are never small, either. *County Fair*, for example, is as loose and smudged as the sweat shirts Peirce

224

SAMUEL GREEN'S "WOODSHED INTERIOR" (1951)

WALDO PEIRCE'S "COUNTY FAIR" (1933)

habitually wears; yet it has something of the magic of the dawn of a big day in rural Maine —the day to get mildly sozzled on beer, win a Kewpie doll, and place a small bet on a harness race. "It's easier to paint a good picture than a bad one," Peirce says. "What's this old wives' tale about Leonardo devoting six years to the *Mona Lisa*? You don't pay a doctor to work six months over your appendix, and music should be played trippingly . . . and the more pleasure [a man] takes in the painting . . . the more pleasure for the spectator."

A bearded lion of a man, Peirce has taken a lion's share of pleasure both in art and in life. The son of a wealthy Maine lumberman, he went to Harvard in the days of Heywood Broun, Harold Vanderbilt, Winthrop Aldrich, Walter Lippmann, and John Reed. By 1910, Peirce and Reed were on their way to England on a cattle boat. As their ship left Boston harbor, Peirce changed his mind, leaped overboard, and swam ashore. He had to take the next boat over, to straighten out the British, who thought he was dead and were holding Reed for murder.

Peirce took second in a canoe race on the Thames ("though a silly sportswriter accused me of having stood up to take advantage of the wind") and later toured Ireland with a French football team ("though I didn't even know their rules"). He joined the American Ambulance Field Service at the start of World War I and won the *Croix de guerre*. Later he toured Spain with Jack Johnson, the former heavyweight champion, and then with Ernest Hemingway, who had just published *The Sun Also Rises*. Hemingway once noted that Peirce could be "damned impressive when he's angry," and he told of Donnybrooks to prove it. To which the painter modestly replied: "If Ernest has a good story, let him stick to it." While in Spain, Peirce painted like Zuloaga. From there he went to Tunis, where he painted like Matisse. Peirce did not find his own bright, unbuttoned style until he returned to Maine in the 1930s.

What clubs a man belongs to usually tells more about his position than his personality, but in this, as in most things, Peirce is an exception. His clubs are Harvard (in New York City), a Tunisian whirling-dervish society known as the Eessaweeya of Hammamet, and the *Grands Buveurs de Calvados de la Vallée de Chevreuse*. As he once wrote of himself:

> . . . He led too many lives
> An' had too many wenches
> An' too many wives
> He had too many vittles
> An' too much licker
> An' too many homesteads
> In France and Africker . . .

Like so many wild men, Peirce always longed to be domesticated. He has entrusted the task to four wives in all. The first was a passing fancy, the second kept him "behind a chintz curtain for eight years," but the third and fourth provided him with a total of five children and the inspiration for hundreds of happy paintings. Now in his seventies, Peirce divides his year between Tucson, Arizona, and Searsport, Maine, and his day between his easel and his present young wife and their two children, eleven and nine. The Peirce children get a wide-angled education, for their towering father constantly thinks aloud. Some sample thoughts, on writing: "Four-letter words are all right when you're talking, but it's no good to put them in print—it would be better to do it with smoke, like in sky-writing." On medicine: "Stay away from hospitals. You know —the white sheets, the cool hand, and the fevered brow. They'll get you in holy bedlock, sure as hell." On art: "I'll give you a tip on painting ladies of today . . . I always let the lady paint her own mouth, which she knows better than I do, and does it two or three times a day on the original countenance."

IN 1947, after brooding over it for three years, Walter Stuempfig put the finishing touches on *Manayunk*. The result looks rather like an Italian hill town painted by the young Corot—except for its prevailing atmosphere of gloom. Actually the picture represents a factory district of Philadelphia near Stuempfig's home. The artist paints only scenes he has long admired: "I have to be in love with a subject to paint it, that's all." The schoolyard and children playing were meant to convey "a closed-in, lonely feeling. I suppose the kids are happy, but who knows?" Stuempfig invented the background steeple and inserted it in the picture simply to add height and spaciousness to the scene.

Stuempfig painted an abstraction—once. "I was told to," he says, "and I did it, in school, where all abstractions belong. But at the Pennsylvania Academy where I studied I tried to resist the tendency of the average art student to like the obvious—the obvious being Matisse and Picasso. . . . Technique, composition, and all that should be unconscious. This whole emphasis on technique is a product of the nineteenth and twentieth centuries; before that, people painted the way they walked. The aim is to create something that moves people." Stuempfig considers his own approach to art romantic. But then, he says, "all good painters are romantic painters. You have to have a certain romantic approach to life or you wouldn't be a painter. . . ."

JOHN Koch is just as traditional, romantic, and successful an artist as Stuempfig, though entirely self-taught. Koch has developed a soft and luminous style of underpainting in egg tempera and glazing with misty oils to create a cool and ingratiating effect vaguely reminiscent of the seventeenth-century Dutch master, Vermeer. He paints mostly portraits of wealthy New Yorkers, at $3,000 and up, set in the elegant interiors that best become them. Mrs. Reginald Marsh posed for Koch's *The Bridge*, which he painted

WALTER STUEMPFIG'S "MANAYUNK" (1947)

JOHN KOCH'S "THE BRIDGE" (1951)

REGINALD MARSH'S "WHY NOT USE THE 'L'?" (1930)

purely for pleasure in his studio overlooking the Queensboro Bridge in New York. "It was a picture I sweated out," Koch frankly recalls, "but the finished canvas looks fresh."

REGINALD Marsh took pleasure in noting that he was born just two hundred and one years after William Hogarth, in 1898. Hogarth had bequeathed to the world a large and sharply drawn view of eighteenth-century London, and Marsh proposed to do the same for twentieth-century New York. Like Hogarth, he stared hardest at his city's seamy side, which prompted John Steuart Curry to ask why he so often took "a worm's-eye view." Marsh's reply was: "You see, as a child I had rickets, and my frantic parents used to trundle me off to the beach and bury me in the warm sand, being convinced it would cure my ailment. But imagine me, buried there, immobilized for hours on end, my only view of humanity being straight up their legs!"

Marsh's childhood burying ground was probably on the Rhode Island coast, where his family had a summer place. The shy, wide, freckled boy went on to Yale, where he barely got through the art courses but made a hit with his illustrations for the *Yale Record*. After graduating in 1920, he drew cartoons for *Vanity Fair*, *Harper's Bazaar*, and the upstart tabloid *Daily News*, for which he made close to 4,000 drawings in three years. Night study with John Sloan and George Luks helped confirm his growing ambition to be an artist, and a trip to Europe settled it. Marsh copied hundreds of European masterpieces in pen and ink, grounding himself so thoroughly that he was afterwards able to teach with great

230

success. "Art is derived from two sources," he would tell his students, "art and nature. All art is a mixture of the two." Then, far from dogmatically fixing proportions for the mixture, he would add: "The greater the degree of each, the greater the art."

Marsh made himself an indefatigable student both of the old masters and of his own New York. "This is a new city," he would say. "Wide open to the artist. It offers itself." Marsh sketched everywhere—in the streets, the burlesque houses, the subways, under the el, and on the beaches where "a million near-naked bodies can be seen at once, a phenomenon unparalleled in history." He drew incessantly, like chain-smoking, and neatly filed the sketches in a steel cabinet in his Union Square studio. His subjects were caved-in bums, bundled-up news vendors, beach athletes, tugboats, trains, pneumatic-looking shopgirls,

cops, operagoers, skyscrapers, burlesque queens, street signs, store windows, Stork Club dancers, and subway kiosks, all of which found their way into the thousand-odd paintings that remained when death took him off the scene at fifty-six.

The chunky, quiet man with the icy sidelong glance had tried hard to make an objective record—perhaps too objective. The people depicted in *Why Not Use the "L"?* and *Negroes on Rockaway Beach* are seen less as individuals than as mere characters in the first case and a crowd in the second—impersonal parts of a harsh and grimy environment. Though the beach picture has a certain forlorn sensuality, like a Gordian knot of human flesh, there is something lonely and remote about the scene. As in much of Marsh's work, the picture lacks the sense of immediacy that Hogarth caught so brilliantly. Yet Marsh's paintings do express much about his city and

MARSH'S "NEGROES ON ROCKAWAY BEACH" (1934)

CHARLES BURCHFIELD'S "SIX O'CLOCK" (1936)

BURCHFIELD'S "SUMMER AFTERNOON" (1917-48)

its people, sweet and sour qualities clear to him, and clearly rendered in his best work.

CHARLES Ephraim Burchfield once wrote that "I will always be an inlander in spirit," and went on to note that the ocean "has a worthy rival in a hay or wheat field on a bright windy day." Burchfield himself turns inward as well as inland, and his finest qualities as an artist are much like those of an unmown field in the wind. Describing the invisible forces of nature, his supple brush can ripple like grass.

Burchfield was born in 1893 in Ashtabula Harbor, Ohio, and raised mainly in the nearby town of Salem. Living on the edge of the woods, he found refuge there almost from the start. As a boy he would wander the wilderness all day by himself, dreamily engrossed in nature's moods, which were often inseparable from his own. After a training stint in World War I, he went straight home to Salem and a clerking job in a mill, so as to be able to paint on weekends the scenes he loved. Although he knew nothing of modern art, instinct somehow led him to make decorative abstractions of what he saw and felt, with little check marks standing for the cicadas' song, wavelike spirals for sensations of fear, vibrating lines for intense heat, and wing shapes for storm clouds. Flat and ephemeral though they were, his early water colors showed genius. But they led to nothing much, for a time, except a job as a wallpaper designer in Buffalo, New York.

233

BURCHFIELD'S "SUN AND ROCKS" (1918-50)

Having a wife and five children to support, Burchfield stuck to wallpaper for most of the 1920s. Home was an old house in a deep, narrow lot in suburban Gardenville, and it more than made up for the boredom of his office work. "I don't believe there are many more flat and banal places than this village," Burchfield wrote. And yet "there is the sky above the village housetops, so vast and mysterious, full of the great loose sunlit, wind-slanted clouds that always come up after a summer storm—through it I have access to infinity, and down below, very tangible, is the yard and garden and how good all things in it seem: the luxuriant tomato plants, now in sharp sunlight. . . . At times the children pass through, intent on their play, seemingly unconscious of my presence; sometimes a wren sings, and there are the various sounds of village activities, all colored by the morning. The dull roar of motors passing on the street seems remote."

Curiously, Burchfield would pass on from this sunny scene to gloomy ones when he felt like painting, and abandoned his lyrical water colors for an austere realism. *Six O'Clock* has human warmth and a cozy sense of the continuity of living, but these are framed in fearful bleakness and ugliness. Curiously again, it was this sort of picture that made Burchfield's fame, enabling him to quit his wallpaper job and to paint full time. In the 1930s he was hailed both as an unflinching realist and as a regionalist, though he had no wish to join the Benton-Wood-Curry camp.

In 1934 Burchfield bought a car, "to take the muse riding." He developed a habit of driving into open country and then parking, to plunge ahead on foot in all kinds of weather. "You cannot experience a landscape," he explains, "until you have known all its discomforts. You have to curse, fight mosquitoes, be slapped by stinging branches, fall over rocks and skin your knees, be stung by nettles, scratched by grasshopper grass and pricked by brambles . . . before you have really experienced the world of nature." This view of nature as experience, and not just a setting, is what distinguishes Burchfield from the more polite landscape painters of Europe and their American followers. It also served, in time, to link him in a skinned-knee procession with John Marin and Winslow Homer. Like them, he concentrated his forces increasingly on nature's works rather than man's. "The faithful interpretation of natural truth," he had decided, "should be a matter of religion—even a bud on a twig wrongly placed would be a sin." He worked on drawing after drawing of a given theme, until "I finally reach a point when, in a rage, I destroy all I have done so far—and at that moment, unknown to myself, I have solved it." Too much literalness and laboriousness were his chief dangers, as he well knew.

After World War II, Burchfield corrected this weakness by an inspired return to the kind of water colors he had made three decades before. *Summer Afternoon* actually incorporated a small water color of his boyhood swimming hole, done in 1917, which he mounted on the middle of a larger sheet. The finished picture combines the moody imagination of youth with a much deepened and enlarged sense of reality. *Sun and Rocks* is even more of a triumph. Here he enlarged a 1918 picture called *The Song of the Peter Bird*, simply because "the longing to hear this bird again on . . . a brilliant day in March in the hollows is so strong at times as to make me ill." Six years of intermittent work almost buried the bird and its voice once more, in favor of Sibelius' *Fourth Symphony*, which Burchfield listened to while painting. "The impressions of the rocks and the music intermingled," he noted, "each magnifying the other, and presently I had a vivid, inner-eye picture of a strange, fantastic scene in some unknown Northland. . . . I put into the sun all the devastating, destroying power of that 'star' that I feel on a March sap day."

With *Oncoming Spring*, Burchfield abandoned both the inspirations of his own early days and of recorded music to tackle nature direct. The picture is partly abstract, for it shows a warm, fructifying wind as yellow streaks whipping into the dark, cold forest. The abstraction invades the comparatively realistic representation of the forest just as thoroughly and naturally as the wind invades the trees. A masterpiece of imagination, organization, and daring, nakedly elemental, the picture puts Burchfield in a class by himself among living water-colorists. The most modest of masters, Burchfield credits *Oncoming Spring*, like all his major works, to forces greater than himself: "Hardly had I set up my easel when a thunderstorm came up. I decided nothing was going to stop my painting, and hurriedly got my huge beach umbrella and my raincoat. I protected my legs with a portfolio, the wind holding it in place. And so I painted with my nose almost on the paper, with thunder crashing, boughs breaking, and rain falling in torrents. A glorious few hours when I seemed to become part of the elements. When I was done at late afternoon, the picture was complete. It seemed as if it had materialized under its own power."

BURCHFIELD'S "ONCOMING SPRING" (1954)

CHAPTER VII

TROUBLED YEARS

I acknowledge the furies, I believe in them, I have heard the disastrous beating of their wings.

—THEODORE DREISER

ALEXANDER BROOK'S
"GEORGIA JUNGLE" (1939)

WHEN Alexander Brook won the Carnegie International Award in 1939 with *Georgia Jungle*, he was asked what led him to pick such a gloomy subject. "I guess I like sad things," Brook replied with a smile. "Most pictures are about sad things. You hardly ever see jolly pictures." Himself a rather jolly fellow, Brook was only voicing the prevailing spirit of the Great Depression. The *Jungle* was a Negro shantytown on a dump heap at the outskirts of Savannah. Coming upon it during a vacation, Brook was both "appalled by the poverty" and intrigued by the artistic possibilities of the scene.

In those troubled years, thousands of artists were kept afloat by federal aid, painting post office murals or copying American antiques. A few hundred chose to go on painting easel pictures that strongly protested the current state of society, and they too got help from Washington. Events proved the wisdom of this impartiality, for three of the most stormily independent men ever on the relief rolls—Philip Evergood, Ben Shahn, and Jack Levine—were to achieve major status in American painting.

PHILIP Evergood once wrote that "on one hand we see gluttony and self-aggrandizement, and on the other self-abnegation, sacrifice, generosity, and heroism, in different members of the same human race." For a time he seemed to feel that all virtue must be on the left-hand side. Politically naive though he was, Evergood's

PHILIP EVERGOOD'S "AMERICAN TRAGEDY" (1937)

moral vision was all too sound; his statement of man's inhumanity to man remains terribly and eternally true. That inhumanity, of course, aroused such masters as Goya and Daumier, whose pictures point to the recurring terrors of life. Evergood's own *American Tragedy* shows the full horror of a police assault on masses of helpless citizens—anywhere.

Behind the picture's bluster are qualities of organization, drawing, and color that make it a masterpiece of protest painting. It commemorates the bloody riot that occurred on Memorial Day, 1937, at Republic Steel's South Chicago plant. The white shirt and springlike green dress of the defiant worker and his pregnant wife in the center foreground are like a momentary break in the hurricane of policeman's blue, edged with pistols and billies, advancing over the sun-baked, blood-slicked asphalt. Contrasting with

the fortress-like factories in the distance, a single straw hat, symbol of carefree individualism, lies pristine under the advancing boots.

That straw hat could even relate to the boater Evergood wore as a student at Eton and Cambridge. His father, an Australian-born painter who lived in Manhattan, was afraid that young Philip might want to follow in his footsteps, and therefore sent him abroad to be made an English gentleman instead. The youth did well at boxing and rowing, but found himself constitutionally "unfitted for that academic rah-rah stuff." Accordingly, he transferred to London's Slade School of Art, where he learned to draw with razor-edged precision. Further study in Paris, and in Manhattan under George Luks, made him one of the best-equipped artists of the day. His art is deceptive. Evergood half-conceals his background, like a man who instructs his

238

tailor to make the knees of his suit a little baggy. His mastery of his tools barely glimmers through a colloquial and occasionally fumbling style.

"When a man is dead," Evergood remarked once, "it only matters if he leaves something acid and something sweet behind him." The Great Depression inspired him to leave plenty of acid, and since then he has produced increasing sweets. In 1954, when Evergood was fifty-three, he surpassed himself with *American Shrimp Girl*. The painter took obvious delight in the picture's abundance of creatures, with all the creative problems they raised. Most difficult to draw, surely, were the hungry sea gulls that circle the girl's head, their eager grace counterpointing her heavy-limbed, foursquare pose. The whole canvas is a New World extension of Hogarth's more modest hymn to feminine vitality, the eighteenth-century *Shrimp Girl*, now at London's National Gallery. Where Hogarth suppressed all detail and strong color to concentrate on his model's glowing face, Evergood does the opposite. His model is no prettier or more sensate-seeming than a doll, with plaster-of-Paris flesh. She calls to mind Gertrude Stein's complaint that "the American girl is a crude virgin." But there is a lot more to her than that. Evergood's big blank heroine dominates her overflowing world like a new pagan deity, a personification of summertime on American shores.

BEN Shahn is a burly man who inclines to be generous in many things, including anger. The first real rage he remembers occurred at the Hebrew school he attended in the Lithuanian town of his birth. The trouble began, he recalls, with the story "about the Ark that was being brought into the Temple, hauled by six white oxen, balanced on a single pole. The Lord knew that the people would worry about the Ark's falling off the pole, so to test their faith He gave orders that no one was to touch it, no matter what happened. One man saw it beginning to totter, and he rushed up to help. He was struck dead. I refused to go to school for a week after we read that story. It seemed so damned unfair. And it still does."

The incident shows Shahn's typical hatred of injustice, distrust of authority, and impatience with mystery, already dominant before the age of eight, when he came with his family to America. Thereafter, he was raised in a Brooklyn slum, where the local toughs forced him to draw their favorite ballplayers in chalk on the pavement. He learned to draw accurately, perforce, and also got a fine edge to his temper. This perfect schooling for protest art was capped, at fifteen, by an apprentice job in a lithography house. There Shahn developed the sureness of line, tone, and detail that still distinguishes his pictures. He worked up to the position of master lithographer, and saved enough money to spend most of the 1920s traveling in Europe and studying the master painters.

When Shahn came home again he was a highly sophisticated artist. He soon resolved to paint contemporary America just as he saw it. "There's a difference," he would argue, "between the way a twelve-dollar coat wrinkles and the way a seventy-five-dollar coat wrinkles. And that has to be right. It's just as important, aesthetically, as the difference in the light of the Ile-de-France and the Brittany coast. Maybe it's more important. If I look at an ordinary overcoat as if I never saw it before, then it becomes as fit a subject for painting as one of Titian's purple cloaks." Shahn's "haves" always look as if they had altogether too much, while his "have-nots" are lean as greyhounds and sad-eyed as spaniels.

Shahn's biting realism is apt to falter when representing a tree in the wind or the curve of a hill. "That part doesn't interest me so much," he says offhandedly. "God can do what He likes, but man is more surprising." By way of collecting surprises, he has built up an enormous file of candid-camera shots of everything from Sunday strollers to trash baskets. This research helped Shahn's Government-sponsored work during the 1930s as well as the posters he painted during World War II. *The Red Stairway* clearly shows the influence of both photos and posters. It combines the starkness of one and the garishness of the other in an unforgettable image.

"You paint something because you like it a lot," Shahn once remarked, "or else because you hate it." *The Red Stairway* obviously came out of hatred. But the genesis of *Spring* cannot be traced to either love or hate alone, and it marked

EVERGOOD'S "AMERICAN SHRIMP GIRL" (1954)

an important deepening of his art. With *Spring*, Shahn achieved bittersweet poetry of a sort that has occupied him a good deal since. The composition is as daring and arresting as most out-and-out abstractions; yet there is nothing abstract about the picture as a whole. "In the spring," it seems to repeat, "a young man's fancy lightly turns to thoughts of love"—and death and inevitable loss as well. Abstractionists complain that paintings such as *Spring* are overly sentimental, while sentimentalists complain about their grimness. Shahn grins like a tiger and complains right back. "Is there nothing," he asks the abstractionists, "to weep about in this world any more? Is all our pity and anger to be reduced to a few tastefully arranged straight lines or petulant squirts from a tube held over a canvas?" And to the sentimentalists he says, on a steadily rising note that ends in a loud explosion: "All the wheels of business and advertising are turning night and day to prove the colossal falsehood that America is smiling. And they want me to add my two per cent. Hell, no!"

LIKE ancient Athens, the self-proclaimed Athens of America also has its back streets. Jack Levine was born on one of them, in Boston's grimy South End, the youngest son of an immigrant shoemaker. But Levine liked the slums. In 1923, when the family moved to suburban Roxbury, eight-year-old Jack was "horrified by the trees and piazzas." To console himself he made "drawings of drunkards and other things I remembered." His drawings caught the eye of a settlement-house art teacher. Soon the Harvard professor, Denman Ross, took Levine under his wing and introduced him to the old masters. "I went through a very conservative adolescence," he says. "Degas, Rembrandt, and Daumier."

When the WPA gave Levine a chance to move out on his own, he discarded conservative painting for expressionist protest pictures stylistically

BEN SHAHN'S "THE RED STAIRWAY" (1944)

241

SHAHN'S "SPRING" (1947)

patterned on Rouault and Soutine. "No matter how much of a wild man you are," he explains, "there's always someone before. So much painting has been done. But, actually, real expressionism wouldn't be acceptable to me; it puts too high a premium on self-expression. I don't want to make a painting that's understandable only to the Museum of Modern Art."

Levine's early pictures of the city's back streets and undercover corruption were clear to anyone. The people he painted looked like withered apples seen through a red mist of rage. "You distort for editorial reasons," Levine says, and then goes on with his built-in, self-deprecating shrug: "Another way of saying caricature." But when attacked as a soapbox painter, Levine has a sharp answer. He is, he asserts, "equipped to punish." Yet the passing years, and a lonely twenty-month World War II tour on Ascension Island, have mellowed him slightly. "Don't call me angry," he likes to say, with a thin smile.

A gemlike product of Levine's maturity is *King Saul*, finished, after years of "fiddling," in 1952. It is a gloomy and even baleful subject, but still a subject and not just a target. The small panel shows a wide range of influences, from Soutine back through Rembrandt to Flemish and Persian miniatures, all beautifully blended to create a new vision. "The problem of being an artist," Levine maintains, "is a problem of the pursuit of real knowledge and freedom. The mature Rembrandt was in pursuit of things that had never been tried or done before—and without his complete mastery of the tradition, his successful pursuit of them would never have been possible." The artist's function, in other words, should be "to bring the great tradition, and whatever is great about it, up-to-date."

While *King Saul* takes its place in the timeless world of legend, the far more ambitious *Election Night* is as up-to-date as a newspaper story. An elaborate satire, coruscating with brilliant bits of

242

JACK LEVINE'S "KING SAUL" (1952)

LEVINE'S "ELECTION NIGHT" (1954)

still life and flabby specimens of human life, all veiled in silvery glancing lights, the painting is designed to hold the mind as well as the eye. It almost calls for a scenario and a director to set the scene in motion.

Now in his early forties, Levine gives promise of becoming one of the nation's finest painters. His growing sense of the complexity of art and life he finds both a hindrance and a help; they make his future especially hard to predict. "I'm a Jew of the American seaboard, looking east," he says. "I've never managed to feel fully indigenous. I've been part of a tolerated minority. That has affected the subject matter as well as the style of my painting." But living in the world's most cosmopolitan city, New York, and being heaped with honors for his art, have inevitably modified Levine's views. "The longer you live and think," he admits with a puzzled frown, "the more things tend to get out of hand."

WITH the coming of World War II, the thunder on the left that had inspired so many American artists was drowned in larger thunders. Soon scores of painters were plunging into the struggle as artist-correspondents. Circumstances did not allow the painstaking mastery of subject that makes for great art, and the majority of American war paintings were in the nature of news reports. Today their interest is largely historical, not aesthetic. But a few artists did succeed in overcoming the immediacy of their subject to describe the sense of battle. Among them were Aaron Bohrod and Bernard Perlin, two of the painters commissioned by *Life* to cover the battlefronts.

Bohrod studied painting under John Sloan, and he determined to do for his native Chicago what Sloan had long since done for Manhattan. During the 1930s, when Bohrod was still in his twenties, he captured the seamy side of Chicago life in canvases that combined slushy colors with bright ones and strong feelings with sharp observation. Today, as an artist-in-residence at the University of Wisconsin, he paints mostly in the fool-the-eye tradition of William Harnett. But World War II vastly widened the range of his subjects to include the South Pacific fighting and the liberation of Normandy. His stormy canvas

of a Normandy village crucifix strung with Signal Corps wires, aptly titled *Military Necessity*, tells a great deal about the nature of all war, and in eternal terms.

Bernard Perlin was twenty-six in the spring of 1944, when he joined the "Sacred Squadron," a British-Greek commando unit, in a raid on the island of Samos. Falling into a German ambush which scattered the squadron, Perlin holed up with two other men in a mountain cave. For twenty-eight hours they huddled in the dark, listening to enemy search parties outside. Then, by great good luck, they escaped back to their ship. *After an Ambush*, showing the painter himself tearing up official papers in the cave foreground, records his adventure in stark, nightmare fashion.

CERTAIN painters find the roots of agony within themselves. Poverty, pain, crime, war, death, and putrefaction are never a surprise to

AARON BOHROD'S
"MILITARY NECESSITY" (1944)

245

BERNARD PERLIN'S "AFTER AN AMBUSH" (1944)

them. Sunshine may be; at least it puts them off, and they prefer the shadows. In the midst of prosperity and peace, therefore, Hyman Bloom and Ivan Le Lorraine Albright keep right on painting private horrors. And their art is too ghastly to ignore; it has all the weird brilliance of beached fish in the dark, exhaling the phosphorescence of decay.

AS Mohammedan legend has it, Jesus was walking in the bazaar with His disciples one day, when they came upon a dead dog. One disciple blurted: "How it stinks!" Another said: "Look at the buzzards wheeling overhead." But Jesus said: "How whiter than pearls are the teeth!" Hyman Bloom likes to retell this story when people complain of his preference for thoroughly dead subjects. Death, he says, "is charged with energy. It is a fruitful area of one's emotional life." When pressed, he falls back upon the irrefutable fact that "everyone dies," adding: "But both the Christians and the Jews believe that the soul is immortal. Probably the difficulty is in applying one's convictions."

Immortality of the soul or no, Bloom brings the ephemeral nature of the flesh brutally forward. The message of *Slaughtered Animal*, for instance, must always escape escapists like the Boston dowager who exclaimed indignantly at a

Bloom exhibition: "When I want raw meat I'll send my chauffeur to the butcher!" But to philosophic people like himself, the canvas is no more irredeemably gloomy than a pitch-dark tunnel that leads to daylight.

Bloom's early career precisely parallels Jack Levine's. Like Levine, he was the son of a Lithuanian Jewish shoemaker who moved his family to Boston; like Levine, he learned about art in a settlement house, and subsequently came under the influence of Harvard's erudite Denman Ross. Bloom and Levine shared a studio in Boston during their WPA days, and remained close friends until almost the end of the 1930s. They differed, as Americans are apt to do, simply over the best means of saving the world. Levine was all for economic and political readjustments, while Bloom felt that "before there can be any change, there must be a moral change in the people." Bloom's search for the means of change led him from Judaism through a host of esoteric sects whose ideas have enriched rather than clarified his art. An Oriental music enthusiast, he himself plays the sitar. The shrill and insistent tonal variations that make Eastern music something of an ordeal for most Western ears have their counterparts in Bloom's lavish use of iridescent color.

Once past the shock of Bloom's pictures, what are their enduring qualities? The first and most

246

HYMAN BLOOM'S "SLAUGHTERED ANIMAL" (1953)

apparent is an austere sincerity—for which he has sacrificed easy wealth and fame to live a ragged, bread-crumb existence in the midst of Boston's primness and plenty. His skills, especially as a draftsman, are as fantastic as they are flamboyant, and he could easily make a pleasant living painting pleasant pictures. The unpleasantness of Bloom's subject matter is about the only adventurous aspect of his art. In style he harks all the way back to the baroque, making grand old cliff-edge gestures that say in effect: "Come on in, the despair is fine."

FOR the past fifteen years, Ivan Le Lorraine Albright has labored over his still unfinished canvas, *Poor Room—There Is No Time, No End, No Today, No Yesterday, No Tomorrow, Only the Forever, and Forever, and Forever, Without End.* This, he explains, is just the temporary working title: "I may call it 'Good Room' when I'm done." The painting already justifies Albright's utter dedication; it is at least as ably painted as it is strangely conceived.

Now sixty, Albright paints in an old wooden house in a down-at-the-heels section of Chicago, largely because "I can think here." An ingenious system of black window shades enables him to throw just the light he desires on each part of his still-life model in turn. The still life stands whole in his studio; he built the moldy brick wall himself, and assembled the array of junk that makes up the rest of the picture. The larger items are on wheels for easy shifting, but Albright seldom shifts them; he lets things lie until they are richly coated with dust, loving them mainly for their melancholy aura of vanished life. "Things are nothing," he says. "It's what happens to them that matters." Through long and intimate association with his inanimate subjects, he comes to know them down to the last minuscule crease, and this is most important to him. "In my pictures," he explains, "knowledge is behind, and feeling is up ahead."

Besides painting each object separately in the light most flattering to it, Albright shows them from different angles. To paint the bottle on the bureau, he will turn the canvas upside down, and then turn it sideways to paint the bureau itself. At first glance, the objects in his pictures seem firmly anchored; then they start spinning. To create his timeless, richly textured wells of withered flesh, wrinkled money, and crinkled tinfoil, Albright uses two main weapons: vast patience and the smallest brushes obtainable. For really fine work he uses one lateral spine from a chicken feather, tied to a handle by a man who specializes in tying trout flies. His first step, which may take him years, is to cover the canvas with an infinitely detailed charcoal drawing—some of which can still be seen, unpainted, in *Poor Room*. After fixing the charcoal with a spray, he starts gently applying thin glazes of oil color, sometimes spending several weeks on a single square inch of the canvas. "When I get sick to death of painting glass," he says, "I paint wood for a while. Then when I get fed up with that, I'll paint bricks—and so forth."

When he gets sick of painting altogether, he taxis home to Chicago's fashionable North Side and his heiress wife, Josephine Medill Patterson, whose father founded New York's *Daily News*. Albright genially confesses that he actually does "not enjoy painting much. I go at it the hard way, with my eyes wide open. But I do like getting the results I want. I'd rather paint one good picture than a hundred bad ones. Anybody can paint bad ones—including me." Among his good ones have been a rotted-looking old woman in underwear, posed for by a young girl and entitled *Into the World There Came a Soul Called Ida*, and a decaying door hung with a funeral wreath entitled *That Which I Should Have Done I Did Not Do*. "I just can't seem to paint nice things," he muses. "I've tried, but it doesn't work. Once I designed a Christmas card and got a prize for it, but no royalties. I think the only copies sold were those I bought myself. It was a stained-glass window— very dirty and dusty. Looked like a funeral. Say, do you think I'm crazy?"

Crazy would be a poor word indeed to apply to so devoted and masterful an artist as Albright. He is not disturbed so much as disturbing. He has brought still-life painting to a new, highly personal pitch of intensity as peculiar in its own way as the horror stories of Edgar Allan Poe. Deriving from no school of art and pointing to none, resembling no other artist, Albright remains simply unique.

IVAN ALBRIGHT'S "POOR ROOM" (1942-   )

CHAPTER VIII

MORTON D. MAY

MAX BECKMANN'S "FISHERWOMEN" (1948)

THE MELTING POT

We are not a nation, so much as a world.

—HERMAN MELVILLE

THE great tides of immigration that deposited so many foreign-born on American shores in the twentieth century have enriched American painting as they have the nation as a whole. Some of the new arrivals came to America with their reputations already assured. Others first turned to painting in their adopted land. But all brought new and varied patterns to American art. So, too, have those Americans who went abroad for their formative years, as well as the native-born descended from the many races that

go to make up America. To this flourishing mixture of cultures and racial strains, the nation's painting owes much of its exuberant vitality.

MAX Beckmann, who arrived in America as one of Europe's best known expressionist painters, liked to repeat the familiar mystical idea that the man who penetrates the visible world deeply enough will see the invisible. In this belief he produced richly symbolic canvases where ferocious men and peach-fleshed women

250

JOSEF ALBERS' "HOMAGE TO THE SQUARE: 'LEGENDARY PASTURE'" (1952)

romp, dream, and torment each other amid the rainbow hues of fiery heavens and icy hells. His *Fisherwomen* shows Beckmann's genius for color as well as his penchant for whipping cruelty and tenderness together in oils. His lamplit girls do not look like the sort that go near the water.

This sort of thing struck the Nazis as "degenerate." Accordingly, they hounded him from his native Germany to Amsterdam, where he painted throughout World War II. Soon after the war, when he was sixty-three, Beckmann came to America to teach—first at Washington University in St. Louis and afterwards at the Brooklyn Museum Art School. Before his death in 1950, Beckmann was to paint more than a hundred canvases for American collections, and imbue at least that many art students with his own explosive mixture of vigor and wonderment.

JOSEF Albers' temperament is the opposite of Beckmann's and yet equally Teutonic. What Albers brought from Germany to his adopted

ABRAHAM RATTNER'S "COMPOSITION WITH THREE FIGURES" (1953)

land was not *Sturm und Drang*, but a passion for simplicity and order. "Emotions," he maintains, "are usually prejudices. When people say my paintings have no emotion, I say, 'O.K. Precision can make you crazy, too.' A locomotive is without emotion—so is a mathematics book, but they are exciting to me."

Two lines of Westphalian craftsmen—tinkers and carpenters on his father's side, blacksmiths on his mother's—went into Albers' making. With Kandinsky, Klee, and Feininger, he taught at Walter Gropius' Bauhaus, a school dedicated to reconciling traditional concepts of art with twentieth-century techniques. When the Bauhaus was closed by Hitler, Germany lost Albers to America. First at Black Mountain College in North Carolina, and since then as chairman of Yale's Department of Design, he has awakened generations of American students to certain basic elements of art. "The concern of the artist," he tells them, "is with the discrepancy between physical fact and psychic effect." If that is not the major concern of most artists, it certainly is in Albers' own case; he looks back on a long career devoted to widening the discrepancy.

"I like to push a grey," Albers explains, "so that it will change its identity." *Homage to the Square: "Legendary Pasture"* is one of a long series of experiments devoted to such color manipulations. In this case the grey becomes purple with prolonged observation, and the sky-blue center begins to radiate light outward through the other colors. This is possible because the human eye never sees colors plain, but always modified by surrounding hues. In Albers' strictly controlled pictures the modification becomes an almost magical transformation. Not even he can tell which tubes his colors have come from without consulting the written records inscribed on the backs of his pictures in a spectacularly minute hand. Using those records, another man could copy Albers' paintings exactly—which he finds a flattering and not at all disturbing thought. He chose squares within squares as the composition for his color experiments over the past decade because "the square is human"—meaning that it is an intellectual form almost never met with in nature. Albers himself is an intellectual creator of a sort almost never met in art.

YASUO KUNIYOSHI'S
"AMAZING JUGGLER" (1952)

FERNANDO GERASSI'S "MAGIC MOUNTAINS" (1951)

ABRAHAM Rattner was born and raised in the United States, and became a camouflage engineer in World War I. But for twenty long years thereafter, he lived and painted in Paris, imbibing the ideas of his friends Picasso, Miró, and Braque. He came home at last in 1940 and later taught at the University of Illinois, bringing the School of Paris straight and unadulterated into the corn belt. *Composition with Three Figures* looks as if it were meant to represent the Crucifixion camouflaged, or seen through stained glass darkly. Rattner does not deny either the religious overtones or the Sainte Chapelle coloring of the painting, but, says he: "It is rather an idea related to the need to give men hope and encouragement and involving the conflicting things that we are confronted with today in our hearts and souls."

YASUO Kuniyoshi painted the hectic, sunset-hued *Amazing Juggler* shortly before his death in 1953. The canvas seems to express the fate—common among artists—of entertaining people without becoming known to them; under the grinning swordfish mask sweats a stranger. This wistful message is conveyed with Oriental delicacy of touch, in colors like those of Japanese kites. Kuniyoshi masked himself in a pork-pie

PETER BLUME'S "SOUTH OF SCRANTON" (1931)

255

SAVO RADULOVIC

SAVO RADULOVIC'S "SURGERY" (1953-56)

256

hat, bulldog pipe, and horn-rimmed spectacles, yet never denied the gloom within. "My paintings are sad," he would say, "because I am a sad man. I feel very lonely."

His loneliness may have dated back to 1906, when he arrived in the United States, a friendless Japanese boy of thirteen, to seek his fortune. He found jobs as dishwasher, engine cleaner, grape picker, ranch hand, and art photographer, and studied painting between times. "I have done nearly everything except commercial art." he once recalled, "but it is not true when they say I worked as a butler." In the 1920s Kuniyoshi's disciplined blending of Eastern and Western art won him a lasting circle of admirers, and leisure enough to take up golf. Thereupon he painted himself carrying a golf club as proudly as if it were a samurai sword. In the 1930s he saw the drift of Japanese militarism, and protested vigorously against it, but that did not prevent his being classified as an enemy alien during World War II. "I am just as much an American in my approach and thinking," he insisted, "as the next fellow." And so he was, but with added values that he had brought with him to America and incorporated in his art.

FERNANDO Gerassi believes that nothing succeeds like failure. "Each time you fail you learn something," he says. "If you have faith in yourself, you accept the failure and go on. The more failures the better." Brought up in Spain, Gerassi first failed at philosophy, which he went to study in Germany. "I wanted to find out the sense of life," he explains. "I found out that you don't find out anything but speculations." A trip to Italy convinced him that painting would lead closer to the sense of life, and since then he has intensely pursued his art. One year older than the twentieth century, Gerassi came to America at the start of World War II. His Ukrainian-born wife now teaches modern languages at the Putney School in Vermont, while Gerassi paints or wanders over the hills. Peaceful, secluded living has heightened the warm and sunny innocence of his art. *Magic Mountains* is at least as removed from reality as the Appalachians are from the Pyrenees. It has the boldness, brightness, and the paradoxical vagueness that six-year-olds

can bring to painting. But behind Gerassi's ebullience lies a highly sophisticated intelligence. Done with rock-bottom economy of means, his picture evokes instead of describing; it has the misty morning splendor of a mirage that stays. The simplicity of the canvas was only accomplished through an arduous process of trial and error—from "failures," as he says.

PETER Blume was born in the Russian town of Smorgon, on the railroad line between Vilna and Minsk. He came with his family to New York in 1911, when he was five. "At first," he recalls, "we lived with my grandmother on the Lower East Side. Her apartment was a refuge for immigrants—there would be twenty or thirty people there at one time." Blume was raised in Brooklyn, and started going to art school at the age of twelve. For the next five years he supported himself as a letterer and jewelry designer while studying art. His icy, crisp approach to the technical problems of painting quickly got the public and critical respect it deserved; ever since the age of eighteen he has managed to earn a living from his pictures.

His first fame came in 1934, when he won the Carnegie International Award with *South of Scranton*. The exhibition director, Homer Saint-Gaudens, implied that the picture was "insane" —hastily adding that "what garlic is to salad, insanity is to art." One Manhattan critic devoted most of his review to describing at considerable length his train trip to Pittsburgh, during which "a sudden lurch" had thrown "an exceedingly handsome young woman" into his arms. "The prize-awarding this year," the critic remarked as something of an afterthought, "has been peculiarly indiscreet."

Actually Blume's picture also describes a trip —from Scranton, Pennsylvania, to Charleston, South Carolina, by Model-T Ford. Blume combined in a single canvas the mountains of waste coal around Scranton, the deep quarries and busily puffing locomotives, a sunset transformed into a red pyramid, a Pennsylvania Main Street, the flat expanse of Charleston Harbor, a German cruiser that happened to be tied up there, and sailors doing calisthenics on deck. A few touches, such as the impossible exuberance of the sailors, carry the whiff of European surrealism, which Gertrude Stein once excoriated as "this thing, this writing, which is the painting everyone is now doing." Far more important is the fact that the painting as a whole describes part of the American scene in a new and striking portmanteau style.

SAVO Radulovic came to the United States with his parents in 1921, at the age of ten. Savo had already earned his keep herding sheep in his native Yugoslavia. At sixteen he was "the youngest coal miner in southern Illinois." Three years later he moved to Detroit and became a tool grinder for Chevrolet. Laid off during the Depression, he joined a sister who had opened a restaurant in St. Louis. The restaurant became an artists' hangout. "There," he recalls with a certain amazement, "music, art, and literature somehow came into my life. I was observing and wanting to know why I'm living. So I took to painting." With time out for World War II, he has been painting ever since, supporting himself in the lean years by teaching, tending bar, and guarding payrolls.

Surgery derives from Radulovic's experiences during the war, including a period of guerrilla fighting in Yugoslavia. "Under war conditions you see surgery in pigpens and cow sheds," he says. "It moved me very much to see the surgeons work under these conditions. But I didn't start the painting until I myself was under surgery after the war, for mastoids and then for ulcers. It was my reaction to anesthesia, which takes you out into space. You will see the moon and the stars."

IN 1916, when Dong Kingman was five years old, his Chinese-American father tired of running a San Francisco hand laundry and moved the family to Hong Kong. Because he showed an instinct for art, the boy was put to studying *hsieh-yi* (to draw a conception) and *hsieh-cheng* (to draw reality). He inclined toward *hsieh-cheng*. At eighteen Kingman came home to California and made his way as a waiter, houseboy, and factory hand. The WPA freed him for painting. Since then he has made himself one of the country's ablest and most original water-colorists, creating

DONG KINGMAN'S "ANGEL SQUARE" (1951)

JACOB LAWRENCE'S "VAUDEVILLE" (1951)

his own vision of America with an unfailing delicacy, precision, fantasy, and wit.

Angel Square looks like a view of Times Square seen through the smoke of Chinese firecrackers. Its tightly dovetailed composition and the subtle interplay of dim and bright colors soften the picture's rather sinister humor without obscuring the fun. "If people take my work too seriously," Kingman says, "I'm disappointed. Of course my pictures are sarcastic, too. I mean, the signs say 'Go Here, Go There,' when you don't really have to. And on Sundays, when there's no traffic, the stop lights keep blinking as if they were crazy. Don't you feel that way?"

AT forty Jacob Lawrence is the world's foremost Negro painter. Yet his draftsmanship would hardly earn passing grades at an academy, his painting technique is flat and dry, and his colors arbitrary in the extreme. What makes Lawrence as a painter is chiefly the fact that he is his own man. He never buys attention with smooth-rubbed clichés; Lawrence's ideas are all fresh minted. "I work long on the *idea* for a painting," he says. "I want the idea to strike right away." The idea for *Vaudeville* came from Lawrence's memories of the Apollo Theater in Harlem: "I wasn't thinking of any particular act. The decorated panel behind? I never saw it; I made it up. You can't just put together things you've seen. I wanted a staccato-type thing— raw, sharp, rough—that's what I tried to get."

Lawrence's own temperament is intense to the point of rawness. Brought up in Harlem during the Depression, he first began attracting attention in 1941 with fierce little pictures of Negro life. Later exhibitions told of his World War II experiences in the Coast Guard and illustrated the life of John Brown. He is now at work on a monumental project depicting American history as a whole. Believing that "the human subject is the most important thing," he is and plans to remain a storytelling artist.

HENRY Koerner leaped into prominence a decade ago, when he was thirty-one, with a picture of autumn woods in which two old people appeared to be thinking things over. They were his parents, liquidated by the Nazis. His canvas spoke the timeless reproach of the dead, who would never again turn to face their persecutors. But Koerner is not a bitter man. His aim, he says, was simply to help his parents "walk once more in the Vienna woods—where we all used to go walking together."

Trained as a commercial artist in Vienna, Koerner spent his summer vacations walking and sketching in Italy, France, Switzerland, and Yugoslavia. At twenty-three he crossed the Alps into Italy for the last time; the Nazis had entered Austria. Although Jewish, his family stayed on behind, "because they loved Vienna very much." Koerner lived for a hungry but inspiring year in Italy, drinking in the glories of Renaissance painting. Then a great-uncle who lived in Brooklyn helped him come to the United States, where he met with instant success as a poster designer. The draft, oddly enough, made a fine artist of him. He began drawing from life on a troopship to England, where there were "8,279 soldiers, all in the same boat. Day in and day out, there was nothing to do but stare into all those faces. During those ten days I saw the human face for the first time." Ever since then he has sketched constantly from life, especially faces.

Demobilized in the spring of 1946, Koerner turned back to Vienna. He found the jagged, windowless walls of his old home and, sticking out of the rubble, an old shoe and the hem of a skirt. That was all. An overwhelming uprush of memories combined with his newfound capacity for clear observation to make Koerner paint. After the success of *My Parents*, he returned to Brooklyn and began a powerful series of canvases blending his New World experience with echoes of the old.

Emerging one evening from the Kings Highway elevated station in Brooklyn, he came face to face with a scene very much like *June Night*. The mural ad (for a photographer who specialized in wedding pictures), the poster with the sleeping baby, even the blimp, were all there. The mural, of course, made him think again of his parents, but it also seemed a gigantic "illusion" of wedded bliss, superimposed on the brick reality of the apartment house and pierced with glimpses into cramped, sweaty lives. Koerner slowly squeezed what he had seen into a tightly

HENRY KOERNER'S "JUNE NIGHT" (1948)

integrated picture, flushed with hot, wet, rosy light. The actual blimp had carried a Goodyear sign; Koerner substituted the flying red horse "because I thought it was a nicer shape." He considerably enlarged the baby's head in the poster and embellished it with sinister rips. By virtue of its size and leaden slumber, the baby almost dominates the picture; he might in fact be dreaming it all. As a whole the painting surpasses mere illustration because it implies so much more than it tells. The very theatricality of the picture seems to say that the "real" man-made world is equally a fabric of illusions.

In recent years Koerner has turned from such imaginative reconstructions to the concrete. He paints entirely on the spot, using tiny slabs of color in a manner reminiscent of France's great Paul Cézanne. "It's amazing how easily you forget reality," he remarks by way of explanation, "and how much richer reality is."

KOERNER'S "MY PARENTS" (1946)

CHAPTER IX

THE DETROIT INSTITUTE OF ARTS

MARK TOBEY'S
"SAN FRANCISCO STREET" (1941)

NORTHWEST PASSAGE

Tell all the truth but tell it slant,
Success in circuit lies,
Too bright for our infirm delight
The truth's superb surprise.

—EMILY DICKINSON

FIVE years ago, Seattle's most admired painter took part in a discussion concerning "the artist in the community." Mark Tobey began by saying the subject really ought to be "the community in the artist."

"Why?"

"In these times of tension," Tobey replied, "the artist's problem is traffic—how to make his color move, how to give it circulation and an avenue through which he can make it come through. And he has the problem of getting away from the central interest."

"How does the artist get away from it?"

"He should move to the right or the left of the canvas. He must move very abruptly or by transition. The artist will have to swing his canvas. Everything has to come through."

"The result?"

"The artist will never be divorced from society. At his best he will translate the unknowns of today so they will be known ten years from now."

STRANGELY enough, the "unknowns" translated by Tobey's own art appear to be gaining increasing acceptance. Although most people are

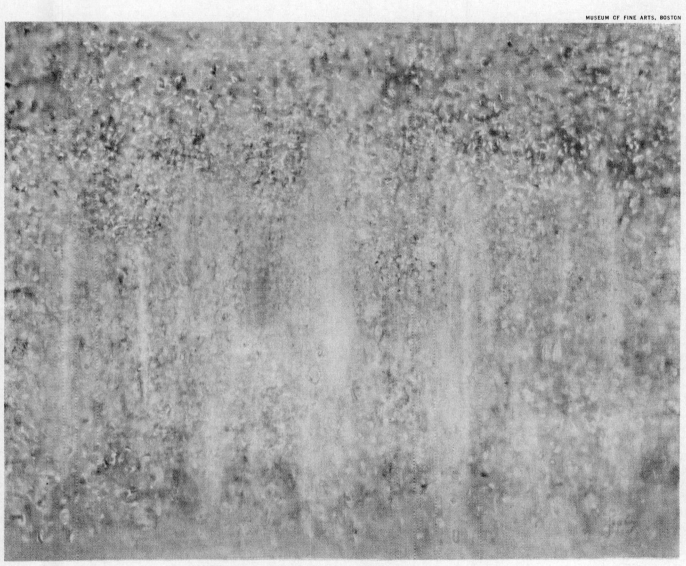

TOBEY'S "FOUNTAINS OF EUROPE" (1955)

TOBEY'S "TRANSIT" (1948)

still far from finding much meaning in Tobey's paintings, they have influenced hundreds of his fellow artists. What Tobey has accomplished is a bland yet pervasive synthesis of Eastern and Western culture. He has opened a Northwest Passage between Occidental painting and Oriental calligraphy, and the results are being felt from Tokyo to Paris.

A splendid figure with white hair and beard, in tweeds and paint-splattered shoes—majestic, abrupt, and assured—Mark Tobey has come a long way from his turn-of-the-century boyhood. In Trempealeau, on the banks of the Mississippi, he "was strictly a barefoot boy—hunting, fishing, and flowers." During adolescence he worshiped Frederic Remington, *Saturday Evening Post* covers, and the American girl—"the most beautiful thing you could put on canvas," he said. Tobey first made a living by illustrating mail-order catalogues in Chicago, and then as a portraitist in Greenwich Village. Because portraiture involved "too damned many dinner parties," he switched to lamps and screens for a time. Then, in 1923, he retreated to an art-teaching job in Seattle, where he has lived on and off ever since. It was a trip to China in 1934 that turned Tobey from a follower into a pioneer. He studied brush drawing in Shanghai, and came home convinced that "we have to know both worlds, the Western and the Oriental." To bridge them, Tobey invented what he calls "white writing"—a way of looping lines of light paint across a dark canvas so that they cannot be resolved either into letters or into a clear picture. "Multiple space bounded by white lines," he explains, "symbolizes higher states of consciousness." Tobey himself does not expect many to understand his explanation. "I can't understand doctors or lawyers," he says, "so why the hell should anyone understand me?"

The truth about Tobey's evident skill and equally evident limitations lies not in what he propounds but in what he paints. In *San Francisco Street* he produced a deep and spacious image of reality, projected in the mind's eye. "Our mind," he once wrote, "is a night sky." *Fountains of Europe* is both flatter and richer, a haze of plashings, flower scents, dusk, and warm drops. With *Transit* Tobey melts down thousands of years of Eastern and Western painting into the

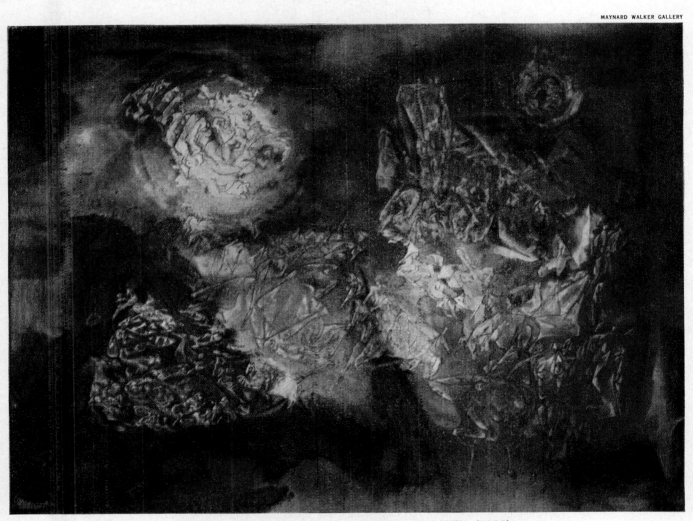

KENNETH CALLAHAN'S "FIERY NIGHT" (1955)

MORRIS GRAVES'S "PREENING SPARROW" (1952)

tentative squiggles from which both, perhaps, arose. Although the picture brings nothing specific to mind, it has a possible analogy in music, a thought which suits Tobey exactly. "When I play the piano for several hours," he says, "everything is clarified in my visual imagination afterwards. Everything that exists, every human being, is a vibration."

KENNETH Callahan, who also lives in Seattle, was long a disciple of Tobey, and named his boy after his idol. Though Callahan and Tobey have drifted apart, their art carries much the same message. The message as expressed in pictures may seem mysterious, but it has a long and clear history in human thought. As the Greek philosopher Heraclitus put it: All is flux.

Callahan once described his ultimate objective in a revealing letter explaining his art: "I have attempted . . . to project an idea of the mass of humanity evolving into and out of nature . . . nature disintegrating and solidifying—solar energy creating life and destroying life—alternately with man's feeble efforts in both cases . . . nature and the infinite controlling everything and composing everything—people locked in small pockets, related and still separated, whirling through life and space, bound in their own little personal, selfish relationships, unseeing and unrealizing they are interrelated, eternally and inevitably flying through mental, physical, and spiritual existences."

The stormy sweep of this concept shapes all of Callahan's art, making him a passionate and curiously naive painter. Neither Tobey's subtleties, nor much travel, nor even a twenty-year tenure as curator of the Seattle Art Museum, has sophisticated Callahan's approach. At the age of fifty he still symbolizes "nature" with cloud-filled whirlwinds of various colors, and draws "man" swarming like lightning bugs within the cloud. Sometimes a wraithlike little horse will gallop soundlessly through Callahan's misty vision, or rock ridges hump into view. *Fiery Night* typically combines these elements.

Callahan's art is "Northwestern" in a sense different from Tobey's; instead of drawing on proximity to the Orient, it reflects the grandeur and violence of the landscape of the Northwest.

Callahan first brought his peculiar style into focus while serving as a fire warden in the Cascade Mountains during World War II. "This is a rugged country," he wrote at the time. "Great, jagged cliffs, tortured and distorted, pile on one another—innumerable waterfalls twist and scatter out of clouds of mist and fog, which swirl and alternately blanket, then disclose, the peaks." Such things seem to loom just below the surface of Callahan's pictures.

MORRIS Graves, too, has based his art on the look of the Pacific Northwest, a land where ocean and rivers and mountains narrowly embrace. An adventurer in the forests and along the shore, Graves pictures the water, the trees, the fish—and most especially the birds—not as he sees them, but as they look to his imagination. His approach springs partly from Tobey's teaching and partly from his own studies in Zen Buddhism. "Zen," Graves explains, "stresses the meditative, stilling the surface of the mind and letting the inner surface bloom." The "inner surface" of Graves's mind is apparently awash with a flood of abstruse symbols and with fragments remembered from art history.

Perhaps the strongest of the three "Northwest School" painters, he is surely the most elaborately cultivated. *Preening Sparrow*, for example, owes a clear debt to the ancient Chinese bronzes that Graves has studied in Seattle, Honolulu, Boston, and New York. It also points an unmeditative moral: the sparrow is too preoccupied with self to realize that the moment of eclipse has arrived—that he is perched on the wing of a bird of prey and will be devoured in another instant. *Sea, Fish, and Constellation* tells an altogether different tale in suitably differing terms. There is something Chinese about the way the smallness of the fish is contrasted with the vastness of the heaving sea, but the sea has a massiveness and feverishness that would shock an Oriental draftsman. Similarly, the lines connecting the stars are drawn from Western astronomy charts and point an emphatically Western moral: that intellectual constructions help keep one's head above water.

Poised, bearded, and birdlike, Graves answers questions with aphorisms such as: "Vision grows in the meadows of obscurity." The Federal Art

Project saw Graves through some thistly meadows as a youth. Since then he has grown famous more or less in spite of himself. Now, at close to fifty, he can afford a palatial mansion in the forest north of Seattle, and also afford to leave it when he wishes to wander as far afield as Japan, France, and Ireland. Like most of the "Northwest School" painters, Graves is an uncertain colorist, but his drawing can be as fine and sure on occasion as a spider's mid-air labors, and some haunting images have been caught in his webs. His concern is less with life's vibrations, as in Tobey, or with its tumultuous flux, as in Callahan, than with its eeriest overtones: the steamboat whistle heard atop a snowy peak, or the rustling of silk in an empty room. To call Graves a mystic would place too much weight on his essentially slender and eclectic art; to call him a fantasist would place too little. He is that rare and valuable in-between creature, the poet.

GRAVES'S "SEA, FISH, AND CONSTELLATION" (1944)

CHAPTER X

ADVENTURES
IN SPACE

Bottomless vales and boundless floods,
And chasms, and caves, and Titan woods,
With forms that no man can discover
For the tears that drip all over;
Mountains toppling evermore
Into seas without a shore;
Seas that restlessly aspire,
Surging, unto skies of fire . . .

—EDGAR ALLAN POE

OUT of the mists of Mark Tobey's Northwest Passage has arisen one of the most extraordinary phenomena in the extraordinary history of modern art. In its Manhattan stronghold the phenomenon is known as "abstract expressionism." In London they call it "action painting," and in Paris, *tachisme* (staining). Like a headland dimly perceived through fog and spray, it looms indistinct, and probably much larger than solid actuality. Surveyors, usually in a passion of approval or disapproval, have violently disagreed as to its hidden welcomes or dangers, its salient features, and the nature of its inhabitants.

ABSTRACT expressionism owes its Oriental overtones to Tobey. Like the great draftsmen of the Orient, the abstract expressionists put much stress on the physical act of painting. Whether working with a brush, a bucket, or a bent spoon, they aim to express their emotions by the very movements with which they lay on the paint. This calls to mind the great Japanese Miyamoto Niten, famed for swordsmanship and draftsmanship, who practiced both in the same spirit. Tobey, of course, appropriated Chinese calligraphy without the calligraphs and Zen Buddhist draftsmanship without its strict attention to subject matter. At its most extreme, Tobey's "white writing" is like a letter without words or meaning, just emotions conveyed by the handwriting itself. That extreme was what appealed to a group of younger American artists, centering on Manhattan, who were to pioneer the new abstract expressionist movement.

But where Tobey tries to "symbolize higher states of consciousness," the younger painters try to limit consciousness to the level of feeling alone. They seldom know in advance what they are setting out to do, and they most emphatically do not want to know. As Mark Rothko once wrote, his paintings "begin as an unknown adventure in an unknown space. It is at the moment of

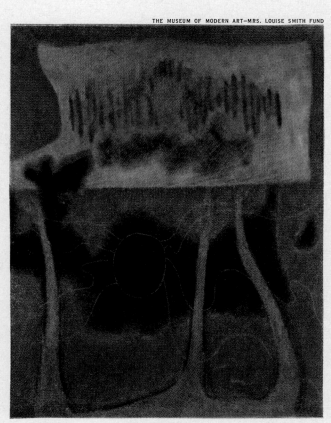

WILLIAM BAZIOTES' "POMPEII" (1955)

completion that, in a flash of recognition, they are seen to have the quantity and function which was intended. Ideas and plans that existed in the mind at the start were simply the doorway through which one left the world in which they occur." And he added: "The most important tool the artist fashions through constant practice is faith in his ability to produce miracles when they are needed." As James Brooks describes such a miracle: "My painting starts with a complication on the canvas surface, done with as much spontaneity and as little memory as possible. It demands a long period of acquaintance. . . . Then it speaks, quietly, with its own peculiar logic." With William Baziotes, too, "each beginning suggests something. . . . As I work, or when the painting is finished, the subject reveals itself." Baziotes goes on to say that he lines his canvases up against a wall of his studio for morning inspection: "Some speak; some do not. They tell me what I am like at the moment."

Judging by *Pompeii*, Baziotes was probably in a glum state about the time it was painted. "The large, grey spiked form rising from the bottom of the picture," he agrees, "is to me the symbol of death and ruin." James Brooks's *R-1953* (a title indicating only that it was his eighteenth painting in the course of the year) seems equally gloomy, though it has the luminous iridescence of the oil slick on a garage floor. Philip Guston's *Summer* (so titled because it was painted in the summertime) follows the declared purpose of his painting: to represent "myself." The better to put himself into his work, Guston often uses canvases measuring close to his own size. But for such self-consciously grandiose efforts, the results look strangely like blown-up details from Claude Monet's water-lily impressions. Mark Rothko's *Orange Over Yellow* exhales unruffled glow, like a cup of cambric tea. Such innocent mildness, typical of Rothko's art, may help explain his curious reluctance to send a painting "out into the world. How often it must be impaired by the eyes of the unfeeling and the cruelty of the impotent, who would extend their affliction universally!" Like some private rain cloud, this odd feeling of persecution seems to dog many of the best-known abstract expressionists, surrounded by a large and loyal following though they may be.

JAMES BROOKS'S "R-1953" (1953)

PHILIP GUSTON'S "SUMMER" (1954)

IF the theoretical and emotional aspects of the abstract expressionists display a certain elusiveness, it is because mere self-expression, as an ideal, begs the question of what the self is trying to express. On the technical and abstract side the movement draws on the techniques of School of Paris painting, and is nothing if not decorative. On that side Hans Hofmann dominates abstract expressionism in Manhattan, not by his painting so much as by his teaching.

Scores of well-known American painters have studied with Hofmann, who was himself thoroughly trained in Europe. "A picture," he says, "must be made, dictated, through the inherent laws of the surface. I invented what I call 'push and pull' force and counter-force. I have been very modest about it, but they are really great discoveries. The highest three-dimensionality is two-dimensionality, which no layman can ever understand." Where Einstein calculated that all space is curved, Hofmann figures it to be flat,

MARK ROTHKO'S "ORANGE OVER YELLOW" (1950)

HANS HOFMANN'S "RED TRICKLE" (1939)

ARSHILE GORKY'S "GARDEN IN SOCHI" (1941)

ROBERT MOTHERWELL'S "WESTERN AIR" (1946-47)

MATTA'S "THE FIFTY PERCENT IRRATIONAL IN MATTER" (1952)

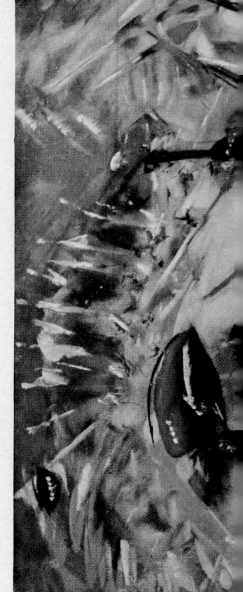

276

but bumpy, as in *Red Trickle*. In fact, a bumpy sort of flatness, large size, and wild color are his three contributions to abstract expressionism. His art "expresses" very little beyond a debt to Wassily Kandinsky and a rather determined gaiety. But he has made a new and boldly decorative mode out of European materials.

The same can be said for a number of Hofmann's peers, including the late Arshile Gorky, who adopted the mannerisms without the emotions of Picasso to paint *Garden in Sochi*. It applies also to Robert Motherwell, whose *Western Air* is cubism smashed flat and provided with a couple of sky holes. Another importer is Matta Echaurren, whose *The Fifty Percent Irrational in Matter* puts the spirit-haunted world of Joan Miró in a weirdly naturalistic light. Instead of imagining dragons, Matta visualizes incandescent insects. John Ferren, too, has a Parisian playfulness. *Red and Blue*, according to one admirer, "looks highly accidental, but to those of us who know better, it represents a good deal of sensitivity."

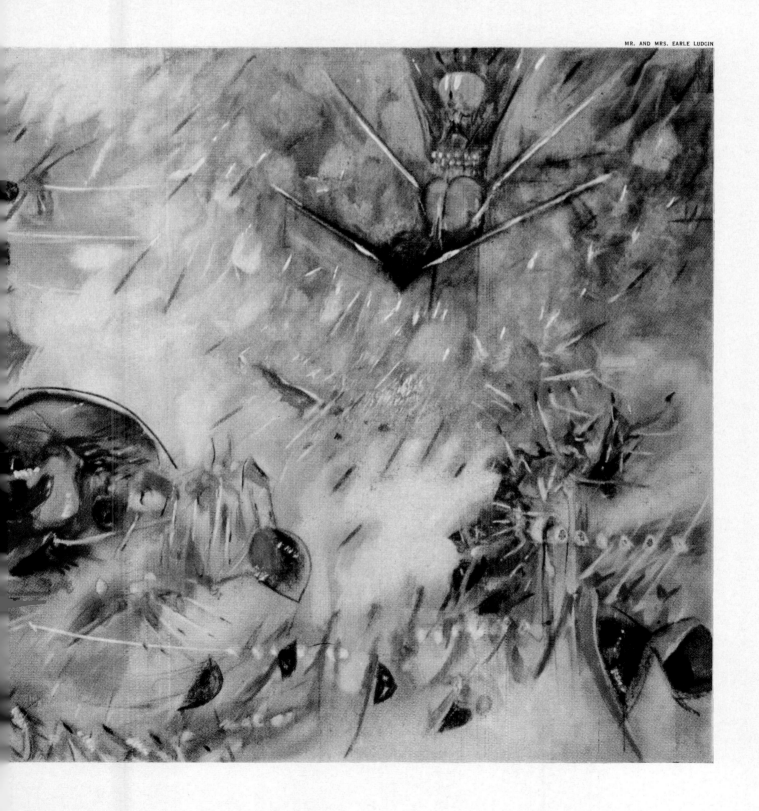

JOHN FERREN'S "RED AND BLUE" (1953)

THE present strength of the abstract expressionist movement lies neither in the dreamy expressionism of a Rothko or Guston nor in the slick abstractionism of a Ferren or a Matta. It comes from an in-between group whose art is both moody and decorative, clumsy on purpose, and above all, powerful. Adolph Gottlieb, Franz Kline, the late Jackson Pollock, and Willem de Kooning keep trying for the stunning blow. Looking at Gottlieb's *Blue at Noon* is rather like watching a snowstorm through a windowpane and remembering Thomas Nash's line: "Brightness falls from the air." Franz Kline's black and white *Cross-Section* packs the snow solid against the pane, now black with night. Both pictures are deliberately stormy and austere.

Jackson Pollock could be twice as stormy, and that made him the champion of the group until his death in an automobile accident in 1956. A burly, bearded individualist out of Cody, Wyoming, Pollock studied first under truculent Tom Benton in the 1930s. He did not develop his

ADOLPH GOTTLIEB'S "BLUE AT NOON" (1955)

FRANZ KLINE'S "CROSS-SECTION" (1956)

own distinctive style until the mid-1940s, when he first spread a vast canvas out on the floor and began walking about it, wildly splashing paint from buckets and trailing it from sticks. When the canvas was hung upright, what gesture and gravity had accomplished looked like an outpouring of Herculean energy. In the years that followed, Pollock proved to have invented a new kind of decoration: flowing, labyrinthine, astonishingly vehement. There was something mild, too, about Pollock. "On the floor," he once wrote, "I am more at ease. I feel nearer, more a part of the painting, since in this way I can . . . literally be *in* the painting. . . . It is only when I lose contact with the painting that the result is a mess. Otherwise there is pure harmony, an easy give and take, and the painting comes out well."

Pollock soon became the most talked-about American artist. But success seemed to sour him. He was a troubled man, vacillating between gentleness and violence, and increasingly ill at ease —on the floor or not—with his own art. For the last few years of his short life he practically stopped painting.

With the passing of Jackson Pollock, Willem de Kooning looms as the most violent and most revered of the abstract expressionists. Amiable and eagle-eyed, he has been painting furiously in Amsterdam and later in America, for most of his fifty-three years. "Art never seems to me peaceful or pure," he says. "I always seem to be wrapped in the melodrama of vulgarity." What De Kooning does is to push a brilliant talent as far in the direction of the wild, woolly, and willful as he can. Since "nothing is positive about art, except that it is a word," he has even gone so far as to paint a few recognizable figures— thereby shocking his followers. In one such canvas, *Woman 1*, a sharp-fanged, horn-bosomed creature sums up all that is frightening about mid-century, middle-aged womanhood.

Gotham News is more typical of De Kooning. He got the title from the faint print that came off on the paint while he was blotting his canvas with a newspaper. Besides blotting, the picture uses a whole arsenal of painting skills to create excitement. It is as juicy as Rubens, gaudy as Delacroix, emphatic as Vlaminck—and utterly ambiguous. If De Kooning's canvas may be said

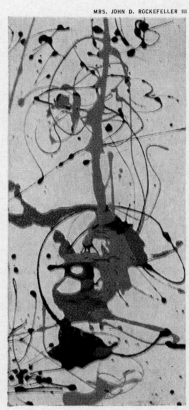

JACKSON POLLOCK'S
"NO. 23" (1949)

POLLOCK'S "SCENT" (1955)

to describe anything, it describes the very effort the artist put into it. The observer's glance is led by the brushstrokes to slide here and there in the calculated chaos, so that looking at the picture recapitulates part of the painting process.

THE general formula of the whole abstract expressionist movement—broad enough to include artists as divergent as Rothko, Hofmann, and De Kooning—might have been drawn from the military strategy of Von Clausewitz: to concentrate the greatest possible amount of force on the smallest possible point. The point is merely to mirror the artist's emotions of the moment; the force varies considerably from painter to painter. The results recall the flickering shadows in Plato's famous allegory of the cave—shadows which the prisoners within mistake for the realities outside. But whether their exclusive concern with their own emotions shackles the abstract expressionists and cuts them off from reality, or whether it can somehow free them for the contemplation of truths beyond ordinary understanding, remains to be proven.

WILLEM DE KOONING'S "GOTHAM NEWS" (1955)

DE KOONING'S "WOMAN 1" (1950-52)

CHAPTER XI

THE REALIST TRADITION

Every correspondence we observe in mind and matter suggests a substance older and deeper than either of these old nobilities.

—RALPH WALDO EMERSON

OVER the past 300 years American painting has followed a course as unpredictable as the changing temper of the times—now savoring the new, now re-examining the old, testing native invention against imports from abroad, or abandoning past experience for the adventure of fresh experiment. Yet American painters have always returned to the tradition that is the mainstream of American art. At mid-century the abstract expressionists dominate the scene—by weight of numbers and the vigor of their advocates. But four of the best American painters to emerge in the first half of the twentieth century remain faithful to the perceptive realism that has occupied the great American masters from Copley to Eakins to the present day.

Each in his own way, Walt Kuhn, Andrew Wyeth, George Bellows, and Edward Hopper have served that same cause, making a clear and convincing translation of reality to canvas. They create not just the appearance of things as they are, but a larger truth that combines the world of visible objects with the invisible world of man's ideas. Informing the purely physical with human thoughts and feelings, they enhance both worlds.

SHORTLY before Walt Kuhn died in 1949, a visitor asked him to describe his working habits. A big, rawboned man with heavy hands and level blue eyes, Kuhn replied by spreading his arms to embrace his dusty Greenwich Village studio, cluttered with stage props and decorated with a few small photographs of archaic Greek statues. When he spoke, it was in the staccato style of a vaudeville veteran describing his act: "I go to bed early if I wanna paint. The weather's gotta be right, I gotta feel right, and the model's gotta feel right, too. . . . Why, if I do one good picture a year I'm tickled to death." Kuhn's art was as specific as his words were general. His paintings were frankly narrow in intent, but a plow also has a narrow blade, and Kuhn could cut a marvelously straight furrow.

Trio is one of Kuhn's "good" pictures, and it stands among the major achievements of modern American art. The one-two-three, red-white-red composition is as buoyantly symmetrical as a triple somersault performed in mid-air—and has much the same mystifying air of inevitability and ease. As an old showman himself, Kuhn naturally chose entertainers for his subject, and by seizing them from the spangled entertainment world into a silent, neutral zone, he made them seem more colorful than ever. By posing them in stiff immobility, he underscored their capacity for action; even though grounded, the trapeze artists seem to soar as a team. Beyond their sharply individual personalities, they share an impersonal dignity, the courage of indomitable transients posing for the audience of eternity.

Kuhn himself climbed a high, twisting ladder to reach such moments of greatness as his *Trio*

WALT KUHN'S "TRIO" (1937)

ANDREW WYETH'S "A CROW FLEW BY" (1949-50)

represents. Born in Greenwich Village in 1880, he got his start making, repairing, and racing bicycles. Since trick bicycles were much used in vaudeville, he found himself in show business, and was soon inventing and producing his own acts. Meanwhile, he "covered a million miles of drawing paper" and dreamed of becoming an artist. In his twenties he sold a few comic drawings, but, as he afterwards recalled: "I was past thirty when I sold my first painting and past forty before I painted a decent picture. I was the gauchest thing you ever saw. But I've had fun! God, I've had fun!" Gauche or not, he played a major part in the selection and promotion of the Armory Show in 1913, studied abroad, made friends with the leading School of Paris artists, and came home to mature his own loud and clear style. In adapting the simplified forms and strident colors of Matisse and Picasso to forthright representation, he suggested one way to reconcile modern means with traditional aims.

Kuhn's particular bridge has found no significant group of American followers, and the split between the moderns and the traditionalists keeps on widening. But the same emphatic and yet mysterious manner in which Kuhn discussed his own pictures stood him in good stead when debating the merits of modern art. "It's gotta stop!" he would announce. "These young fellows don't know where the Sam Hill they're at!" Simmering down, he would give a wink: "In this business, guts and a sense of humor are the main ingredients."

WHEN Andrew Wyeth was born in 1917, the American artists he most admires were already dead. But the spirit of Eakins and Homer remains alive and fruitful in his art. Like them,

286

Wyeth paints man and nature directly, with loving, gloomy intensity. Like them, too, he is a craftsman of the first order, somewhat weak in color but strong in drawing and characterization. Like them, he peers humbly and resolutely into the mysteries of life and death.

Natural cataclysms were what moved Homer most, and human courage was Eakins' chief subject; Wyeth turns to intimations of mortality, with deathly calm. In fact this calm so imbues his art as to render it somewhat static. To overcome the difficulty Wyeth employs a device more common in Oriental art than in the West, which is the painter's equivalent of the photographer's high-angle and low-angle shots. His pictures are seldom straight-on visions: a viewer either gazes down upon them from a hovering position or looks up to them from the ground.

A Crow Flew By is viewed from near the ceiling, which gives an added ghostliness to the scene. The title, Wyeth says, was an incidental afterthought; yet it is appropriate. Crows are birds of ill omen, and the old Negro leaning fearfully into the light cannot have long to live. The crow soaring somewhere outside appears symbolically within the picture as well, for the man's blue denim jacket gleams like plumage and his work-worn hands are talonlike. The figure is crossed by one sword-flick of light— which brings inevitable darkness to mind.

Wyeth's own beginnings were crossed with darkness and light. A sickly, spindly boy, he was

WYETH'S "YOUNG AMERICA" (1950)

287

taken out of first grade after three months and never went back to school. He reluctantly submitted to a little learning at home, but even now he has trouble with his spelling. Mostly, during the long days when his stronger and brighter-seeming brother and sisters were away at school, young Andy just mused, played with tin soldiers, or wandered the countryside. Storms of illness and the chill rains of solitude slowly nurtured his imagination.

But the rains could have done nothing at all for him without the sunshine that Wyeth's father provided. Newell Convers Wyeth was himself a brilliant artist; his illustrations for Robert Louis Stevenson and James Fenimore Cooper have enriched the imaginations of millions of children. And he knew how to give a warmly legendary air not only to literature but to everyday life as well. Given this inspiration, the boy spent his twelfth year with cardboard, scissors, and paint,

making a miniature theater and players for a performance of Arthur Conan Doyle's medieval romance, *The White Company*. The show, staged singlehanded for the family, opened the elder Wyeth's eyes. "Tomorrow morning," he told Andy, "you're going to start studying. Come into the studio."

Wyeth had the inestimable and increasingly rare advantage of learning his craft thoroughly while he was young. His father drilled him hardest in drawing, until the youth could report in sketch form the precise shape and feel of any object set before him. His health and spirits rose together with his growing abilities, so that something of the father's genial light came to shine in turn from the son.

Wyeth married, had two sons of his own, and settled into much the same pattern of life his father had led—painting at Chadds Ford, Pennsylvania, in the winter and at Cushing, Maine,

WYETH'S
"CHAMBERED NAUTILUS"
(1956)

in the summertime. But instead of taking his subject matter from the world of imagination, he paints only the people and places he knows best. Realistic art can be superficial, he reasons, only if the painter's response to what he is painting does not run very deep. "What the subject means is the important thing." *Young America*, for instance, is a straightforward representation of a Chadds Ford boy riding a shiny new bicycle—but there is something more. "Somehow he seemed to express a great deal about America," Wyeth says. "I thought to myself, 'Now he thinks his bicycle is wonderful, but in a year he'll earn enough to buy himself a car.' I was struck by the freedom he represented—by distances in this country, the plains of the Little Bighorn and Custer and Daniel Boone and a lot of other things. I was excited by the motion of the bicycle, too. The moving wheels were one of the most difficult things I ever painted."

Wyeth welcomes the kind of technical problems that almost any other painter would run from, and by mastering the small elements he confers authority on the large. "Just because something is tightly done doesn't mean anything," he explains, "but I feel that the more you get into the textures of things the less you have to clutter up the composition with a lot of props. When you lose simplicity you lose drama." The drama in *Chambered Nautilus* is characteristically simple, muted, and concerned with mortality. Wyeth's mother-in-law posed for the picture at seventy-two, when much weakened by disease. Her illness, Wyeth felt, had given her "a fleeting, youthful, timeless quality." This he brought out by contrasting the old lady's fine fragility with the massive, shiplike bed. And by filling the bed curtains with a faint breeze, he gave a sense of sailing into the unknown. Instead of symbolizing the unknown by means of darkness, Wyeth does it with the fog-blank light pressing through the window. Between the wicker basket, with its cargo of Bible and Christian Science reader, and the shell of a chambered nautilus, the coverlet softly flows like the tide.

"When I paint," Wyeth explains, "I try to obliterate Andy Wyeth." With pictures rich in concept and precise in execution, he succeeds far beyond his stated ambition. For in losing himself in his subject, Wyeth finds himself as an artist.

BECAUSE he bloomed so early, the greatest alumnus of the old Ashcan School, and died so young, the victim of sudden illness, George Bellows is usually thought of as a painter of an earlier generation. Actually, he was born in 1882, the same year as Edward Hopper, and, like Hopper, he is one of those who has carried the tradition of the late nineteenth-century masters into the present.

Bellows came of pioneer stock; an eighteenth-century ancestor founded the Vermont town of Bellows Falls. He grew up in a congenial, quietly prosperous family in Columbus, Ohio. At the state university he was a star shortstop and long-ball hitter. Young Bellows, strong, confident, genial, and direct, was the sort voted "most likely to succeed" in school yearbooks. Nobody would have taken him for an artist. Yet in 1904,

289

GEORGE BELLOWS' "STAG AT SHARKEY'S" (1907)

his junior year at college, Bellows made up his mind to become one. "What this world needs is art," he was to declare. "Art and more art." This conviction alone may have settled Bellows' career. Baseball, beer, and beauty were perhaps the foremost of his many enthusiasms. American life as he found it could assuage his appetite for the first two; the third he decided was in short supply, and resolved to replenish.

Accordingly, Bellows drew a small financial contribution from his reluctant parents, packed up some thoroughly amateurish drawings, and left for New York. His aim was to enroll under the banner of the great teacher Robert Henri, whose general views on life and art agreed with his own. Master and pupil, twenty years apart in

age, hit it off at once. Henri encouraged him not to fret over preliminary plans and sketches but to paint fast and forthrightly whatever moved his heart. This brought out Bellows' athletic instinct for timing and attack. He plunged into picture-making with a vigor to astonish even his fellow students, and became the rambunctious golden boy of Henri's class. Meanwhile he found he could support himself by weekend earnings from playing professional baseball and basketball. All sports fascinated him. He took to frequenting Tom Sharkey's boxing club, just across Lincoln Square from his studio. The sweaty and bloody struggles on club nights gave young Bellows the material for his first great picture, which made him a celebrity at once. No one ever painted a

290

BELLOWS' "CHILDREN ON THE PORCH" (1919)

BELLOWS' "GRAMERCY PARK" (1920)

BELLOWS' "AUNT FANNY" (1920)

better prize-fight canvas than *Stag at Sharkey's*. It is both brutally and beautifully true.

Along with boxing, Bellows painted memorable pictures of swimming, tennis, and polo. (He never tackled his own two favorite sports, baseball and basketball, which are notoriously difficult to paint.) Turning to landscape, he painted the Hudson River with a sweep and sparkle to put the historic Hudson River School painters in the shade. His New York cityscapes were as true to the tall, empurpled town as the best of the Ashcan School. And the great qualities of Bellows' art were self-evident; he was popular from the start. His elders generously welcomed the prodigy; he became the youngest member of the National Academy and also joined the Society of Independent Artists. Like Kuhn, he was among the organizers of the Armory Show; yet the exhibition had no perceptible effect on Bellows' own art. He was a bear for work, but not much interested in the work of others and too busy ever to travel abroad. He did some art teaching, and what he chiefly imparted to students was self-confidence. Doubts and subtleties were alien to Bellows; he settled for insights that came to him naturally.

Marriage and two beautiful daughters slowly mellowed his art. Like so many parents, Bellows came to feel the wistful intuition that children are as much a part of nature as they are part of a family, and he painted them so. His dreamily intent *Children on the Porch* might be birds of passage who have wandered in for a while from the dunes. His daughter Anne, in the foreground of Manhattan's Gramercy Park, seems almost a creature of sunshine.

In 1920, when Bellows was thirty-eight, he combined the dark vigor of his early style with the tenderness of his family canvases to paint the superb *Aunt Fanny*—a picture steeped in the love and awe that favorite aunts inspire. Elegant, indomitable, worn, and patient above all, Aunt Fanny waits for the painting and posing to be over and done with. This posing was by no means the first service she had performed for her nephew. While he was still in his baby carriage, she swore, she taught him to whistle. The story would be scarcely credible except that its hero always was in such a tearing hurry.

As things turned out, Bellows had reason to hurry, for all his robust health. At only forty-two, he died of a ruptured appendix.

WHAT have I to say to the young?" asked the poet Robert Frost, and then answered himself: "Just this: If you're looking for something to be brave about, consider the fine arts." Edward Hopper looked, and found them. Of much the same temperament as Frost, Hopper dedicates himself to his calling with the same deliberate and austere intensity.

Hopper feels closer to Thomas Eakins than to any other American predecessor, though he considers that "Eakins had much more humanity than I do." It is true that the people in Hopper's canvases are less individualized than the buildings, as if the artist wished not to intrude. His own unalterable reserve makes him as surprising, in an age of clattering egos, as a tree growing in the middle of Main Street. He is, as he himself admits, biting off the words, "a self-seeker."

Hopper's hard and lonely road into the self began at the town of Nyack, up the Hudson River from Manhattan. A bookish, gawky boy, he built his own sailboat at the age of twelve. "It didn't sail very well," he recalls laconically. "Kept heading into the wind." When he was seventeen, Hopper enrolled in Robert Henri's art classes, where he found the guiding philosophy agreeable but had trouble accommodating himself to Henri's dark and flamboyant technique. "The only real influence I've ever had," he says, "was myself." His classmate, George Bellows, headed a political faction called the "Strenuous Life Party." Hopper, all for peace and quiet, cast his lot with the "Simple Life Party." The strenuous young Bellows was headed for quick fame, Hopper for obscurity—and the really simple life.

In 1906 Hopper went to Paris to study. He kept to himself, sketching and painting along the Seine and in the parks. "I'd heard of Gertrude Stein," he recalls, "but I wasn't important enough for her to know me." The light and not the life of Paris was what took Hopper's eye: "The light was different from anything I had known. The shadows were luminous—more reflected light. Even under the bridges there was a certain luminosity. Maybe it's because the

EDWARD HOPPER'S "MANHATTAN BRIDGE LOOP" (1928)

294

HOPPER'S "EARLY SUNDAY MORNING" (1930)

HOPPER'S "NIGHT HAWKS" (1942)

clouds are lower there, just over the housetops, I've always been interested in light."

Light, in fact, is the protagonist in all of Hopper's art—not the soft, refulgent light of Paris, but America's clean glare slanting from high blue skies. *Manhattan Bridge Loop* and *Early Sunday Morning*, two of his first great pictures, play that relentless light across Hopper's preoccupation, the American scene. Archetypes of the commonplace, such masterpieces can sum up a thousand separate sights.

Before he was ready to create his archetypes, Hopper himself had to make an archetypical withdrawal into the desert—he took up commercial art. The advertising and publishing houses that bought his drawings of storybook characters "posturing and grimacing" were desert sands to him. "Sometimes I'd walk around the block a couple of times before I'd go in, wanting the job for money and at the same time hoping to hell I wouldn't get the lousy thing." His yearning was simply to "paint sunlight on the side of a house." But his oils lacked the gusto then in fashion. They betrayed an elaborate fear of the flourish. No one wanted them, and for a whole decade he practically ceased painting them. His empty easel was wasteland, and within himself, too, lay wilderness.

By the very fact of being so cut off from his mission, Hopper was able to bring it into being. Protected from the slow ravages of compromise —either with the public's taste or with his own immaturity—he developed his style invisibly along with his character. At last he produced

HOPPER'S "CAPE COD MORNING" (1950)

some etchings that had a wholly new quality, the quality of himself. This was his true beginning as an artist, for as he once said, "What lives in a painting is the personality of the painter." There followed a hesitant shower of equally personal water colors, and finally more oils. In 1924 he had his first one-man show of new work—which sold out. Marrying a girl who had also studied with Henri, Hopper shook the dust of commercial illustration from his feet and began, at forty-three, the career he was born for.

"Recognition doesn't mean so much," Hopper says. "You never get it when you need it." But unlike some more easily gained reputations, his own, once made, held fast. For upwards of thirty years Edward Hopper has held a place among the nation's most honored artists. For the past decade he has even known moderate prosperity. But the Hoppers still lead an astonishingly frugal life. Their Washington Square studio is a fourth-floor walk-up apartment, and their meals are of the lunch-counter sort. Everything in their life is geared to painting. When he is gestating a new picture, Hopper just goes to movies, wanders the streets, alone, tours the highways with his wife, or reads. "I like Emerson to read," he says, adding cautiously: "I guess."

One remark of Emerson's applies very well to Hopper's paintings: "In every work of genius we recognize our own rejected thoughts: they come back to us with a certain alienated majesty." Hopper's quality is of this kind. He paints not only what Americans have seen from the corners of their eyes, but also what they have dimly thought and felt about it all. *Night Hawks*, for example, is a stark equation, with brick, asphalt, night, and loneliness on the one hand, and light, food, and casual, quiet fellowship on the other. *Cape Cod Morning* brings together a traditional house, tender light, and a lonely lady. The clean, bare interior of *Rooms by the Sea* seems a fragile shell suspended against the elements. *Sunlight on Brownstones* balances blessings and blemishes: the golden light against the awkward stoops and the couple's youthfulness against their apparent apathy. Such everyday subjects are what Hopper chooses to make immutable and unforgettable on canvas. He stares with sober passion at the most ordinary things about America, sights that others take for granted. The fascination of his subject matter lies partly in the fact that much of it is man-made and common-man-made. It is the expression of human striving in all its loneliness, ugliness, and nobility.

Now in his seventies, Hopper expresses present American life with the heartfelt attachment of youth. The tradition he practices has nothing to do with convention; it involves no set approach and never stoops to slavish copying. He seldom sketches on the spot, and has not painted an oil direct from nature in fifteen years. Still, what he paints grows from what he sees. "I look all the time," he explains, "for something that suggests something to me. I think about it. Just to paint a representation or a design is not hard, but to express a thought in painting is. Thought is fluid. What you put on canvas is concrete, and it tends to direct the thought. The more you put on canvas the more you lose control of the thought. I've never been able to paint what I set out to paint."

What Hopper has been able to do is to open a new chapter in American realism. He presents common denominators in a somehow final way. The results can have the poignancy of familiar scenes witnessed for the very last time. "To me," he says, "the important thing is the sense of going on. You know how beautiful things are when you're traveling." To create that kind of beauty he uses paint reticently and flatly, giving his pictures a single overall surface, like a picture window. By suppressing all details that would not be noticed at a glance and by arranging his scene to suggest that it extends far beyond the frame, he puts his picture window in motion. Looking at his paintings is like drifting past people's backyards on a slow local, in a state of intimate awareness. Slowly the train glides on, through dreams and decades. The tall, stooped conductor keeps silent. In silence he gestures toward the windows, and America beyond.

It is a changing scene that Hopper shows, as it was for Eakins, Copley, and for all the country's greatest painters. Rising to the challenges of continual change, American art has been a running accompaniment to the nation's history. For change and progress are the stuff of life, especially in America. And life itself, especially in America, is the heart and soul of painting.

HOPPER'S "SUNLIGHT ON BROWNSTONES" (1956)

HOPPER'S "ROOMS BY THE SEA" (1951)

ONE HUNDRED COLLECTIONS

OF

AMERICAN PAINTING

The following guide is limited to permanent collections of American painting open to the public. All contain a number of paintings by artists whose work is included in this book. Many more collections, both public and private, own some American works, and most museums, galleries, and universities have, in addition, periodic loan exhibitions of American art.

ARIZONA

TEMPE

The Arizona State College Collection of American Art has all of its 93 paintings permanently on display in the Matthews Library. Beginning with portraits by the early limners, the collection includes works from most periods and schools of American painting. Of special interest are Stuart's *Mrs. Stephen Peabody*, Audubon's *The Otter and the Salmon*, Inness' *Late Afternoon, Montclair, N.J.*, Ryder's *The Canal*, Demuth's *A Sky After El Greco*. Hours: 8 to 10 Monday through Friday; 8 to 5 Saturday; 2 to 5 Sunday.

TUCSON

The University of Arizona Art Gallery normally has about half of its collection of 169 American paintings on view. The collection begins with the late 19th century but is particularly strong in paintings of the 1930s and 1940s. Hours: 10 to 5 Monday through Saturday; 2 to 5 Sunday.

CALIFORNIA

LOS ANGELES

The Los Angeles County Museum owns 748 paintings by American artists, of which about 150 are usually on view. The 19th and 20th century painters are well represented, especially the realists and impressionists of the late 19th century. Outstanding pictures are Cole's *River Scene*, Homer's *Lost on the Grand Banks* and *After the Hunt*, and Bellows' *Cliff Dwellers*. Hours: 10 to 5 Tuesday through Sunday. Closed Monday.

PASADENA

The Pasadena Art Museum has some 350 paintings by American artists in its permanent collection, of which about 20 are generally on view. Although the collection is principally devoted to the work of 20th century painters working in Southern California, it also contains fine minor examples of 19th century and other 20th century artists. A group of 10 water colors by Feininger is of special interest. Hours: 10 to 5 Tuesday through Saturday; until 9 Friday evening; 2 to 5 Sunday. Closed Monday and holidays.

SAN DIEGO

The Fine Arts Gallery owns about 100 paintings by American artists, of which about 40 are usually on view. Its best

pictures are from the late 19th and 20th centuries, including works by Homer, Johnson, Henri, Cassatt. Hours: 10 to 5 Tuesday through Saturday; 1 to 5:30 Sunday. Closed Monday and during September.

SAN FRANCISCO

The California Palace of the Legion of Honor owns 153 American paintings, with contemporary painters best represented. Among its best known works are Harnett's *After the Hunt* and Benton's *Susanna and the Elders*. Hours: 10 to 5 daily.

M. H. de Young Memorial Museum has approximately 350 paintings by American artists in its permanent collection, of which about 100 are usually on view. The strength of the collection is in the 19th century, with early California painters well represented. Of special interest are Vanderlyn's *Marius Amidst the Ruins of Carthage*, which won Napoleon's Gold Medal in 1808, and Cole's *Evening in the White Mountains*. Hours: 10 to 5 daily.

The San Francisco Museum of Art owns about 400 American paintings, of which at least 10 are always on view. Most of the collection's American paintings are by Bay Area artists, and Kingman is represented by 14 water colors. Apart from local artists, the chief strength of the collection lies in works from 1930 to the present. Hours: 12 to 5 Monday; 12 to 10 Tuesday through Saturday; 1 to 5 Sunday and holidays.

SANTA BARBARA

The Santa Barbara Museum of Art usually has on view about 25 paintings from its American collection. Although some of the paintings date from the 18th and 19th centuries, the collection is strongest in 20th century works, including Weber's *Winter Twilight* and Kuniyoshi's *Weathervane and Sofa*. Hours: 11 to 5 Tuesday through Saturday; 12 to 5 Sunday. Closed Monday.

COLORADO

COLORADO SPRINGS

The Colorado Springs Fine Arts Center has about 100 American pictures, mostly contemporary, in its permanent collection, and always has at least 10 on view. The collection includes the work of Dove, Hartley, Marin, Graves, and 22 paintings by Kuhn. Its most important single picture is Kuhn's *Trio*. Hours: 9 to 5 Tuesday through Saturday; 1:30 to 5 Sunday. Closed Monday from September until June.

DENVER

The Denver Art Museum owns about 150 American paintings, ranging from an early portrait by Copley to Marin, but is strongest in contemporary works. Until its building program is completed, the museum has inadequate room to show its collection, but American paintings may usually be seen in the contemporary galleries of the South Wing. Hours: 9 to 5 Tuesday through Saturday; 2 to 5 Sunday; 2 to 5 and 7 to 9 Monday. No evening hours during July and August.

CONNECTICUT

HARTFORD

The 114-year-old Wadsworth Atheneum has about 1,000 American pictures, from Copley's *Mrs. Seymour Fort* to Shahn's *Vacant Lot*. Some 200 are on view most of the time. The collection is strong in 18th century works, including those of Smibert, West, Stuart, Trumbull, and Earl, and has fine coverage of the Hudson River School. It also has good 20th century examples (Sloan, Davis, Blume, Hopper, Glackens, Marin). Hours: 12 to 5 Tuesday through Friday; 9 to 5 Saturday; 2 to 5 Sunday. Closed Monday and major holidays.

LITCHFIELD

The Litchfield Historical Society owns 65 paintings by American artists, plus 32 miniatures. The miniatures and 35 of the paintings are always on view. The collection is best known for its 10 portraits and 1 landscape by Earl. Hours: June to September, 2:30 to 5:30 Monday through Saturday, except Thursday 11 to 1. Closed Sunday. October through May, 11 to 1 and 2:30 to 5:30 Thursday only.

NEW BRITAIN

The Art Museum of New Britain Institute is devoted entirely to American paintings, of which it owns about 400, with about 300 on view at all times. The collection represents all periods of American painting, starting with Smibert and anonymous itinerant painters. It is particularly strong in the works of the late 19th century painters, of the Ashcan School, and of contemporaries (including the *Arts of Life in America*, murals painted by Benton for the Whitney Museum). Hours: 2 to 5:30 Tuesday through Sunday. Closed Monday and major holidays.

NEW HAVEN

The Yale University Art Gallery has more than 1,450 paintings by American artists. About 200, including miniatures, are usually on view in the gallery, and another 500 are normally on display in university buildings. The collection includes works from 1670 to the present, but is particularly strong in the 18th and early 19th centuries. Copley, West, C. W. Peale, and Stuart are all well represented, and Yale owns the world's largest and finest collection of the works of Trumbull, including his *Declaration of Independence*, *Capture of the Hessians at Trenton*, and some 60 miniatures painted from life as studies for later paintings. Other outstanding works are Smibert's 1729 painting of Bishop Berkeley and his entourage and Earl's portrait of Roger Sherman. Hours: 10 to 5 Tuesday through Saturday; 2 to 5 Sunday. Closed Monday.

NEW LONDON

The Lyman Allyn Museum owns 155 paintings by American artists, with about 50 on view the year round. The collection includes some 18th century works, but is strongest in 19th century landscapists and other painters of the period. Hours: 1 to 5 Tuesday through Saturday; 2 to 5 Sunday. Closed Monday.

DELAWARE

WINTERTHUR

The Henry Francis duPont Winterthur Museum is a 100-room mansion restored and furnished to show how Americans lived at different periods from 1640 to 1840. Its 300 paintings, chosen primarily to fit in a particular setting, include works by early New York Dutch, New England, and Southern painters, as well as paintings by Copley, C.W. and Rembrandt Peale, Vanderlyn, and Stuart. Tours for up to 60 visitors a day on written application Tuesday through Saturday. Closed Sunday, Monday, and major holidays. Twenty museum rooms and the DuPont gardens open without advance reservations Tuesday through Saturday during the last week in April and the first 4 weeks in May.

DISTRICT OF COLUMBIA

WASHINGTON

The Corcoran Gallery of Art owns 450 American paintings, of which about 250 are usually on view. The collection covers the period 1700-1957 with important examples by most of the foremost painters. It excels in early 19th century painting, including Morse's *The Old House of Representatives* and outstanding examples of the Hudson River School. It is also strong in late 19th century works. Hours: 10 to 4:30 Tuesday through Friday; 9 to 4:30 Saturday; 2 to 5 Sunday. Closed Monday and major holidays.

The American paintings in the Freer Gallery of Art of the Smithsonian Institution were collected by Charles Lang Freer. Three of his favorite artists are exceptionally well represented: Whistler by 133 paintings, Tryon by 72 paintings (including *Springtime*), and Thayer by 16 paintings (including *The Virgin*). Hours: 9 to 4:30 daily.

The National Collection of Fine Arts of the Smithsonian Institution includes about 800 American paintings, of which some 400 are always on display. The collection covers the 18th and 19th centuries and is richest in late 19th century paintings, especially the works of Ryder (18 oils) and Thayer (25 oils). Hours: 9 to 4:30 daily.

The National Gallery of Art of the Smithsonian Institution owns 335 paintings by American artists. About 110 American paintings, from the collection or on loan, are usually on display. The gallery owns 184 American primitive paintings, the gift of Edgar William and Bernice Chrysler Garbisch. Early portraitists are well represented, particularly Stuart (with 36 paintings, including *The Skater* and the Vaughan *Washington*) and Sully (with 16, including *Lady with a Harp: Eliza Ridgely*). Other outstanding works include West's *Guy Johnson*, Ryder's *Siegfried and the Rhine Maidens*, Cassatt's *The Boating Party*, and Homer's *Right and Left* and *Breezing Up*. Hours: 10 to 5 Monday through Saturday; 2 to 10 Sunday. Closed Christmas and New Year's Day.

The Phillips Collection contains more than 1,000 American paintings, of which about 60 are usually on view. The collection is strongest in works of the 20th century, in keeping with the founder's aim to create a "museum of modern art and its sources." Among the painters represented by several works are Avery, Burchfield, Dove, O'Keeffe, Gatch

(*Industrial Night*), Hartley, Knaths, Marin (*Spring No. 1*), Prendergast, Ryder, and Sloan (*Wake of the Ferry*). Hours: 11 to 6 Monday through Saturday; 2 to 7 Sunday and holidays. Closed July 4, Labor Day, and Christmas.

The United States Capitol art collection includes 161 American paintings, all usually on view. Portraits by Copley, C. W. Peale and Rembrandt Peale, Stuart, Vanderlyn, and Sully are hung there as well as 8 large historical paintings in the rotunda (4 of them by Trumbull, 1 by Vanderlyn). Hours: 9 to 4:30 daily. Closed Thanksgiving, Christmas, and New Year's Day.

The United States National Museum of the Smithsonian Institution owns about 450 oil paintings of the West by Catlin, including all those appearing in this book. At least 25, often more, are usually on view. Hours: 9 to 4:30 daily. Closed Christmas.

FLORIDA

WEST PALM BEACH

The Norton Gallery and School of Art owns about 150 American paintings. The collection includes scattered examples from Copley on, but its main strength lies in its fine group of 20th century works. Hours: 10 to 5 Tuesday through Saturday; 1:30 to 5:30 Sunday. Closed Monday and holidays.

GEORGIA

ATHENS

The Eva Underhill Holbrook Collection of the University of Georgia's Georgia Museum of Art includes 327 paintings by Americans from Morse and the Hudson River School to the moderns, of which about 60 are usually on display. Hours: 9 to 5:30 Monday through Friday; 9 to noon Saturday. Closed Sunday.

ATLANTA

The Atlanta Art Association's High Museum of Art owns 250 American paintings, of which about 100 are usually on view in the new galleries. Emphasis is on 19th century and contemporary art. Hours: 10 to 9 Tuesday; 10 to 5 Wednesday through Saturday; 2 to 6 Sunday. Closed Monday, Thanksgiving, and Christmas.

ILLINOIS

CHICAGO

The Art Institute of Chicago owns about 300 oils and 300 water colors by American artists, of which about 75 are generally on view. The collection covers all periods and styles from the mid-18th century to the present. Outstanding are groups of several dozen water colors each by Homer and Marin, a good collection of Demuths and Prendergasts, as well as a number of oils by Inness. Important recent pictures: Wood's *American Gothic*, Curry's *Hogs Killing a Rattlesnake*, Hopper's *Night Hawks*, Levine's *Trial*, De Kooning's *Excavation*, Pollock's *Grayed Rainbow*. Hours: 9 to 5 Monday through Saturday; 12 to 5 Sunday and holidays.

URBANA

The University of Illinois owns approximately 150 paintings by American artists, about 15 of which usually hang in the corridors of the Architecture Building; others may be seen in the continuous gallery exhibitions in the same building. The American collection is particularly strong in the contemporary field. Hours: 9 to 5 Monday through Saturday; 2 to 5 Sunday.

INDIANA

INDIANAPOLIS

The John Herron Art Institute owns 364 paintings by American artists, with about 45 always on view. Indiana painting is emphasized, but many painters of national importance, from Copley to Wyeth, are represented. Hours: 9 to 5 Tuesday through Saturday; 1 to 6 Sunday. Closed Monday.

IOWA

DES MOINES

The Des Moines Art Center owns more than 100 paintings by Americans, of which 25 are usually on view. The collection is strongest in 20th century works, including *Aunt Fanny* by Bellows and *Amazing Juggler* by Kuniyoshi. Hours: 11 to 5 Tuesday through Saturday; until 9 Thursday evening; 1 to 6 Sunday. Closed Monday.

KANSAS

WICHITA

Most of the American paintings in the Wichita Art Museum are in the Roland P. Murdock Collection, of which 70 are usually on display. Painters from Feke onward are represented, but the collection is strongest in Marin, Sloan, Hopper, Kuniyoshi, Prendergast. Hours: 10 to 5 Tuesday through Saturday; 1 to 5 Sunday. Closed Monday.

LOUISIANA

NEW ORLEANS

The Isaac Delgado Museum of Art owns more than 100 paintings by American artists, most of which are on view at some time during the year. The collection is strongest in early 19th century pictures, especially those associated with the life of Louisiana, and in post-World War II works. Hours: 12 to 5 Monday through Saturday; 1 to 6 Sunday. Closed Mardi Gras, Thanksgiving, and Christmas.

MAINE

BRUNSWICK

The Walker Art Museum at Bowdoin College usually has close to 50 American paintings on view. The collection is particularly interesting for its early works, including 5 portraits of the Bowdoin family by Feke, and 7 Stuarts. Hours: 10 to noon and 2 to 4 Monday through Saturday; 2 to 4 Sunday and holidays. During July and August, 9 to 1 and 2 to 4 Monday through Saturday; 2 to 4 Sunday. Closed major holidays.

MARYLAND

BALTIMORE

The Baltimore Museum of Art owns 265 American paintings, of which about 40 are usually on view. The collection is broad historically, ranging from a number of early portraits by the Peales and Hesselius to a wide sampling of moderns. Hours: during the winter, 2 to 5 and 8 to 11 Tuesday; 10 to 5 Wednesday through Saturday; 2 to 6 Sunday. Closed Monday. During the summer, 11 to 5 Tuesday through Saturday; 2 to 6 Sunday. Closed Monday.

The Walters Art Gallery owns some 265 American paintings, with up to a dozen usually on view. Outstanding are 200 water colors of the West by Miller. Hours: 11 to 5 Monday through Saturday; 2 to 5 Sunday.

MASSACHUSETTS

AMHERST

The Amherst College Art Collection, housed in the Mead Art Building, where the paintings are exhibited in rotation, contains some 350 American paintings. The collection is strongest in the early portrait painters (including Copley, Stuart, Sully) and in the landscapists of the 19th century. Hours: 9 to 5 Monday through Saturday; 11:30 to 5 Sunday. Closed holidays. Summer admission by application to the college guide.

ANDOVER

The Addison Gallery of American Art collection at Phillips Academy includes about 300 oils and water colors, with the paintings rotated for display. The collection is well balanced historically, from colonial days (Copley, West) to the present (Hartley, Marin, Pollock, and living artists). Among the outstanding paintings: *Eight Bells* by Homer, *Coming Storm* by Inness, *The Spielers* by Luks, *Manhattan Bridge Loop* by Hopper. Hours: 9 to 5 Monday through Saturday; 2:30 to 5 Sunday.

BOSTON

The Isabella Stewart Gardner Museum owns 190 paintings by Americans, all usually on view. Outstanding is the group of 28 paintings by Sargent, which includes *El Jaleo* and many of his water colors. Hours: 10 to 4 Tuesday, Thursday, and Saturday; 2 to 5 Sunday; until 10 the first Thursday evening of each month. Closed Monday, Wednesday, Friday, holidays, and during August.

The Massachusetts Historical Society owns about 300 American paintings, of which 80 are usually on exhibition. Early portraits include the work of Smibert, Copley, Trumbull, Stuart, Harding, and Sully, and the portrait of Ann Pollard by an anonymous limner. Hours: 9 to 4:45 Monday through Friday. Closed Saturday and Sunday. October through May, closed the second Thursday of the month.

The Museum of Fine Arts owns some 1,200 oils and 600 water colors by American artists, with about 250 usually on view. The collection excels in 18th century portrait painters and has the nation's largest group of paintings by Copley (46) and Stuart (50). It also includes the Karolik Collection of 232 paintings of the period 1815 to 1865, and important works by Allston, Homer, and Sargent. Among the museum's masterpieces: Copley's *Paul Revere* and *Brook Watson and the Shark*, Allston's *Moonlit Landscape*, Cassatt's *At the Opera* and *A Cup of Tea*, Sargent's *Daughters of Edward D. Boit*. Hours: 10 to 5 Tuesday through Saturday; until 10 Wednesday evening; 1:30 to 5:30 Sunday. Closed Monday and holidays.

CAMBRIDGE

The Fogg Art Museum at Harvard adjusts its exhibition program to the university curriculum, but tries to keep one gallery for American art, where at least 10 or 12 pictures are always on view. Its collection of some 2,500 paintings represents almost every period of American art, with emphasis on Copley (20 oils), Whistler (16 oils and 5 water colors), Sargent (13 oils and 19 water colors), Homer (2 oils and 21 water colors), and Hassam (4 oils and 11 water colors). Hours: 9 to 5 Monday through Saturday. Closed Sunday and holidays, on Saturday during the summer, and for 3 weeks in late August and early September.

NORTHAMPTON

The Smith College Museum of Art owns 200 American paintings, of which about 30 are generally on view. The collection covers major styles and trends from the 18th century to the present. The late 19th century is strongly represented, including most of the major artists of the day. Hours: 9 to 5 Monday through Saturday; 2:30 to 4:30 Sunday during the academic year. Closed Thanksgiving and Christmas.

PITTSFIELD

The Berkshire Museum has 106 American paintings in its permanent collection, of which 45 are usually on view. The collection is strongest in the 19th century and includes the landscapists Cole, Durand, Bierstadt, Church, Inness, Blakelock. Hours: 10 to 5 Tuesday through Saturday; 2 to 5 Sunday. Closed Monday and holidays.

SALEM

The Essex Institute owns more than 400 American paintings, of which about 70 are usually on view in the portrait gallery. Portraits of New Englanders from the mid-17th century to the end of the 19th century make up the bulk of the collection, which includes a number of Smiberts and Greenwoods. Hours: 9 to 4:30 Tuesday through Saturday; 2 to 5 Sunday and holidays. Closed Monday and July 4, Thanksgiving, and Christmas.

SPRINGFIELD

The Springfield Museum of Fine Arts owns some 350 American paintings, of which 85 are usually on view. The largest part of the collection is contemporary, but it includes a sizable group of late 19th century works, among them Field's *Monument of the American Republic*. Hours: 1 to 5 Tuesday through Saturday; 2 to 5 Sunday. Closed Monday.

WILLIAMSTOWN

The Sterling and Francine Clark Art Institute owns 25 American paintings, of which at least 15 are usually on view. Of special interest: a Stuart *Washington*, 12 Sargents, and 7 fine Homers. Hours: 10 to 5 Tuesday through Sunday. Closed Monday.

WORCESTER

The Worcester Art Museum owns some 400 American paintings, of which about 125 are usually on view. Best represented are the years 1750-1830 and 1890-1910. Among the standouts are Smith's late 17th century self-portrait, 16 water colors by Homer, and a rare early landscape, *Looking East from Denny Hill*, by Earl. Hours: 10 to 5 Monday through Saturday; 2 to 5 Sunday and holidays.

MICHIGAN

BLOOMFIELD HILLS

The Galleries of the Cranbrook Academy of Art own 85 paintings by American artists, of which about 15 are usually on view. The collection concentrates on the 20th century, but includes paintings dating back to West. Among its landscapes are Cole's *Niagara Falls*, Blakelock's *Deepening Shadows*, and Inness' *Summer*. Hours: April through October, 2 to 5 Tuesday through Sunday. Closed Monday. November through March, 2 to 5 weekends only.

DETROIT

The Detroit Institute of Arts has some 740 paintings by American artists in its permanent collection, of which about 200 are usually on view. The collection shows the whole development of American painting with examples by most leading American painters from colonial times to the present. Among them: C. W. Peale's *Lamplight Portrait*, Rembrandt Peale's *Court of Death*, Allston's *Flight of Florimell*,

Mount's *Banjo Player*, Whistler's *Falling Rocket*, Tobey's *San Francisco Street*. Hours: 1 to 10 Tuesday through Friday; 9 to 6 Saturday and Sunday. July and August, 9 to 6 Tuesday through Sunday. Closed Monday and holidays.

MINNESOTA

MINNEAPOLIS

The Minneapolis Institute of Arts owns 155 paintings by American artists, of which at least 30 are always on view. The collection is strongest in paintings from the colonial period (Copley's *Mrs. Nathaniel Allen*) and the late 19th century. Hours: 12 to 9 Tuesday through Friday; 10 to 5 Saturday; 2 to 6 Sunday and holidays. Closed Monday.

The Walker Art Center owns about 165 American paintings, with about 60 generally on view. Although some 19th century painters are represented, the collection concentrates on 20th century works, including Davis' *Colonial Cubism*, Hofmann's *Elegy*, Sloan's *South Beach Bathers*, Weber's *Woman Carrying Picture*. Hours: 10 to 10 Tuesday, Wednesday, Thursday; 10 to 5 Friday and Saturday; 12 to 6 Sunday. Closed Monday.

MISSOURI

KANSAS CITY

The William Rockhill Nelson Gallery of Art and the Atkins Museum of Fine Arts (combined in one building) have 269 American paintings dating back to Copley and West. The 19th century is best represented, though the 20th century collection is growing. Of special interest: 11 paintings by Bingham, Missouri's earliest painter of note. Hours: 1 to 5 Tuesday through Saturday; 2 to 6 Sunday; until 10 Thursday evening, October through May. Closed Monday and major holidays.

ST. LOUIS

The City Art Museum of St. Louis owns 265 oil paintings by American artists, of which 140 are usually on view. The collection has good examples of most American periods and styles, but emphasizes 19th century artists of the region, such as Bingham (11 paintings) and Wimar (19). Outstanding pictures include Bingham's *The Wood-Boat* and Greenwood's *Sea Captains Carousing at Surinam*. Hours: 10 to 5 Tuesday through Sunday; 2:30 to 9:30 Monday. Closed Christmas and New Year's Day.

MONTANA

GREAT FALLS

The C. M. Russell Gallery has 70 paintings by Russell in its collection, nearly all on permanent display. Hours: during the summer, 10 to 4 Tuesday through Saturday; 1 to 4:30 Sunday. Closed Monday. During the winter, 2 to 4:30 Tuesday, Thursday, Saturday, Sunday only.

HELENA

The Historical Society of Montana's New State Museum at Helena specializes in Western Americana and includes about 100 paintings and sculptures by Russell. Hours: during the summer, 7 to 6 daily. During the winter, 8 to 5 Monday through Friday; Saturday and Sunday afternoons.

NEBRASKA

LINCOLN

The University of Nebraska Art Galleries contain about 350 paintings by American artists, with between 50 and 75

usually on display, chiefly in Morrill Hall but also in other university buildings. The collection, largely limited to 20th century works, is strongest in the romantic realism of the mid-1930s and the abstract expressionism of the mid-1950s. Morrill Hall hours: 8 to 5 Monday through Saturday; 5 to 10 Tuesday and Thursday evenings, October through May; 2 to 5 Sunday and holidays.

OMAHA

The Joslyn Art Museum owns more than 350 paintings by American artists, of which 50 or more are usually on view. The museum is adding to its paintings from earlier periods of American history, is at present strongest in regional paintings and works from the 1920s to the present day. Hours: 10 to 5 Tuesday through Saturday; 2 to 6 Sunday. Closed Monday and holidays.

NEW HAMPSHIRE

HANOVER

The Carpenter Gallery of Art at Dartmouth College owns 300 paintings by American artists, of which some 150 are generally on view in the gallery and in other college buildings. Some 18th and 19th century painters are represented (among them: Stuart, Morse, Vanderlyn, Remington, Healy, Inness, Eakins), but the collection is strongest in works of the 20th century, including a fine group of Sloans. Hours: 2 to 5 daily, except holidays and during school vacations, when admission can be arranged upon application to the art department.

NEW JERSEY

MONTCLAIR

The Montclair Art Museum owns about 250 American paintings, which are rotated so that nearly all are shown during the year. The collection includes a fine group of Innesses and one painting from each member of the Ashcan School. Hours: 10 to 5 Tuesday through Saturday; 2 to 5:30 Sunday. Closed Monday and during July and August.

NEWARK

The Newark Museum shows about 150 American paintings each year from its own collection, which includes works by leading painters from the 18th through the mid-20th centuries. It is strong in 19th century landscapes, including several each by Durand, Bierstadt, and Inness. Among the moderns, it owns 5 Stellas, including *The Bridge*. Hours: 12 to 5:30 Monday through Saturday; 7 to 9:30 Wednesday and Thursday evenings; 2 to 6 Sunday. During the summer, 12 to 5 Monday through Saturday. Closed July 4, Thanksgiving, and Christmas.

NEW YORK

BUFFALO

The Albright Art Gallery owns 179 American paintings, of which about 50 are usually on view. Although the gallery is strongest in 20th century works (including Shahn's *Spring*, Burchfield's *Sun and Rocks*, De Kooning's *Gotham News*), the collection is fairly comprehensive and dates back to Stuart. Hours: 10 to 5 Tuesday through Saturday; 2 to 6 Sunday and Monday.

CANAJOHARIE

The Canajoharie Library and Art Gallery owns some 230 American paintings, of which 30 are usually on view. The collection includes a scattering of early and contemporary works, but it is strongest in the late 19th and early

20th centuries (including 19 paintings by Homer). Hours: 10 to 5:15 Monday through Friday; 7 to 9 Monday evening; 10 to 2 Saturday. Closed Sunday.

COOPERSTOWN

The New York State Historical Association owns about 250 American paintings, of which 90 are generally on view in Fenimore House. Its major collection of American folk art includes *General Putnam's Leap* and *The Murder of Jane McCrea*. The collection also has a large group of portraits of New York State leaders, genre paintings and landscapes, many of them of the Hudson River School. Hours: during the summer, 9 to 6 daily. During the winter, 9 to 5 daily. Closed Thanksgiving, Christmas, and New Year's Day.

KINGSTON

The Senate House Museum collection of American paintings is especially interesting for its portraits and landscapes by Vanderlyn, Kingston's native son. About 50 of his works are always on view. Hours: 9 to 5 Monday through Saturday; 1 to 5 Sunday.

NEW YORK CITY

The Brooklyn Museum's American painting collection consists of about 450 oils and 180 water colors. About 275 are always on view, making it the only historically comprehensive American painting collection in New York City on permanent display. It includes an excellent group of early colonial portraits, with Feke and C. W. Peale well represented, a strong sampling of 19th century painters, especially the Hudson River School, Sargent, Ryder (including his *Grazing Horse*), Homer, Eakins, the Ashcan School, and contemporary works. Hours: 10 to 5 Monday through Saturday; 1 to 5 Sunday and holidays.

City Hall, noted also for its pure colonial architecture, houses more than 100 portraits by American painters, including 13 by Trumbull, 5 by Vanderlyn, 5 by Inman, 2 by Sully, and 3 by Morse, notably his *Marquis de Lafayette*. Hours: 9 to 5 Monday through Saturday. Closed Sunday.

The Cooper Union Museum for the Arts of Decoration owns about 230 paintings by Americans, including 20 landscapes by Homer, a few portraits by early American painters, and some 200 landscape sketches by Church. About 20 paintings are usually on view. Hours: 10 to 5 daily; until 9 Tuesday and Thursday evenings, October through April. Closed Saturday (during the summer) and holidays.

Although its display space for American painting is limited, the Metropolitan Museum of Art owns more than 3,000 oils and water colors by Americans, dating back to the early limners. West, Copley, Stuart, and later portraitists are well represented. Bingham's *Fur Traders Descending the Missouri* is an outstanding example of the mid-19th century painters of the West. Homer is represented by 15 oils (including *Gulf Stream* and *Prisoners from the Front* and a number of water colors), Eakins by 7 oils (including *Max Schmitt in a Single Scull*), Sargent by more than 100 water colors and 13 oils (including *Mme. X*), Marin by 60 water colors. In recent years the collection of contemporary works has been greatly increased, and a number of newly renovated galleries show part of the collection. Hours: 10 to 5 Monday through Saturday; 1 to 5 Sunday and holidays.

The Museum of Modern Art owns approximately 600 20th century paintings by Americans, though only about 30 can be shown regularly because of limited gallery space. Among the painters best represented are Prendergast, Dove, Feininger, Marin, Hartley, Davis, Shahn, Blume, Burchfield, Hopper, Gorky, Bloom, Matta, and Baziotes (including his *Pompeii*). The museum also owns Sterne's *After the Rain*, Motherwell's *Western Air*, De Kooning's *Woman 1*, Levine's *Election Night*. Hours: 11 to 6 Monday through Saturday; 1 to 7 Sunday.

The New-York Historical Society owns more than 2,000 American paintings, mostly early portraits. Some 500 of them, including miniatures, are on permanent exhibition, as well as about 25 from the society's collection of 500 water color drawings by Audubon for his *Birds of America*. Early Dutch colonial painters are well represented, as well as C. W. and Rembrandt Peale, Mount, Trumbull, Inman, Cole, and Durand. Notable pictures: C. W. Peale's *The Peale Family*, the five-picture series by Cole called *The Course of Empire*, *Wild Turkey* by Audubon. Hours: 1 to 5 Tuesday through Sunday. Closed Monday and during August.

The Solomon R. Guggenheim Museum owns about 300 American paintings of the 20th century which are shown in regular exhibitions. Paintings of the '40s and '50s are well represented by De Kooning, Pollock, Gottlieb, Kline, and others; a group of Feiningers dates back to 1911 and includes *Gelmeroda No. 4*. Hours: 10 to 6 Tuesday through Saturday; 12 to 6 Sunday and holidays. Closed Monday.

The Whitney Museum of American Art has some 800 20th century paintings in its permanent collection, of which about 250 are generally on view. Most modern American painters of importance are included, with Bellows, Hartley, Sloan, Sheeler, Burchfield, and Hopper particularly well represented. Among the museum's major works: Hopper's *Early Sunday Morning*, Sloan's *Backyards, Greenwich Village*, Demuth's *My Egypt*, Levine's *Gangster Funeral*. Hours: 1 to 5 daily. Closed July 4, Thanksgiving, and Christmas.

OGDENSBURG

The Remington Art Memorial contains hundreds of Remington's oils, water colors, sketches, and bronzes left in his study after his death. Hours: 2 to 5 Monday through Saturday. Closed Sunday and holidays.

POUGHKEEPSIE

Vassar College owns about 200 American paintings, some of which are always on view in the Art Gallery and in other college buildings. Church, Inness, and Ryder are well represented, and such contemporaries as Marin (by 5 water colors). Gallery hours: 8:30 to 5 Monday through Saturday; 2:30 to 5 Sunday.

ROCHESTER

The Rochester Memorial Art Gallery of the University of Rochester owns about 325 American paintings, which are rotated so that about 60 are usually on view. The collection covers the main trends in American art from the pioneer portraitists to the abstract expressionists, and includes 1 Copley, 2 Stuarts, and from the 19th century an early industrial commission: Catlin's *Shooting Flamingoes* (ordered by the Colt Firearms Co.). Hours: 10 to 5 Monday through Saturday; 2 to 5:30 Sunday.

STONY BROOK

The permanent collection of the Suffolk Museum numbers 500 paintings, including 30 by Mount, Stony Brook's lifetime resident, which are permanently on view in a gallery devoted to his works. Hours: mid-March through December, 10 to 5:30 Wednesday through Sunday. Closed Monday and Tuesday.

UTICA

The Munson-Williams-Proctor Institute owns more than 450 American paintings, about 40 of which are usually on display. The collection excels in 20th century painting and includes a few early American examples. Hours: 10 to 10 Monday through Friday; 10 to 6 Saturday; 2 to 6 Sunday.

YONKERS

Philipse Manor Hall houses 67 American paintings, mainly portraits of U.S. Presidents from Washington to Coolidge. Painters include West, Copley, Stuart, C. W. and Rembrandt Peale, Morse, Vanderlyn. Hours: 9 to 5 Monday through Saturday; 1 to 5 Sunday. Closed on major holidays.

OHIO

CINCINNATI

The Cincinnati Art Museum owns about 700 paintings by American artists. About 130 American paintings are usually on exhibition. The late 19th and early 20th centuries are best represented, with 2 to 6 examples each by Johnson, Inness, Cassatt, Whistler, Sargent, Homer, and Hassam. Hours: 10 to 5 Monday through Saturday; 2 to 5 Sunday. Closed Thanksgiving and Christmas.

CLEVELAND

The Cleveland Museum of Art owns 205 oils by American painters (plus a sizable group of works by local artists), about half of which are usually on view. The collection includes such early painters as Feke, Smibert, Hesselius; Ryder's *The Race Track;* Bellows' *Stag at Sharkey's;* and a comprehensive group of contemporary painters. Hours: 9 to 5 Monday through Saturday; until 10 Wednesday and Friday evenings, October through May; 1 to 6 Sunday.

COLUMBUS

The Columbus Gallery of Fine Arts owns some 300 American paintings, of which 100 are usually on view. Although there is a good sampling of 19th century work, the collection is strongest in 20th century paintings. Bellows is represented in his home town by 13 of his works. The collection also includes a number of paintings by Prendergast, Hartley, and Marin. Hours: noon to 5 daily; 7 to 10 Friday evening.

TOLEDO

The Toledo Museum of Art owns about 300 oils and water colors by American artists, of which 130 are usually on view. The collection ranges from the art of early colonial days (Smibert, Feke, Greenwood) to contemporary. The late 19th century is well represented by 6 Innesses and several Sargents and Homers. Hours: 9 to 5 Tuesday through Saturday; 1 to 5 Sunday, Monday, and holidays.

YOUNGSTOWN

The Butler Institute of American Art owns more than 750 paintings by American artists, of which about 300 are on permanent display. Beginning with portraits by Copley, Earl, and Stuart, the collection represents all periods of American painting. Among the best known pictures: Homer's *Snap the Whip*, Sloan's *Recruiting, Union Square,* Hopper's *Pennsylvania Coal Town.* Hours: noon to 5 Tuesday through Saturday; 1 to 5 Sunday. Closed Monday.

OKLAHOMA

TULSA

The Thomas Gilcrease Institute of American History and Art owns more than 3,000 American paintings, of which

200 are usually on view. The collection begins with colonial painters, including Smibert, Feke, and Copley, and includes most major 19th century artists, but its Western works are outstanding (several hundred by Catlin, 130 by Cross, 81 by Remington, a number by Russell, Leigh, Bierstadt, Blakelock, Miller). Hours: 9 to 5 Monday through Saturday; 1 to 5 Sunday and holidays.

OREGON

PORTLAND

The Portland Art Museum owns 60 American paintings, of which about half are usually on view. The leading painters of the late 19th and early 20th centuries are represented, with several works by Inness, Ryder, Hassam, Speicher, Lawrence, Kuniyoshi, Tobey, and Graves. Hours: noon to 5 Tuesday through Sunday; until 10 Wednesday evening. Closed Monday.

PENNSYLVANIA

PHILADELPHIA

The Historical Society of Pennsylvania owns 775 American paintings, the best ones on permanent display throughout the building. The collection excels in the period from about 1750 to 1840 and includes 8 Wests, 14 C. W. Peales, 40 Sullys, and 12 Neagles. Hours: 9 to 5 Monday through Saturday. Closed Sunday and during August, and Christmas Eve, Christmas, New Year's Eve, and New Year's.

The collection at Independence Hall and its neighboring buildings (which make up Independence National Historical Park) consists of 300 American paintings, 150 of which are permanently on view. It excels in 18th and 19th century portraiture, including 88 C. W. Peale portraits, many of them shown in the same part of Independence Hall that once held Peale's museum. Also in Independence Hall (though owned by the Pennsylvania Academy) is West's *Penn's Treaty with the Indians.* Hours: 8:45 to 5:15 daily.

The Pennsylvania Academy of the Fine Arts has been showing the work of American painters in its annual exhibitions since 1805; of its collection of approximately 2,000, some 300 American paintings are usually on view, dating from 1750 to the present. Among the best represented painters are C. W. Peale (20), Rembrandt Peale (23), Stuart (31), Sully (50), Inman (13), Neagle (28). Well-known paintings include several huge historical works by West (*Christ Rejected*) and Allston (*The Dead Man Revived in the Tomb by Touching the Bones of the Prophet Elisha*), *Benjamin Franklin* by C. W. Peale, the Lansdowne portrait of Washington by Stuart, *Ariadne* by Vanderlyn, *Walt Whitman* by Eakins. Hours: 10 to 5 Tuesday through Saturday; 1 to 5 Sunday. Closed Monday and major holidays.

The Philadelphia Museum of Art has some 250 American paintings in its permanent collection, of which about 115 are generally on view. Although the comprehensive collection dates back to the days of West, its principal strength lies in the late 19th century. The museum's collection of more than 60 paintings by Eakins includes his *William Rush Carving His Allegorical Figure of the Schuylkill River, Between Rounds, Concert Singer,* and *The Fairman Rogers Four-in-Hand.* Among other paintings of special interest: C. W. Peale's *Staircase Group.* Hours: 9 to 5 daily.

PITTSBURGH

The Department of Fine Arts at the Carnegie Institute owns 211 American paintings, of which 60 are usually on view. The permanent collection consists chiefly of work by artists prominent in the annual Carnegie Institute International Exhibitions, with emphasis on Americans. Hours: 10 to 5 Monday through Saturday; 2 to 5 Sunday. Closed major holidays.

RHODE ISLAND

PROVIDENCE

The Rhode Island School of Design owns 348 oils by American painters, mainly from the colonial period, the days of the early Republic, and the late 19th century. About 70 American pictures are usually on view. Stuart is represented in his native state by 6 fine portraits, including a Washington. Hours: 10:30 to 5 Tuesday through Saturday; 2 to 5 Sunday. Closed Monday and holidays.

SOUTH CAROLINA

CHARLESTON

The collection of the Carolina Art Association at the Gibbes Art Gallery includes 322 paintings by American artists, of which about 260 (including 160 miniatures) are on regular view. Best represented are 18th and early 19th century works by artists native to, or at some time resident in, the South. Hours: 10 to 5 Monday through Saturday and until 9 Tuesday evening; 3 to 6 Sunday.

TEXAS

DALLAS

The Dallas Museum of Fine Arts owns 360 paintings by American artists, which are rotated so that most are seen at least once a year. The museum concentrates on paintings by Southwestern artists, but it also has representative works in most periods of American painting, particularly late 19th century and early 20th century works. Hours: 10 to 5 Tuesday through Saturday; 2 to 6 Sunday. Closed Monday and holidays.

HOUSTON

The Museum of Fine Arts of Houston is particularly strong in Remington, owning about 70 of his paintings (including *Fight for the Water Hole*), some of which are permanently on view. Hours: 9:30 to 5:30 Tuesday through Sunday. Closed Monday.

SAN ANTONIO

The Marion Koogler McNay Art Institute owns 81 paintings by American artists, all on exhibition at least once a year. The collection, dating back to the impressionists, includes a representative group of modern works, particularly water colors. Hours: 9 to 5 Tuesday through Saturday; until 9 Thursday evening; 2 to 5 Sunday. Closed Monday.

VIRGINIA

RICHMOND

The Virginia Museum of Fine Arts owns 207 works by American artists of all periods. About 60 are generally on view. Contemporary works of special interest: Kuniyoshi's *Nevadaville*, Burchfield's *Old House and Elm Tree*, Hopper's *House at Dusk*, Shahn's *Africa*, Davis' *Little Giant Still Life*. Hours: 11 to 5 Tuesday through Thursday; 2 to 5 and 8 to 10 Friday; 11 to 5 Saturday; 2 to 5 Sunday. Closed Monday.

WILLIAMSBURG

The Abby Aldrich Rockefeller Folk Art Collection is outstanding in its field, with more than 400 American paintings, mostly by anonymous or little-known 19th century folk artists. Hours: noon to 9 Tuesday through Sunday. Closed Monday.

WASHINGTON

SEATTLE

The Seattle Art Museum concentrates on the contemporary art of the Northwest. The collections, in which about 175 American artists are represented, include 28 paintings by Tobey, 28 by Callahan, and 18 by Graves. Hours: 10 to 5 Tuesday through Saturday; 7 to 10 Thursday evening; noon to 5 Sunday. Closed Monday and holidays.

WISCONSIN

MILWAUKEE

The Milwaukee Art Institute and Layton Art Gallery own some 150 paintings by Americans, of which about 25 are usually on view. The collection excels in late 19th century works, including 3 Blakelocks and 3 Johnsons (one being *The Old Stage Coach*). Hours: 9 to 5 Monday through Saturday; until 9 Thursday evening; 2 to 5 Sunday.

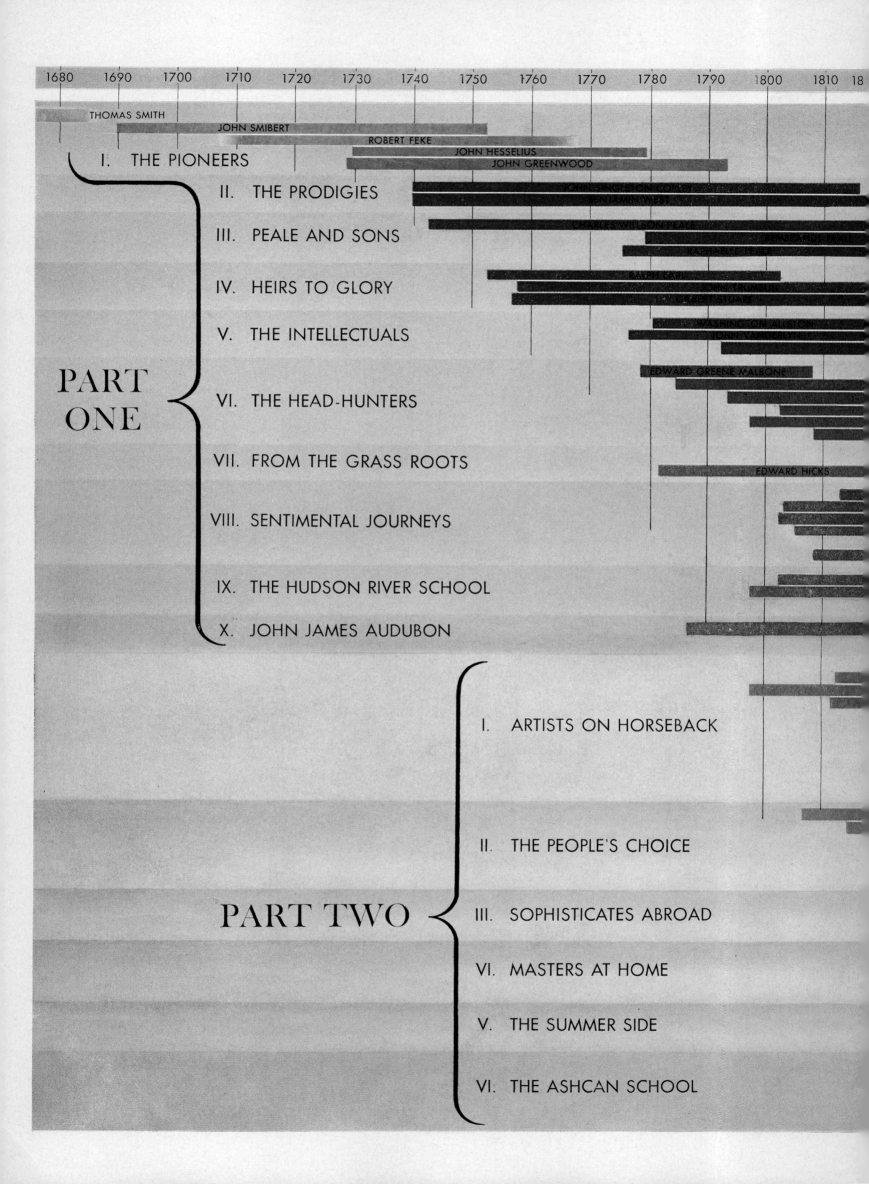

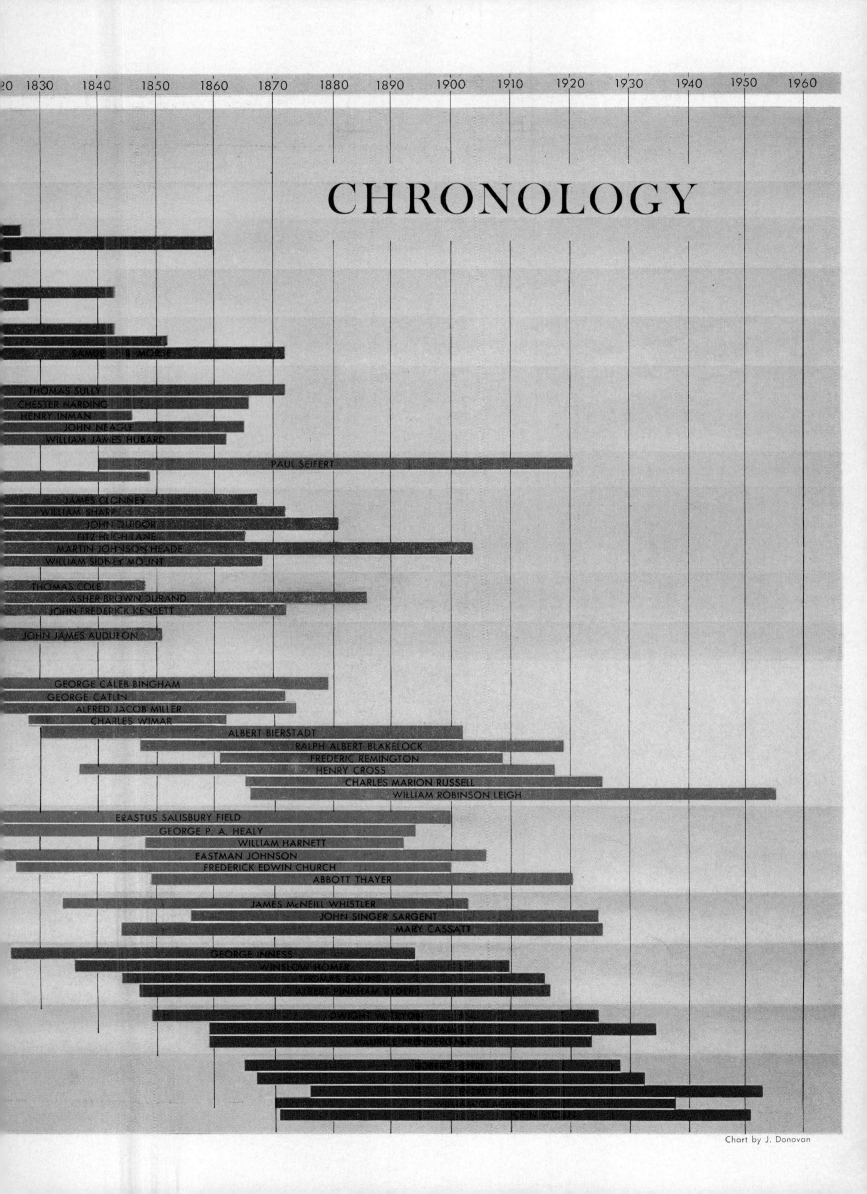

CHRONOLOGY

SAMUEL F. B. MORSE

THOMAS SULLY
CHESTER HARDING
HENRY INMAN
JOHN NEAGLE
WILLIAM JAMES HUBARD

PAUL SEIFERT

JAMES CLONNEY
WILLIAM SHARP
JOHN QUIDOR
FITZ HUGH LANE
MARTIN JOHNSON HEADE
WILLIAM SIDNEY MOUNT

THOMAS COLE
ASHER BROWN DURAND
JOHN FREDERICK KENSETT

JOHN JAMES AUDUBON

GEORGE CALEB BINGHAM
GEORGE CATLIN
ALFRED JACOB MILLER
CHARLES WIMAR
ALBERT BIERSTADT
RALPH ALBERT BLAKELOCK
FREDERIC REMINGTON
HENRY CROSS
CHARLES MARION RUSSELL
WILLIAM ROBINSON LEIGH

ERASTUS SALISBURY FIELD
GEORGE P. A. HEALY
WILLIAM HARNETT
EASTMAN JOHNSON
FREDERICK EDWIN CHURCH
ABBOTT THAYER

JAMES McNEILL WHISTLER
JOHN SINGER SARGENT
MARY CASSATT

GEORGE INNESS
WINSLOW HOMER
THOMAS EAKINS
ALBERT PINKHAM RYDER

DWIGHT W. TRYON
CHILDE HASSAM
MAURICE PRENDERGAST

ROBERT HENRI
GEORGE LUKS
EVERETT SHINN
WILLIAM GLACKENS
JOHN SLOAN

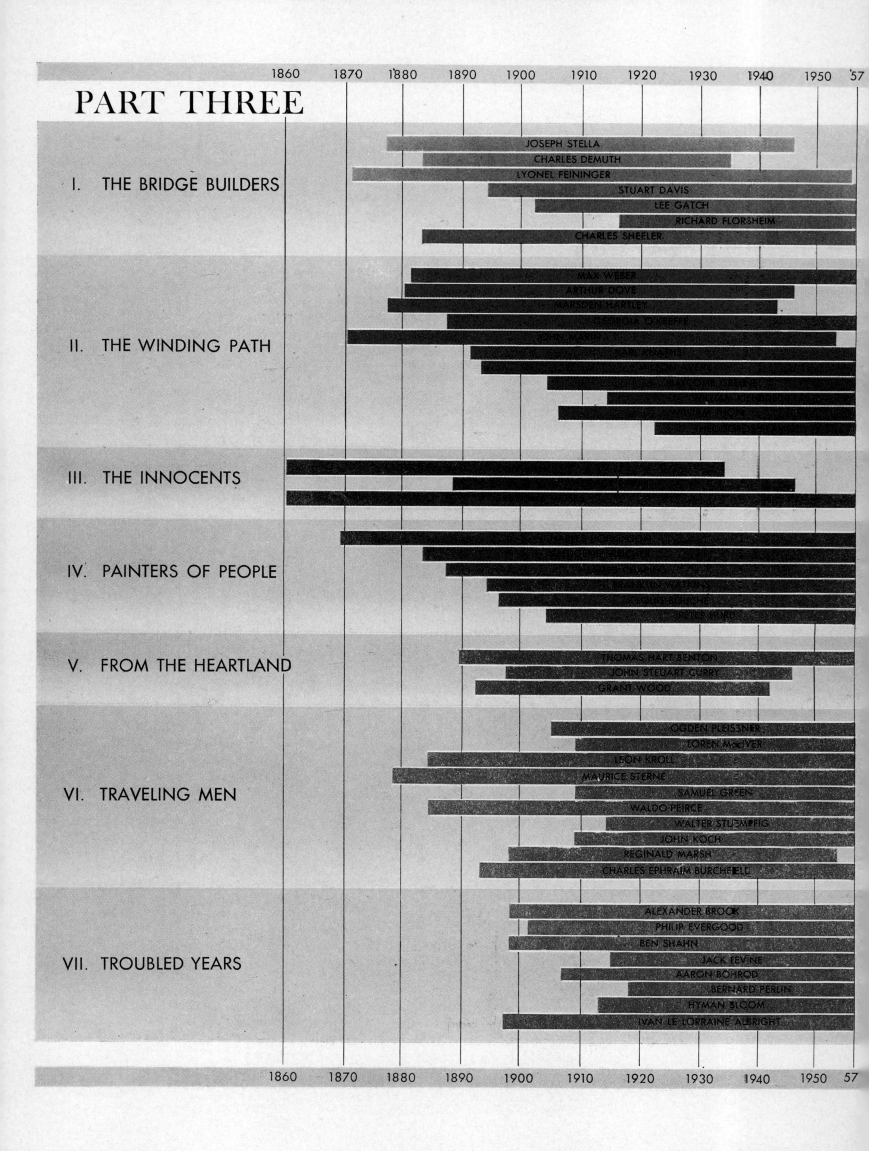

PART THREE

I. THE BRIDGE BUILDERS

JOSEPH STELLA
CHARLES DEMUTH
LYONEL FEININGER
STUART DAVIS
LEE GATCH
RICHARD FLORSHEIM
CHARLES SHEELER

II. THE WINDING PATH

MAX WEBER
ARTHUR DOVE
MARSDEN HARTLEY
GEORGIA O'KEEFFE
JOHN MARIN
KARL KNATHS
MILTON AVERY
BALCOMB GREENE
WILLIAM KIENBUSCH
WILLIAM PHON
THEODORE STAMOS

III. THE INNOCENTS

IV. PAINTERS OF PEOPLE

CHARLES HOPKINSON
EUGENE SPEICHER
JAMES CHAPIN
FRANKLIN WATKINS
LOUIS BOUCHE
PETER HURD

V. FROM THE HEARTLAND

THOMAS HART BENTON
JOHN STEUART CURRY
GRANT WOOD

VI. TRAVELING MEN

OGDEN PLEISSNER
LOREN MacIVER
LEON KROLL
MAURICE STERNE
SAMUEL GREEN
WALDO PEIRCE
WALTER STUEMPFIG
JOHN KOCH
REGINALD MARSH
CHARLES EPHRAIM BURCHFIELD

VII. TROUBLED YEARS

ALEXANDER BROOK
PHILIP EVERGOOD
BEN SHAHN
JACK LEVINE
AARON BOHROD
BERNARD PERLIN
HYMAN BLOOM
IVAN LE LORRAINE ALBRIGHT

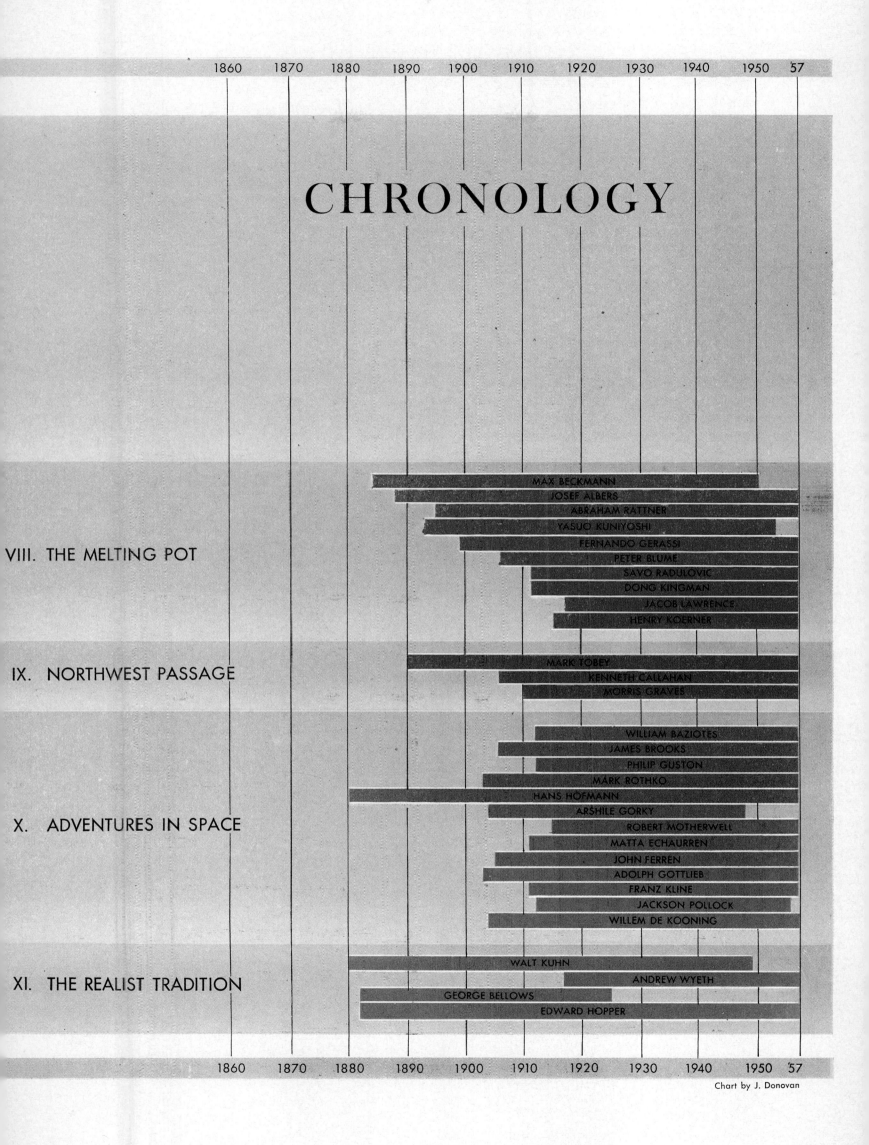

CHRONOLOGY

VIII. THE MELTING POT

MAX BECKMANN
JOSEF ALBERS
ABRAHAM RATTNER
YASUO KUNIYOSHI
FERNANDO GERASSI
PETER BLUME
SAVO RADULOVIC
DONG KINGMAN
JACOB LAWRENCE
HENRY KOERNER

IX. NORTHWEST PASSAGE

MARK TOBEY
KENNETH CALLAHAN
MORRIS GRAVES

X. ADVENTURES IN SPACE

WILLIAM BAZIOTES
JAMES BROOKS
PHILIP GUSTON
MARK ROTHKO
HANS HOFMANN
ARSHILE GORKY
ROBERT MOTHERWELL
MATTA ECHAURREN
JOHN FERREN
ADOLPH GOTTLIEB
FRANZ KLINE
JACKSON POLLOCK
WILLEM DE KOONING

XI. THE REALIST TRADITION

WALT KUHN
ANDREW WYETH
GEORGE BELLOWS
EDWARD HOPPER

Chart by J. Donovan

BIBLIOGRAPHY

The following selective bibliography, grouped as general and biographical references, includes the principal books and catalogues consulted in the preparation of this volume. Standard reference works such as the *Dictionary of American Biography* and periodicals (indexed in the *Art Index*) were also used. The resources of the Frick Art Reference Library in New York were frequently called upon, as well as TIME's own files. General references are listed alphabetically by author, biographical references alphabetically by artist.

GENERAL

BARKER, VIRGIL. *American Painting: History and Interpretation.* New York: The Macmillan Co., 1950.
A Critical Introduction to American Painting. New York: Whitney Museum of American Art, 1931.
BAUR, JOHN I. H. *Revolution and Tradition in Modern American Art.* Cambridge, Mass.: Harvard University Press, 1951.
BAUR, JOHN I. H., AND SHINN, EVERETT. *The Eight.* New York: The Brooklyn Museum, 1943.
BOLTON, THEODORE. *Early American Portrait Painters in Miniature.* New York: Frederic Fairchild Sherman, 1931.
BORN, WOLFGANG. *American Landscape Painting: An Interpretation.* New Haven, Conn.: Yale University Press, 1948.
Still Life Painting in America. New York: Oxford University Press, 1947.
BOSWELL, PEYTON, JR. *Modern American Painting.* New York: Dodd, Mead & Co., 1939.
BROWN, MILTON W. *American Painting from the Armory Show to the Depression.* Princeton, N.J.: Princeton University Press, 1955.
BURROUGHS, ALAN. *Limners and Likenesses: Three Centuries of American Painting.* Cambridge, Mass.: Harvard University Press, 1936.
CAHILL, HOLGER. *American Folk Art; The Art of the Common Man in America, 1750-1900.* New York: The Museum of Modern Art, 1932.
CAHILL, HOLGER, AND BARR, ALFRED H., JR. (eds.). *Art in America, A Complete Survey.* New York: Reynal & Hitchcock, 1935.
CONSTABLE, W. G. (ed.), BAUR, JOHN I. H. *M. and M. Karolik Collection of American Paintings, 1815 to 1865.* Published for the Museum of Fine Arts, Boston. Cambridge, Mass.: Harvard University Press, 1949.
DE VOTO, BERNARD. *Across the Wide Missouri.* Boston: Houghton Mifflin Co., 1947.
DRESSER, LOUISA. *Seventeenth-Century Painting in New England.* Worcester, Mass.: Worcester Art Museum, 1935.
DUNLAP, WILLIAM. *A History of the Rise and Progress of the Arts of Design in the United States.* New edition, ed. Frank W. Bayley and Charles E. Goodspeed. 3 vols. Boston: C. E. Goodspeed, 1918.
FIELDING, MANTLE. *Dictionary of American Painters, Sculptors & Engravers.* New York: Paul A. Struck, 1945.
FLEXNER, JAMES THOMAS. *America's Old Masters.* New York: The Viking Press, 1939.
First Flowers of Our Wilderness, American Painting. Boston: Houghton Mifflin Co., 1947.
The Light of Distant Skies, 1760-1835. New York: Harcourt, Brace & Co., 1954.
A Short History of American Painting. Boston: Houghton Mifflin Co., 1950.
FORD, ALICE. *Pictorial Folk Art, New England to California.* New York and London: The Studio Publications, Inc., 1949.
GENAUER, EMILY. *Best of Art.* New York: Doubleday & Co., 1948.
GOODRICH, LLOYD. *A Century of American Landscape Painting, 1800-1900.* New York: Whitney Museum of American Art, 1938.
GROCE, GEORGE C., AND WALLACE, DAVID H. *The New-York Historical Society's Dictionary of Artists in America, 1564-1860.* New Haven, Conn.: Yale University Press, 1957.

GRUSKIN, ALAN D. *Painting in the U.S.A.* New York: Doubleday & Co., 1946.
HAGEN, OSKAR. *The Birth of the American Tradition in Art.* New York: Charles Scribner's Sons, 1940.
HALE, ROBERT BEVERLY (Intro.). *100 American Painters of the 20th Century.* New York: The Metropolitan Museum of Art, 1950.
HARTMANN, SADAKICHI. *A History of American Art.* Revised edition. Boston: L. C. Page, 1932.
ISHAM, SAMUEL. *The History of American Painting.* New edition with a Supplement by Royal Cortissoz. New York: The Macmillan Co., 1927.
JANIS, SIDNEY. *Abstract and Surrealist Art in America.* New York: Reynal & Hitchcock, 1944.
They Taught Themselves—American Primitive Painters of the 20th Century. New York: The Dial Press, 1942.
JONES, LOUIS C., AND DAVIDSON, MARSHALL B. *American Folk Art in Fenimore House, Cooperstown, N.Y.* New York: The Metropolitan Museum of Art, 1953.
KOOTZ, SAMUEL M. *Modern American Painters.* New York: Brewer & Warren, Inc., 1930.
LA FOLLETTE, SUZANNE. *Art in America.* New York: Harper & Bros., 1929.
LARKIN, OLIVER W. *Art and Life in America.* New York: Rinehart & Co., 1949.
LEE, CUTHBERT. *Early American Portrait Painters: The Fourteen Principal Earliest Native-Born Painters.* New Haven, Conn.: Yale University Press, 1929.
LIPMAN, JEAN. *American Primitive Painting.* New York: Oxford University Press, 1942.
LIPMAN, JEAN, AND WINCHESTER, ALICE. *Primitive Painting in America, 1750-1950, An Anthology.* New York: Dodd, Mead & Co., 1950.
McCAUSLAND, ELIZABETH, AND WILLIAMS, HERMANN WARNER, JR. *American Processional, 1492-1900.* Washington, D.C.: The Corcoran Gallery of Art, 1950.
McCRACKEN, HAROLD. *Portrait of the Old West.* New York: McGraw-Hill Book Co., Inc., 1952.
MELLQUIST, JEROME. *The Emergence of an American Art.* New York: Charles Scribner's Sons, 1942.
MILLER, DOROTHY C. (ed.). *Americans 1942—18 Artists from 9 States.* New York: The Museum of Modern Art, 1942.
14 Americans. New York: The Museum of Modern Art, 1946.
15 Americans. New York: The Museum of Modern Art, 1952.
12 Americans. New York: The Museum of Modern Art, 1956.
MOHOLY-NAGY, L.; KNATHS, KARL; MORRIS, GEORGE L. K.; LEGER, FERNAND; GALLATIN, A. E.; MONDRIAN, PIET; ALBERS, JOSEF. *American Abstract Artists.* New York: The Ram Press, 1946.
MOTHERWELL, ROBERT; ROSENBERG, HAROLD; CHAREAU, PIERRE; CAGE, JOHN (eds.). *Possibilities 1.* Statements by six American artists. New York: Wittenborn, Schultz, Inc., 1947.
MUMFORD, LEWIS. *The Brown Decades, A Study of the Arts in America, 1865-1895.* New York: Harcourt, Brace & Co., 1931.
NATIONAL GALLERY OF ART. *American Primitive Paintings from the Collection of Edgar William and Bernice Chrysler Garbisch.* Parts 1 and 2. Washington, D.C.: National Gallery of Art, 1954, 1957.

PEARSON, RALPH M. *Experiencing American Pictures*. New York: Harper & Bros., 1943.
　The Modern Renaissance in American Art. New York: Harper & Bros., 1954.
RATHBONE, PERRY T.; VAN RAVENSWAAY, CHARLES; LEONARD, H. STEWART. *Mississippi Panorama*. St. Louis: City Art Museum of St. Louis, 1949.
RATHBONE, PERRY T.; VOELKER, FREDERICK E.; FILSINGER, CATHERINE; EISENDRATH, WILLIAM N., JR. *Westward the Way*. St. Louis: City Art Museum of St. Louis, 1954.
READ, HELEN APPLETON. *Robert Henri and Five of His Pupils*. New York: The Century Assn., 1946.
RICHARDSON, E. P. *American Romantic Painting*. New York: E. Weyhe, 1944.
　Painting in America: The Story of 450 Years. New York: Thomas Y. Crowell Co., 1956.
RODMAN, SELDEN. *Conversations with Artists*. New York: The Devin-Adair Co., 1957.
　The Eye of Man. Form and Content in Western Painting. New York: The Devin-Adair Co., 1955.
SAINT-GAUDENS, HOMER. *The American Artist and His Times*. New York: Dodd, Mead & Co., 1941.
SOBY, JAMES THRALL. *Contemporary Painters*. New York: The Museum of Modern Art, 1949.
　Modern Art and the New Past. Norman, Okla.: University of Oklahoma Press, 1957.
SOBY, JAMES THRALL, AND MILLER, DOROTHY C. *Romantic Painting in America*. New York: The Museum of Modern Art, 1943.

SWEENEY, JAMES JOHNSON. *Younger American Painters, A Selection*. New York: Solomon R. Guggenheim Museum, 1954.
SWEET, FREDERICK A. *The Hudson River School and the Early American Landscape Tradition*. Chicago: Art Institute of Chicago, 1945.
　Sargent, Whistler and Mary Cassatt. Chicago: Art Institute of Chicago, 1954.
SWEET, FREDERICK A., HUTH, HANS. *From Colony to Nation: an exhibition of American painting and architecture from 1650 to the War of 1812*. Chicago: Art Institute of Chicago, 1949.
TUCKERMAN, HENRY T. *Book of the Artists: American Artist Life*. New York: G. P. Putnam's Sons, 1867.
UNIVERSITY OF ILLINOIS. *Exhibition of Contemporary American Painting*. Urbana, Ill.: College of Fine and Applied Arts, University of Illinois, catalogues for 1950, 1951, 1952. *Exhibition of Contemporary American Painting and Sculpture*. Urbana, Ill.: College of Fine and Applied Arts, University of Illinois, catalogues for 1953, 1955, 1957.
WALKER, JOHN, AND JAMES, MACGILL. *Great American Paintings from Smibert to Bellows, 1729-1924*. New York: Oxford University Press, 1943.
WATSON, FORBES. *American Painting Today*. American Federation of Arts, Washington, D.C. New York: Distributed by Oxford University Press, 1939.
WEHLE, HARRY B., AND BOLTON, THEODORE. *American Miniatures, 1730-1850*. Garden City, N.Y.: Garden City Publishing Co., 1937.
WIGHT, FREDERICK S. *Milestones of American Painting in Our Century*. Published for The Institute of Contemporary Art, Boston. New York: Chanticleer Press, 1949.

BIOGRAPHICAL

ALBERS, JOSEF. Hamilton, George Heard (ed.). *Paintings, Prints, Projects*. Catalogue by Sewell Sillman. New Haven, Conn.: Yale University Art Gallery, 1956.
ALLSTON, WASHINGTON. Richardson, E. P. *Washington Allston, A Study of the Romantic Artist in America*. Chicago: University of Chicago Press, 1948.
AUDUBON, JOHN JAMES. Rourke, Constance. *Audubon*. New York: Harcourt, Brace & Co., 1936.
BELLOWS, GEORGE. Boswell, Peyton, Jr. *George Bellows*. New York: Crown Publishers, 1942.
　George Bellows—Paintings, Drawings and Prints. Articles by Eugene Speicher, Frederick A. Sweet, Carl O. Schniewind. Chicago: The Art Institute of Chicago, 1946.
BENTON, THOMAS HART. Benton, Thomas Hart. *An Artist in America*. New York: Halcyon House, 1939.
BINGHAM, GEORGE CALEB. Christ-Janer, Albert. *George Caleb Bingham of Missouri*. New York: Dodd, Mead & Co., 1940.
BLAKELOCK, RALPH ALBERT. Goodrich, Lloyd. *Ralph Albert Blakelock*. New York: Whitney Museum of American Art, 1947.
BLOOM, HYMAN. *Hyman Bloom*. With an Essay by Frederick S. Wight and a Postscript by Lloyd Goodrich. Boston: The Institute of Contemporary Art, 1954.
BURCHFIELD, CHARLES EPHRAIM. Baur, John I. H. *Charles Burchfield*. Published for the Whitney Museum of American Art. New York: The Macmillan Co., 1956.
CASSATT, MARY. Breeskin, Adelyn D. *The Graphic Work of Mary Cassatt*. New York: H. Bittner & Co., 1948.
　Watson, Forbes. *Mary Cassatt*. New York: Whitney Museum of American Art, 1932.
CATLIN, GEORGE. Donaldson, Thomas. "The George Catlin Indian Gallery" in *Smithsonian Institution Report*. Washington, D.C.: 1885.
　Haberly, Lloyd. *Pursuit of the Horizon. A Life of George Catlin, Painter and Recorder of the American Indian*. New York: The Macmillan Co., 1948.
COLE, THOMAS. Seaver, Esther I. *Thomas Cole*. Hartford, Conn.: Wadsworth Atheneum, 1949.
COPLEY, JOHN SINGLETON. Flexner, James Thomas. *John Singleton Copley*. Boston: Houghton Mifflin Co., 1948.

CURRY, JOHN STEUART. Schmeckebier, Laurence E. *John Steuart Curry's Pageant of America*. New York: American Artists Group, 1943.
　John Steuart Curry 1897-1946. Lawrence, Kans.: The University of Kansas Museum of Art, 1957.
DAVIS, STUART. *Stuart Davis*. New York: American Artists Group, 1945.
　Sweeney, James Johnson. *Stuart Davis*. New York: The Museum of Modern Art, 1945.
DEMUTH, CHARLES. Ritchie, Andrew Carnduff. *Charles Demuth*. New York: The Museum of Modern Art, 1950.
DOVE, ARTHUR G. *Arthur G. Dove 1880-1946*. With a Foreword by Duncan Phillips and an Essay by Alan R. Solomon. Ithaca, N.Y.: Andrew Dickson White Museum of Art. Cornell University, 1954.
EAKINS, THOMAS. Goodrich, Lloyd. *Thomas Eakins, His Life and Work*. New York: Whitney Museum of American Art. 1933.
EARL, RALPH. Sawitzky, William. *Ralph Earl, 1751-1801*. New York: Whitney Museum of American Art, 1945.
EVERGOOD, PHILIP. *20 Years—Evergood*. With a Foreword by Herman Baron, an Essay by Oliver Larkin, and a Statement by Philip Evergood. New York: A C A Gallery Publication, 1946.
FEININGER, LYONEL. *Lyonel Feininger—Marsden Hartley*. Miller, Dorothy C. (ed.). New York: The Museum of Modern Art, 1944.
　The Work of Lyonel Feininger. With a Preface by Leona E. Prasse and an Essay by Frederick S. Wight. Cleveland: The Cleveland Museum of Art, 1951.
FEKE, ROBERT. Goodrich, Lloyd. *Robert Feke*. New York: Whitney Museum of American Art, 1946.
GLACKENS, WILLIAM J. Pène du Bois, Guy. *William J. Glackens*. New York: Whitney Museum of American Art 1931.
GRAVES, MORRIS. Wight, Frederick S.; Baur, John I. H.; Phillips, Duncan. *Morris Graves*. Berkeley and Los Angeles: University of California Press, 1956.
GREENWOOD, JOHN. Burroughs, Alan. *John Greenwood in America (1745-1752)*. Andover, Mass.: Addison Gallery of American Art, 1943.

HARNETT, WILLIAM. Frankenstein, Alfred. *After the Hunt— William Harnett and Other Still Life Painters, 1870-1900.* Berkeley and Los Angeles: University of California Press, 1953.

HARTLEY, MARSDEN. McCausland, Elizabeth. *Marsden Hartley.* Minneapolis: University of Minnesota Press, 1952.

HEALY, G.P.A. De Mare, Marie. *G.P.A. Healy, American Artist.* New York: David McKay Co., 1954.

HENRI, ROBERT. Henri, Robert. *The Art Spirit.* New edition. Philadelphia: J. B. Lippincott Co., 1951.

HICKS, EDWARD. Ford, Alice. *Edward Hicks, Painter of the Peaceable Kingdom.* Philadelphia: University of Pennsylvania Press, 1952.

HOFMANN, HANS. Wight, Frederick S. *Hans Hofmann.* Berkeley and Los Angeles: University of California Press, 1957.

HOMER, WINSLOW. Goodrich, Lloyd. *Winslow Homer.* Published for the Whitney Museum of American Art. New York: The Macmillan Co., 1945.

HOPPER, EDWARD. *Edward Hopper.* New York: American Artists Group, 1945.
Goodrich, Lloyd. *Edward Hopper—Retrospective Exhibition.* Published cooperatively by the Whitney Museum of American Art, New York, the Museum of Fine Arts, Boston, and the Detroit Institute of Arts, 1950.

INNESS, GEORGE. Inness, George, Jr. *Life, Art and Letters of George Inness.* New York: The Century Co., 1917.
McCausland, Elizabeth. *George Inness, an American Landscape Painter, 1825-1894.* New York: American Artists Group, 1946.

JOHNSON, EASTMAN. Baur, John I. H. *An American Genre Painter, Eastman Johnson, 1824-1906.* New York: The Brooklyn Museum, 1940.

KANE, JOHN. Kane, John. *Sky Hooks—The Autobiography of John Kane.* Philadelphia: J.B. Lippincott Co., 1938.

KUNIYOSHI, YASUO. Goodrich, Lloyd. *Yasuo Kuniyoshi.* New York: Whitney Museum of American Art, 1948.

LEVINE, JACK. The Institute of Contemporary Art, Boston. *Jack Levine.* With a Foreword by Lloyd Goodrich and an Essay by Frederick S. Wight. New York: Whitney Museum of American Art, 1955.

MacIVER, LOREN. Baur, John I. H. *Loren MacIver—I. Rice Pereira.* Published for the Whitney Museum of American Art. New York: The Macmillan Co., 1953.

MARIN, JOHN. Helm, MacKinley. *John Marin.* Published in association with the Institute of Contemporary Art, Boston. New York: Pellegrini & Cudahy, 1948.
Marin, John. *The Selected Writings of John Marin,* ed. Dorothy Norman. New York: Pellegrini & Cudahy, 1949.
Williams, William Carlos; Phillips, Duncan; Norman, Dorothy; Helm, MacKinley; Wight, Frederick S. *John Marin.* Berkeley and Los Angeles: University of California Press, 1956.

MARSH, REGINALD. Goodrich, Lloyd. *Reginald Marsh—Exhibition Catalogue.* New York: Whitney Museum of American Art, 1955.

MORSE, SAMUEL F. B. Larkin, Oliver W. *Samuel F. B. Morse and American Democratic Art.* Boston: Little, Brown & Co., 1954.

MOSES, GRANDMA. *Grandma Moses—My Life's History,* ed. Otto Kallir. New York: Harper & Bros., 1952.

MOUNT, WILLIAM SIDNEY. Cowdrey, Bartlett, and Williams, Hermann W., Jr. *William Sidney Mount, an American Painter.* Published for the Metropolitan Museum of Art. New York: Columbia University Press, 1944.

O'KEEFFE, GEORGIA. Rich, Daniel Catton. *Georgia O'Keeffe.* Chicago: The Art Institute of Chicago, 1943.

PEALE, CHARLES WILLSON. Sellers, Charles Coleman. *Charles Willson Peale.* 2 vols. Philadelphia: American Philosophical Society, 1947.

PEIRCE, WALDO. *Waldo Peirce.* New York: American Artists Group, 1945.
Varga, Margit. *Waldo Peirce.* New York: The Hyperion Press, Harper & Bros., 1941.

PIPPIN, HORACE. Rodman, Selden. *Horace Pippin—A Negro Painter in America.* New York: The Quadrangle Press, 1947.

POLLOCK, JACKSON. Hunter, Sam. *Jackson Pollock.* New York: The Museum of Modern Art, 1956.

PRENDERGAST, MAURICE. Brooks, Van Wyck (Intro.). *The Prendergasts; Retrospective Exhibition of the Work of Maurice and Charles Prendergast.* Andover, Mass.: Phillips Academy, 1938.

REMINGTON, FREDERIC. McCracken, Harold. *Frederic Remington, Artist of the Old West.* Philadelphia and New York: J. B. Lippincott Co., 1947.

RUSSELL, CHARLES M. Adams, Ramon F., and Britzman, Homer E. *Charles M. Russell, the Cowboy Artist.* Pasadena, Calif.: Trail's End Publishing Co., 1948.

RYDER, ALBERT PINKHAM. Goodrich, Lloyd. *Albert Pinkham Ryder.* New York: Whitney Museum of American Art, 1947.

SARGENT, JOHN SINGER. McKibbin, David. *Sargent's Boston.* With a complete check list of portraits. Boston: Museum of Fine Arts, 1956.
Mount, Charles Merrill. *John Singer Sargent.* New York: W. W. Norton & Co., Inc., 1955.

SHAHN, BEN. Rodman, Selden. *Portrait of the Artist as an American. Ben Shahn: A Biography with Pictures.* New York: Harper & Bros., 1951.

SHEELER, CHARLES. *Charles Sheeler—A Retrospective Exhibition.* With a Foreword by William Carlos Williams and Essays by Bartlett H. Hayes Jr. and Frederick S. Wight. Los Angeles: Art Galleries, 1954.
Rourke, Constance. *Charles Sheeler—Artist in the American Tradition.* New York: Harcourt, Brace & Co., 1938.

SLOAN, JOHN. Brooks, Van Wyck. *John Sloan, A Painter's Life.* New York: E. P. Dutton & Co., 1955.

STELLA, JOSEPH. *Joseph Stella. Catalogue of Paintings and Drawings in a Retrospective Exhibition.* With an Introduction by Arthur F. Egner. Newark, N.J.: The Newark Museum, 1939.

STERNE, MAURICE. *Maurice Sterne—Retrospective Exhibition 1902-1932.* With Essays by H. M. Kallen and Maurice Sterne. New York: The Museum of Modern Art, 1933.

STUART, GILBERT. Flexner, James Thomas. *Gilbert Stuart: A Great Life in Brief.* New York: Alfred A. Knopf, 1955.
Morgan, John Hill. *Gilbert Stuart and His Pupils: Together with the Complete Notes on Painting by Matthew Harris Jouett from Conversations with Gilbert Stuart in 1816.* New York: The New-York Historical Society, 1939.

TOBEY, MARK. *Retrospective Exhibition.* With an Essay by Jermayne MacAgy. New York: Whitney Museum of American Art, 1951.

TRUMBULL, JOHN. Sizer, Theodore. *The Works of Colonel John Trumbull, Artist of the American Revolution.* New Haven, Conn.: Yale University Press, 1950.
Trumbull, Colonel John. *The Autobiography of Colonel John Trumbull,* ed. Theodore Sizer. New Haven, Conn.: Yale University Press, 1953.

WEBER, MAX. Goodrich, Lloyd. *Max Weber.* Published for the Whitney Museum of American Art. New York: The Macmillan Co., 1949.

WHISTLER, JAMES McNEILL. Pearson, Hesketh. *The Man Whistler.* New York: Harper & Bros., 1952.

WOOD, GRANT. Garwood, Darrell. *Artist in Iowa—A Life of Grant Wood.* New York: W. W. Norton & Co., 1944.

INDEX

Italicized page references indicate illustrations.

316

PRINTED AND BOUND BY

The Lakeside Press · R. R. DONNELLEY & SONS COMPANY

CHICAGO, ILLINOIS AND CRAWFORDSVILLE, INDIANA.

PAPER BY THE MEAD CORPORATION, DAYTON, OHIO.